The Lost Village of Mardale

OLD MEASAND SCHOOL

Memories of Old Mardale

The most primitive and secluded dale, the most charming and restful to be found in all Lakeland.

Isaac Hinchliffe, of Manchester (1921).

I don't know whether it was the exceptional beauty of those still autumn days or the knowledge that, in a few years' time, this valley would be under water, that gave our stay at Measand a poignancy that can still affect me over forty years later.

Heaton Cooper, in his book "The Lakes".

At Haweswater the reservoir that has submerged the little lake now lies, hygienically glittering, in its suitably sterilized hollow.

E M Ward, "Days in Lakeland" (3rd edn., 1948).

No one who walked up the valley [Mardale] in 1936 and saw the fields carpeted with wild-flowers and the hedges in a glory of bloom, and the great rhododendron bushes clustering round the *Dun Bull Inn,* could fail to regret that it was their last flowering before the water began to flood in during the following winter.

Maxwell Fraser, "Companion into Lakeland", (1937).

Haweswater . . . in the throes of being converted into yet another waterworks for Manchester. Surely the people of Manchester must be the cleanest, within and without, in the British Isles.

Doreen Wallace (1940).

We were never lonely, even though Mardale was a backwater of Lakeland.

Maggie Lancaster, of Flake How.

The Lost Village
of
Mardale

by W R Mitchell

CASTLEBERG
1993

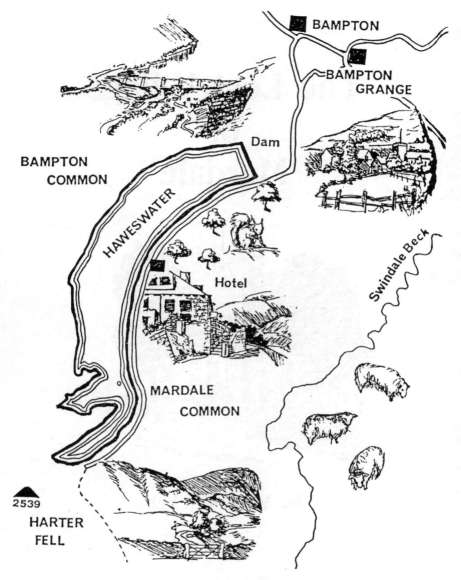

Published by Castleberg, 18 Yealand Avenue, Giggleswick,
Settle, North Yorkshire, BD24 0AY

Typeset in Clearface and printed by Lamberts Printers,
Station Road, Settle, North Yorkshire, BD24 9AA

ISBN: 1 871064 92 9

Contents

Illustrations

Line drawings by Peter Fox—1 and 3. From "A Backwater in Lakeland" (1925)—33, 68, 71. Courtesy of John Alcock—73. Other line drawings by E Jeffrey mostly based on photographs by the author.

Cover pictures: front—Bob Swallow; back—W R Mitchell.

Acknowledgements

John Alcock, Canon T E H Baily, T Barbour, Mrs Lucy Bell, W C Cannon, P Delap, Raymond Duckett, Mike Hitchmough, Mr and Mrs John Graham, Nigel Holmes (Radio Cumbria), John Hurst (*Cumberland and Westmorland Herald*), Kendal Reference Library, P Kitching, North West Water, Penrith Library, Mr and Mrs Jack Taylor, Syd Wear.

5

Why Mardale Was Drowned

THE Lakeland, an area of great beauty, has been developed as a major source for three reasons:

It is one of the wettest parts of the country—annual rainfall average 2,360 mm (93 inches)—with Thirlmere recording the country's highest on October 30, 1977, at more than 178 mm (seven inches); its comparative remoteness reduces major pollution risks; its raised lakes and valleys provide vast storage.

from a document issued by North West Water.

Foreword

by
John Hurst
(Editor, *Cumberland and Westmorland Herald*)

CALL for a snack at Tebay East or Tebay West, the service stations alongside the M6 motorway, in a mountainous area of Cumbria, and you will be impressed by eye-catching pictures of Isaac Cookson, a burly, bearded shepherd, who is shown carrying a sheep across his shoulders.

These are among the few surviving photographic fragments from the heyday of Mardale Shepherds' Meet, the annual gathering which used to focus attention on a hamlet now lying under the surface of Haweswater. Mardale was submerged over half-a-century ago, when the valley was turned into a reservoir to provide the citizens of Manchester with part of their water supply.

Isaac Cookson was one of the Lakeland flockmasters who turned up at Mardale's *Dun Bull* Inn, first to sort out the stray sheep which had been assembled and then to join in a convivial evening of tatie pot and hunting songs.

"When the fire's in the hearth and good cheer abounds, we'll drink to Joe Bowman and his Ullswater hounds..."

Mardale Shepherds' Meet lives on, though with another Lakeland pub as the venue, but other aspects of the lost hamlet, deep beneath the lapping water, remain only in fading memories and the yellowing pages of out-of-date history books.

The late Fred Barclay, who used to repair watches for the people of Penrith, as well as winding up the town's public clocks, had

7

a favourite tale of taking part in a cycling trip to Mardale on a scorching Sunday afternoon in the 1920s. Fred recounted how the group stopped at the *Dun Bull* and persuaded the landlord to sell them pints of shandy with which to quench their thirsts. The little party was ended when a policeman paid an unexpected call and the young cyclists had to pay dearly for their drinks, later being fined half-a-crown apiece by the magistrates at Shap for out-of-hours drinking.

William Whellan, in his history and topography of Cumberland and Westmorland, takes us even further back with a few details of the hamlet midway through the nineteenth century, when Mardale chapel occupied a picturesque situation, surrounded by beautiful old yew trees and in the background were the "everlasting hills".

Many will look forward to Bill Mitchell's book on the long-lost hamlet, for the very mention of Mardale sparks a special enchantment. Although the place disappeared from the landscape so long ago, it remains a frequent and fascinating talking point.

Old folk share tales of the last church service before the flooding of the remote valley, while younger ones are drawn many miles to get a glimpse into the past when a drought once again reveals the remnants of cottages and field walls.

ECCLESIASTICAL

LAST SERVICE AT MARDALE

Bishop of Carlisle and the Future

Newspaper heading of 1935.

An Introduction

Haweswater is a lesser Ullswater, with this advantage, that it remains undefiled by the intrusion of bad taste.

William Wordsworth, Guide to the Lakes
(The Fifth Edition, 1835).

...the lake is well stocked with fish of various kinds, but chiefly reserved for the table of Lowther Castle.

Jonathan Otley (1830).

Mardale Green...lost its life by drowning...All that is left are ghosts.

Alfred Wainwright, guide book writer.

I first saw Haweswater almost forty years ago while following the road which winds hesitantly between Shap and Bampton, flanked by limestone walls made without a dab of mortar.

It was late spring, with the sky "packy", as the dalesfolk call one which is bright but holds plenty of cloud. Curlews arched themselves like feathered kites and then glided earthwards, bubbling over with song.

Glancing to the west, I saw mountains tinged blue-grey by mist. In the foreground were irregular fields, spread across the landscape like a patchwork quilt. Then my eyes focussed on the dam which had transformed Haweswater, a natural lake, into a reservoir—a water cistern for Manchester—and displaced the farming community of Mardale.

Mardale had first come into my thoughts at Shap, where I had a cup of coffee and a buttered scone in Mrs Bell's cafe, meanwhile scanning old photographs of Mardale, which adorned the walls. Mrs Bell told me how the dale had been drowned by Manchester Waterworks.

At Bampton Grange, I conversed with a retired farmer about the weather, fatstock prices—and Old Mardale, which I gathered was a "bonny, quiet spot" until "they [Manchester] wanted t'watter."

A tremor of excitement used to pass through the Bamptonians when the salmon were running. Sixty and more years ago, so many salmon came up the river on their spawning run, and were illegally removed by local people, that fish which could not immediately be eaten—and there were no "freezers" then—were boiled as hen food.

An Airedale dog, named Sam, belonging to the Misses Moody, was adept at grabbing a fish in the river, killing it expeditiously by holding its head tightly with its teeth and carrying it on to the grassy bank. One of Sam's fish weighed thirteen pounds.

I also heard about Isaac Cookson, a fellside equivalent of Santa Claus, with a long white beard, furrowed brow and eyes quick and clear as those of a fox. Isaac, who attended Mardale Shepherds' Meet for sixty years and more, lived in Heltondale.

He did not often leave his farm. One Friday evening, Albert Graham of Rosgill, saw Isaac having a wash, the basin being supported on a form of the type used at sheep-shearing time. Isaac explained to Albert: "I'm thinking o' going to Penrith on Tuesday."

On my first trip to Mardale, I skirted Burnbanks, the old shanty village which in navvy-time, a mere quarter of a century before, housed several hundred workmen. Now, this "temporary" place had a decidedly permanent look about it, providing homes for officials, maintenance men and their families.

In navvy-time, Burnbanks had its resident policeman—Constable Ostle—a man almost due for retirement who was given the task of supervising Burnbanks and the site of the dam. No one quarrelled with PC Ostle because he had a faithful and potentially aggressive companion: an Alsatian dog.

Beyond Burnbanks, I was in a green aisle between trees. Visitors to Haweswater, using the old road, were to recall the sudden dramatic appearance of the lake.

A Manchester journalist with the ability to make words sing observed: "A little lift on the road, a sharp turn, and the lake is below, the slopes on either hand, and beyond the grey blue heights of the High Street range, blindly stretching out deep-cut spurs like so many sprawling limbs."

I followed a road which lay on a ledge blasted from living rock, extending from Naddle Gate to the dalehead, chuckling at the recollection of an early encounter with a local man. I commented that "this road's fairly high up." He replied, in a quiet Cumbrian way: "Well, it's above t'high watermark anyway." Syd Wear, a farmer's son who was born in Deepdale, Patterdale, but moved to Haweswater as a skilled joiner in 1929, says there was just a rough track through to Naddle Farm.

Syd recalls: "I was married and travelled from Penrith for a year on my motor bike. Some people working at Haweswater travelled eight miles from Tirril every day—on push bikes... When I came, the engineers were just making trial holes and there was only one compressor. The work closed down due to recession in 1931 and opened up again in 1934. It was completed in 1941 and it overflowed in 1941, but I don't think it was *officially* opened till later."

The explosives used by the road-makers disturbed the ancient peace of Naddle Forest, a resort of red squirrels and red deer. Nature soon put a green dressing on the sores and the deer returned behind the screen of new growth. Jack Holden's gang built the roadside walls. Syd Wear says that Jack, who lived at Butterwick, was a lile chap who was "a glutton for work".

Manchester Waterworks Committee—they who arranged for explosives to be used in the re-shaping of the valley and the construction of the new lakeside road—nonetheless went to a great deal of trouble to make the Haweswater area presentable.

A reporter for *The Herald* of Penrith, writing in 1937, affirmed that Manchester did not want to affront the susceptibilities of those who suspect blots on the landscape. "I believe that all sorts of suggestions made by Professor Abercrombie and other scenic experts have received respectful consideration at all points."

In cutting a ledge on the craggy eastern side of Mardale, the waterworks men chose the proper season so they might "dig up the luxurious clumps of fern, so beautiful now with their delicate lace-like fronds and their uncurling brown bishop's croziers, now growing on the old road to Mardale, and replant them above the Plimsoll Line on the other side of the lake or in the lanes and woods below the dam. Manchester proposes digging up seedling trees in much the same way and replanting them."

The Herald compared the new *Haweswater Hotel* with the "Castle of Chillon". Forty years ago, I had the pleasure of coffee and being served by Eric Sangster, who succeeded Harold Hazelhurst as the manager. It was Harold who opened up the new hotel in 1937, so the tales of Old Mardale were still easy to recall.

A model of old Mardale Church, in a glass-sided case, had been placed in the entrance hall of the hotel when it was opened and had remained there ever since.

Jack Taylor, of Penrith, worked for a time on the new hotel. "I was working for Lowther Estate as a builder. Things were running down a bit so I left and got a job helping to build the hotel. I left the work when it was up to the first floor.

"There were two gangs of men, one from Baines of Kendal and another made up of local men who knew a lot more about working with blue stone. Each gang had to make two samples of walling to see which was the best way to go about it. The Manchester Corporation man who inspected them decided our type of wall was the one they wanted. The stone was quarried on the site. It was blown out rather than properly quarried but it has turned the weather all these years."

Syd Wear, who by his own admission was inquisitive, regularly cycled from his home at Burnbanks to keep his eye on progress of the building work.

Guests at the *Haweswater Hotel* watched red squirrels gavorting in the deciduous trees and, from the front terrace, if they were lucky, to see a golden eagle crossing a watery sky or spiralling upwards until it was little more than a black dot against the cloudbase.

England's first nesting pair of eagles for a century or two chose to build on a ledge in one of the recesses of Mardale. I was to see the local pair of eagles flying in the same limited air space as a pair of peregrine falcons, which were scolding the larger birds. A friend picked up a cast wing feather from beneath a thorn tree on which an eagle had been roosting.

Syd Wear, one of those who remembers when Haweswater was a lake of modest size, says the water extended from a point a quarter of a mile above the present dam for a distance of two and a-half miles. The reservoir is now four miles long.

The Yellow Earl (Lord Lonsdale) was the major landowner and decided who might fish Haweswater. He had emissaries in the Mardale area. There was a boatman. Isaac Dufton, Lordy's gamekeeper, "finished his time off at the waterworks."

Haweswater char, one of the piscatorial celebrities, has been here since the Ice Ages, when the re-shaping of the landscape ended the migratory life of many fish and they adapted to life in Lakeland, being found in the deep water of several lakes and coming to shallow water to spawn.

Long before this area became a wardened nature reserve, with all the trappings, I joined friends on quiet deer-watching excursions, watching lordly animals which had crossed over from Martindale, the only deer stalking forest in England. When a Meet of the North West branch, British Deer Society, was based on the *Haweswater Hotel*, one autumn, the first item was coffee in the lounge.

One of the deer experts began talking about aspects of managment but it was difficult to concentrate on what was being said because we had real-life deer in view. The picture window framed a tract of fellside to the west of Haweswater. White water surged down the becks. The bracken had died back to a coppery hue. Sheep were in their usual routine of grazing or chewing the cud.

Into sight came a small group of red hinds and calves of the year. They fed where much grazing had kept the grass short and sweet. The russet hue of deer coats was accentuated by the low, hard autumn sunlight.

Later, in neighbouring Swindale, more deer were seen, along with felltop birds—a raven, the "croaker", wearing its suit of undertaker-black, and a peregrine falcon, stooping at a green bird which was identified through binoculars as a parrot, doubtless a free-ranging bird on a day trip from Lowther Wildlife Park.

The peak time for visiting Haweswater is in a drought year when the water level falls to reveal traces of the "lost" village. It was hardly a village, being just a scattering of farms, with church, school and the hotel.

A correspondent of *The Manchester Guardian* (1918) wrote: "Four or five farmhouses lie here and there amid the lower meadows; a tiny church, plain-built in a Puritan century, squats amid its yews; the only touches of modernity are the schoolhouse and vicarage, but subdued grey stone and spreading leafage have blended these into natural harmony."

The "new road", as Mardalians still call the one built sixty years ago, replaced a narrower, more winding way direct from Burn-banks, keeping west of the water. Syd Wear remembers when it was kept tidy as part of the area covered by three Council roadmen—Bob Langstaff, his son Arthur and Jim Martin. All lived at Knipe and "made a good job of maintaining the roads."

Syd recalls many a journey along that road as part of his work helping to maintain local properties. He helped to "dismantle" Mardale school. It was a substantial stone building, including ac-commodation for the teacher and, outside, a coal house and privvy.

Whelter, a farm at one time, was latterly used as a dwelling by Dr Connell, a surgeon at the Cumberland Infirmary in Carlisle. There was no bathroom in the property so periodically the doctor stood under one of the local waterfalls.

The last tenant of the vicarage, Mr Barham, was "one of the nicest chaps you could meet. We were putting him a new gate in when a roadster or milestone inspector [tramp] went by. Mr Barham called out to him and handed him some money." The roadster went on his way rejoicing.

Syd Wear says: "Once you went past the old *Dun Bull,* you were in wild country." The dalehead has a horseshoe-shaped range of hills, including the fissured face of Harter Fell. Edward Baines, a tourist in 1829, wrote of Harter's "stupendous and furrowed precipices" which "frown over the head of the dale."

This and other eminences—Branstree, Mardale Ill Bell, High Street and Kidsty Pike—give Mardale a hemmed-in appearance. The old through routes—Nan Bield and Gatescarth passes, on either side of Harter Fell—linked Penrith with Kendal via Mardale.

Edward Baines, our early tourist, had ridden a horse from Longsleddale to Mardale, where he roused "mine host" of the *Dun Bull* from his bed. Baines described Mardale as "a lively, fertile and beautiful valley, with very few habitations." He went on to attain the summit plateau of High Street—a broad tract of land, covered with short grass, where once horse racing took place. An alternative name for High Street is Racecourse Hill.

I have a special memory of the Rigg, leading on to High Street. A fell-walker suggested a meeting here, high above Riggindale, on a summer's dawn, to see a blood-red sun rise from beyond Cross Fell. The redness would be seen in the reservoir and the fells. We might even see some red-red deer!

Dawn came with the sun obscured by cloud. We clambered to the summit of High Street and settled down for a snack meal not far from the line of the footpath which was once the "Brettestreete", or route of the Britons and later became a Roman road linking the forts of Brougham and Ambleside.

My first ascent of High Street was in the company of Dick Hilton, who had been grievously wounded when he trod on a land mine during the Italian campaign of the 1939-45 war but recovered his health and made up for the loss of one leg with a wooden substitute. We walked on to High Street via Blea Tarn and

I still clearly recall the *thwack, thump* of boot and wooden leg as Dick followed me up.

Once, walking from High Street to the head of Nan Bield in mist and drizzle, I experienced one of those transformation scenes with which all Lakeland fell-walkers are familiar: the quickening wind, a movement in the cloud, the appearance of a patch of ultramarine blue, "big enough to patch a Dutchman's trousers".

Suddenly, in a blaze of sunlight, Smallwater changed from grey to blue, its crater-like rim being banded by yellow. In the mid-distance of the view, Haweswater sparkled with silver highlights.

I can never think about Haweswater without brooding over the lost buildings. Mardale church had a sturdy, battlemented tower and an interior half full of old woodwork. "It was a very pleasant little church, but usually cold." In winter, the light came from paraffin lamps.

Until the eighteenth century, those who died in Mardale were interred at Shap, eight miles away. A corpse was conveyed, on the back of a fell pony, up the zig-zags of an old peat track which became known as the Corpse Road. The cortege passed through Swindale.

When the reservoir builders came to clear out the graveyard of Mardale church, they attended to one hundred and four graves, which was relatively few considering its use for two centuries.

On my first visit to Haweswater, I chatted with several people who remembered Old Mardale. In succeeding years, as Editor of *Cumbria* magazine, I added to my store of information about a closely-knitted company of dalesfolk who spent their short lives in the sort of seclusion we cannot imagine in the high-tech, high speed, world of today.

The best-remembered years are those when the watermark is low and traces of the "lost" village appear to view. In the spring and summer of 1984, which were said to be the driest of the century, it was calculated that less than a million gallons of water were entering Haweswater each day and eighty million gallons were flowing out.

As the arid weeks passed, and the foundations of Mardale Green came into view, media men arrived with their notebooks and cameras. The man-made concrete cliff of the dam was almost fully exposed. Crowds of people, anxious to see what remained of Mardale Green and the farms, clogged the road.

Eventually that road had to be closed to traffic. The vendors of ice cream and hot dogs had a lively trade.

Re-built bridge in Wet Sleddale.

Mardale in History

THE Lake District is a monument to the Ice Ages—to a million years of recurrent glaciation. It was the playground of masses of slow-moving, powder-blue ice which planed the summits of the ridges and gave the valleys their characteristic U-shaped cross-sections. A lake like Haweswater was created by a gouging out and damming of the valley ends with the terminal moraines.

The ice sheets melted some ten thousand years ago. Much of the land was smothered in a stiff porridge which congealed into the boulder-clay which is still the main substrata of much of our landscape.

As the land stabilised after the ice, a tundra cover developed, traces of which—both botanical and zoological—persist on the high fells. A Pleistocene chilliness is still to be detected on the highest ground, where patches of snow might linger into June.

Trees crept northward as the climate permitted, with birch, willow, alder and pine covering the area to an elevation of some one thousand five hundred feet.

There followed a climax blanket of oak which persisted into historic times. The attack on the forest cover began with the appearance of man. Wordsworth wrote: "When the first settlers entered this region, they found it overspread with wood; forest trees, the fir, the oak, the ash and the birch had skirted the fells, tufted the hills and shaded the valleys, through centuries of silent solitude . . ."

Bronze Age folk may have established a defensive position on Birks Crag, to the west of Haweswater, where they were sheltered from the prevailing wind. Neolithic man had wielded the Great

Cumbrian Axe, its head formed of a particularly hard smooth rock quarried at the head of Langdale. By the Bronze Age, the axe, slashing and burning had produced substantial bare patches on the fells.

The early peoples, making their homes west of Haweswater, were on the sunny side of the dale and sheltered from the prevailing wind. The lake which would become known as Haweswater yielded fish and waterfowl. The district held abundant red deer, some of which would be a nuisance, grazing any cultivated land in the twilight.

Dark-haired Britons took refuge, in times of stress, on the headland known as Castle Crag, at an elevation of 1,250 feet. A rampart protected their living quarters. The Norsefolk, arriving along the western seaboard, penetrated the dales but are not known to have settled much beyond Measand, where they had a shieling. The name Mardale has a Norse connection, meaning the dalr (valley) of the mere.

In Norse times, a pattern of open sheep-runs was established and Norse terms were to remain in general use with the farming community of a valley like Mardale. Norse farmers had their winter homes and their saeters (summering areas) on high ground, where their stock continued the process of denuding the landscape of timber by grazing hard and close, preventing its natural regeneration.

Into the fell-locked valley, this fingermark of green and brown and blue on the eastern face of Lakeland, came monks from Heppe (now Shap) and an oratory was established—founded, some say, by Rudolphus Holme. Monastic establishments developed a lively trade in wool. The number of sheep increased.

For seven centuries, Mardale was the little kingdom of the Holme family. In a detailed obituary in the *Penrith Observer* following the death of Miss Holme, the last of the family, in

December, 1915, we are told: "There can be no doubt as to the great antiquity of the Holme family without in any way accepting the story of the origin."

The writer had in mind the somewhat fanciful story of Hugh Holme, whose forbears had reached England with William the Conqueror. Hugh found himself implicated in the Canterbury Conspiracy against King John and he fled north, intending to go to Scotland.

Hugh arrived in Mardale and, liking the area, lived for a time in a cave under Kidsty Pike—a cave known to this day as Hugh's Cave—and eventually, feeling it was safe to take part in social life, he married a local girl and they founded the Holme dynasty, which became known as "Kings of Mardale".

The Holme connection is evident from the frequent mention of the family in the Shap registers, Mardale being an ancient chapelry of Shap. When the Mardale register was begun in 1684, the second name entered was that of Elizabeth Holme. It was said that the family so largely occupied the book that it might almost have been kept for its benefit.

The name Holme occurs in the list of local vicars. Thomas Holme built the vicarage in 1860. The male line continued until 1885. The "Kings" were never knighted, much less crowned, for it needed no tickle from a real king's sword to heighten their status in Westmorland.

Plumes of smoke rose from Naddle in medieval times. The remains of small settlements have been found. The charcoal-burners had their pitsteads here until the middle of the nineteeth century. A tract of mixed indigenous woodland was clear-felled each thirty years or so and the wood carefully stacked and covered with earth to control the burning and prevent it from bursting into flame. The attendants lived in simple wooden huts and took it in turns to attend to the smouldering heap until charcoal was available to be bagged and transported for industrial purposes.

Tucked away in the memories of the oldest "amang us" are details of life in Mardale as it was early this century. A former Mardalian, who was at school prior to 1911, remembered Miss Holme, the last of the family, "a grand old lady", as she described her in an interview with Nigel Holmes of Radio Cumbria.

Radio listeners also heard memories of the time when Lord Lonsdale, a considerable landowner, held the fishing rights in Haweswater. Periodically, he and his posh friends gathered for the custom of "dragging the lake". They took the unsporting course of catching fish using a large net, which stretched from boat to shore. Any surplus fish were "dished out" among the folk of the valley. A Mardalian recalls: "We thought it was great. They were nearly always dragging the lake opposite the school. How we enjoyed watching them!"

The old boatman, Mr Kitching, who lived at Measand, and had a wife and fifteen children, was so impressed by Lordy and his society friends that he named his children after them. "They had some awful long strings of Christian names, such as Albert Ashington Donald Sykes and Elsie Violet Constance Fothergill May."

Mardale was on the packhorse route between Penrith and Kendal. The strings of sturdy animals, with loads ranging from wool to salt, passed over the Gatesgarth or Nan Bield passes for centuries before the transport revolution early in the nineteenth century. The leading horse in a train wore a bell on its harness which gave warning of its approach. Among the favoured ponies used were the black or brown variety bred on the eastern fells of Lakeland: a type of pony still to be seen around Haweswater.

Those same routes were possibly used by Scottish raiders intent on looting in the Kendal area. A Mardale tradition claims that a party of Scots was ambushed and slain by the Kendal Bowmen.

They were buried beside the track in an unmarked grave.

The restless spirit of Jimmie Lowther haunted the district, despite the efforts of the vicar to exorcise the ghost. Jimmie, a wild character who was frequently drunk, broke his neck while indulging in his favourite activity of steeplechasing. So sudden was his death, there was no time for him to repent of his sins. His restless ghost was a torment to local people until Jimmie's mortal remains were dug up for burial in a remote spot—on Hugh Laithes Pike, the highest part of Naddle Forest.

In the early days of tourism, when Lakeland was being "discovered" by people "of taste and leisure", Mardale Green was not so much lost as forgotten. Mrs E Lynn Linton, writing in 1864, about a walk from Ullswater, taking in Haweswater and High Street, found Mardale was "all very primitive and rough"; it was easy to understand how "fine gentlemen and ladies who travel with 'comforts' would shrink from the only place of entertainment at Hawes Water as they would shrink from an Indian's wigwam; and for some of the same reasons."

She mentioned the narrowness of the approach road and the diplomacy needed if two carriages met, for one would have to be backed into a gateway. Mardale Church was "by no means a rustic cathedral" and the *Dun Bull* "a wretched wayside public-house, where you can get eggs and bacon and nothing else—except the company of a tipsy parson lying in bed with his gin-bottle by his side." (Clearly, the authoress did not care for parsons).

The dominant event in the recent history of Mardale was its transformation into Manchesterdale, a process spread out between 1919 and 1941, when the Haweswater dam was brought into use. H H Symonds, an energetic walker, mentioned the old view of Haweswater and "the neat and seemly works of man against the craggy background of the fells." Now, with Manchester in control, "no bright hayfields, no houses, barns and cows are left."

To Symonds, the new motor road—"parapetted and dyked and drained"—was a disaster: an "irremediable line, a piece of desperate and level slicing gouged across nature's own gradual curves. This embattled road glowers down on the dalehead."

Norman Nicholson, author and poet, did not know Mardale before the Flood and he was not one of those who rushed into the dying valley to have a last drink at the *Dun Bull* or to pull on the bell rope of a stricken church. To him, the shores of the new Haweswater had "a kerb of detritus" reminding him of "a half-empty swimming pool". When we chatted at his home in Millom, he mentioned the loss of the intermediate land when the surface of the water rose with the completion of the dam. What remained were high hills standing up to their waists in cold water!

In 1937, when the transformation was occurring, the authors of a book entitled *The Lakeland Landscape* (Clark and Thompson) visited the area and wrote lyrically of the old Mardale, this "pastoral paradise graced by its lovely lake and happily farmed by generations of dalesmen, each sheltering in a picturesque stone farmhouse standing in the midst of the typical lakeland holding, part valley, part fell...

"Today a huge dam is being constructed across the northern end of the valley, and soon the waters will rise to those uncanny marks on the sides of the hills. The church has been demolished and the tower blown up. The friendly *Dun Bull* is to drown..."

Visiting Mardale was a haunting experience with, south of the dam, the farmhouses "standing abandoned, empty ghosts, where happy families once enjoyed a hard, free life. It is like travelling in a country stricken with the plague..."

The Natural Scene

It is sad that our children will never see the world as we see it. Each generation leaves its mark on its surroundings and, as civilisation advances and population increases, wild nature is tamed more and more to man's service...
The Manchester Guardian, October 1, 1918.

It nearly always rained when I was there. I'd look out of the window of Flake How and see the rain coming down in sweeps.
Ethel Taylor, 1993.

AT THE dalehead, the eye is claimed by the solemn bulk of Harter Fell. On the other side, there's a steady climb to the summit. Looking up from the car park at the head of Haweswater, the fell is everyone's idea of a mountain, pyramidal and well-fissured.

Much less imposing is High Street, to the right, which is so flat on top it looks as though it has been made using pencil and ruler. Interest is added by the fell's angular spurs. My memories of High Street are mainly of the springtime, when a cock ring ouzel—our north-country nightingale—is uttering its cool, clear notes in the echo-chamber around Blea Tarn.

I scramble on to Riggindale Crag, with more ring ouzels for company, and behold a stark scene, with bare ridges and an uncluttered dale being grazed by sheep, deer and fell ponies. The stocky black ponies give Riggindale an Icelandic appearance.

High Street? At 2,700 feet, I reach the ancient trackway running for a dozen miles or so at an elevation of over 2,000 feet. To the Romans, it was a handy if breezy connection of 26 miles, easily covered in one day, between their forts at Brocavum [Brougham] and Galava [Ambleside].

High Street is the sort of terrain I associate with the dotterel, a plover-like bird, one of the rarest nesting species in Britain. I have seen small "trips" of passage migrants on several northern hills, and towards the end of April my eyes ache as I look for them on High Street where, in the wicked old days, gunners were active, hoping to meet the brisk demand by anglers for feathers they could use when tying "flies".

Once when having a snack meal on Kidsty Pike, I heard the call of a peevish crow and, sneaking a view over the edge, saw it was harassing a golden eagle. So near was the bird I saw the tips of its primary feathers were widely separated, like rows of lean brown fingers. The eagle, unflap-

The Dotterel.

able in fact as well as manner, spiralled upwards to become little more than a black dot against a cloud.

The eagle is a magnificent addition to the fauna of the Haweswater area. The Scottish naturalist, Seton Gordon, wrote (1955): "There is no reason why, if not molested, the golden eagle should not return to the high hills of the Lake District and of North Wales, from which strongholds it has long been exterminated."

In discussions with Ernest Bleazard, who was then the curator of natural history at Tullie House, Carlisle, we were conscious that in a southward spread of the golden eagle, a pair was now nesting just north of Solway Firth, within easy viewing range of Lakeland's northern fells.

Confusion has existed in Lakeland between the golden eagle and its cousin, the white-tailed eagle, a massive bird which a friend of mine likened to "a flying barn door". A pair of white-tails used to nest on Wallow Crag, Haweswater, also on Buck Crag in adjacent Martindale. The indomitable Mr Thorpe, photographer, found it difficult to obtain pictures of these birds because "in each instance, the birds nested in the shadow of a great rock, so that no gleams of sunlight could reach their gloomy eyrie."

I imagine that "Heron Crag" above Riggindale is a name derived from erne, or white-tailed eagle. Any number of "eagle" sightings in Lakeland were, in fact, of buzzards, which are relatively common. A useful maxim is: "If you are in doubt, it's a buzzard!"

Golden eagles nested in the Mardale area in 1970 and 1971. When I was editing the magazine *Cumbria,* R D Humber wrote me a piece in which he recalled Conservation Year, 1970, and the high hopes we had that an eagle pair would raise young in our district. By March 31 there was one egg in the nest. By mid-April, the hen bird was sitting two eggs. Early in June, one eaglet had hatched.

On June 28, Bob Humber was in that area when his companion saw the eagle coming right over them. "I searched the blue sky and saw the great bird sailing like a bronzed shield above a whirling flight of rooks which were in the fell country feeding on antler moth caterpillars."

For a time the smaller male eagle seemed intent on catching a rook. "It dropped one wing and descended at terrific speed. The rooks...scattered like black rags in a gale. The eagle flickered the tips of its wings and shot away with an astonishing burst of speed."

Of scarce terrestrial animals, the pine marten is most elusive. MacPherson, in his *Fauna of Lakeland* (1892), mentions the former widespread distribution of the pine marten in woodland.

Persecution and the loss of timber led to the survivors existing on the open fells. "The marten is almost compelled to live on the roughest and most broken ground that it can find," wrote McPherson. "On an open, level plain it could easily be run down even by a fast cur-dog."

So the marts of the nineteenth century frequented "the high mountains of Central and Western Lakeland", the list including Haweswater and Mardale. We are told that "the marten usually prefers to live on the sunny side of a fell" and that "foxes and martens do not flourish very well on the same ground, for 'when foxes is rank, marts is scarce'."

MacPherson records that the dalesmen hunted pine martens only in the winter-time, "and generally find the quarry hiding up in a brossen rock where there is a deal of heather."

At Naddle, overlooking the lower end of Haweswater, the summer light slants between thin and tattered groups of trees— between birch, ash, hazel, rowan and sessile oak. Such mixed deciduous woodland is one of the glories of Lakeland.

Naddle is composed of several woods, with Low Forest and Guerness Wood forming the largest timbered tract and extending southwards along a boulder-strewn slope above the reservoir as far as Guerness Gill. In the east, where the slopes above Naddle Beck have an easier gradient, lie High Forest and Mirkside.

A wood like Naddle contains the two characteristic and widely distributed wild cherries, the gean and the bird cherry, known to Dorothy Wordsworth, sister of the illustrious Wordsworth, as the heckberry. The bareness of winter is relieved by two common everygreens—holly and yew.

William Wordsworth, in his *Guide to the Lakes* (1820) mentions that the old type of woodland had wych elm, "with underwood of hazel, the white and black thorn and hollies; in moist places alders and willows abound." He also made the perceptive observation that such woodland would at one time extend far up the fells, into areas which have long been bare.

In Naddle, mosses are arrayed on rocks and trees. Among the species of moss is the rare Ostrich Plume *(Ptilium crista-castrensis).* Naddle's easterly position and associated climatic factors influence the composition of the rich bryophyte and lichen flora, which differ markedly from those of the more "oceanic" sites in the western and central Lake District.

Naddle, this relic area of the indigenous woodland of Old Lakeland, has a proportion of trees which must be over two centuries old. It is an ageing wood, with few saplings to follow on because of over-browsing by sheep and deer. Shepherding is not made easy for the farmers by a mini-jungle of ferns, obscuring holes and crevices.

Most of the sheep around Haweswater live on open fells. Now mainly of the Swaledale breed, they survive where many species of sheep would starve. I have seen a thousand sheep—yows and lambs—being shepherded at one time on the Naddle side of Haweswater.

At Naddle, the Hill Farming Research Organisation has investigate the impact of sheep grazing on the ecosystem. By manipulating stock rates, and by seasonal use, it is hoped that the wood will be helped to regenerate naturally and continue to play host to a limited number of sheep and deer.

Naddle supports many birds, including buzzards, pied flycatchers and wood warblers. Woodcock sit motionless on their eggs amid a litter of dead leaves on the woodland floor. One old chap told me he could detect a crouching woodcock by the sparkle in its eye. Both roe and red deer flit like shadows through the twilight.

Naddle House is "a good sheep spot", though the old farm was much changed with the completion of the Haweswater dam and the flooding of much valuable low ground. The sheep stocks belonging to Grove Brae, Chapel Hill, Flake How and Naddle were henceforth bound to Naddle House.

These north-country sheep deliver their lambs towards the end of April and into May. Riggindale and Waters stocks have actually lambed on the fell, the others being brought down to low ground. Sheep are naturally inclined to fall back into Riggindale during starvation-time [early spring] and they tend to go higher when their lambs are strong at foot and the hill-ends are greening-up after snow.

Haweswater, which is said to have taken its name from a Norse settler called Hafr, was in pre-reservoir days the highest of English lakes (at 694 feet above sea level).

The western area (High Water) and the eastern end (Low Water) were divided by the delta of Measand Beck—a fan-like tract which gave Old Haweswater a waist like a wasp. The natural lake had an average depth of about forty feet, with a maximum of just over a hundred feet.

Now that Haweswater is a reservoir, it is often choppy and chilling, like an inland sea, and the dam fits the northern end like a cork in a bottle. At the other end are scenic changes, related to variations in the water level. The ridge from High Street ends at the waterside with The Rigg, a finger of land pointing at the island called Wood Howe, near which old Mardale Church and other buildings of the "lost" village once stood.

When a party of folk from Penrith visited the area in the autumn of 1918, having heard of the proposal to create a reservoir, they were keen to sample its beauty before the Flood. The Penrithians stood aside to allow a flock of fifty or sixty geese to pass on their way from Bampton Common, "a big flat basin under the hills where thousands are bred during the season".

Suddenly, out of the sunshine, the visitors "passed into the shadow of dark scowling hills and a gentle, rippling expanse of lake lay before our eyes. On its farthest side, no road approached and the steel-grey mountains sprang sheer from its edge."

No boat crossed the "lonely waters" save that of fishermen who had Lord Lonsdale's permission to be there. The grassland abutting the lake was "a stretch of greensward waving with the bronze tassels of the wild burnet and the blue heads of scabious."

Where the ground was sodden, bog asphodel brightened the turf with its coral-red seed spikes. In the mortared walls grew tufts of parsley fern. "The whole area was vocal with the musical brawling of thousands of watercourses racing down the hillsides. Sometimes, they hid themselves underground, to boil out again as little crosspatch cascades."

Anglers now arrive at Haweswater intent on luring trout. Also surviving in the cold depths are two piscatorial curiosities of Lakeland—skelly and char. It has been estimated that seventy per cent of the fish in the reservoir are skelly, twenty five per cent are trout and there are just a few char.

It is theorised that the ancestors of the present char, once migratory, were trapped in several lakes at the time of the Ice Age. Though spending most of their lives in deep water, they enter the shallows to spawn. MacPherson (1892) was surely exaggerating when he recorded that when skellies lay in shallow water [presumably at spawing time] "vast numbers are taken at one draught" to be transported by horse and cart to the nearest towns. "They weigh about five ounces each and eight hundred are commonly reckoned as many as one horse can draw."

Skelly became scarce in Ullswater but remained moderately common in Old Haweswater. The Rev T Hodson told McPherson that although the fish were procured with nets almost exclusively, he had recently caught a fine specimen of a Haweswater skelly with a fly.

Lord Lonsdale and his guests went fishing with a very large net. An image was fixed by Jacob Thompson, a Penrith-born artist, who was staying with the Bland family of Measand Hall. On Thompson's picture are recognisable figures—Lord Lonsdale himself, Lord Justice and Lady Brett, the Earl of Malmesbury, Captain F W Lowther and a Mr Robinson, who was Lonsdale's secretary.

The artist wrote to a friend: "At Haweswater, shut out from intrusive visitors who only kill time, working on pictures you may shortly see in London, and sharing with those who are dear to me the pleasures of intellectual retirement, we spend happy lives among the mountains. Among scenes like these, man feels the power and goodness of God more intensely than in the din and bustle of a crowded city. We shall leave Haweswater with regret."

A G Bradley (1901) wrote of Haweswater as being the best trouting lake in the land, if you were not over-critical as to the size of fish caught. "But the trout here are really free risers, an admirable quality which the strictest preservation cannot always ensure.

"Memories of a soft and breezy June day spent upon Haweswater, and of its sporting little trout, will remain with me for a long time..."

His Lordship's bailiff released some rainbow trout in Small Water and had then to plod up to the tarn with a net when fish of this type were needed for the table at Lowther Castle. The trout of Blea Water were said not to keep for long after being taken from the water. Within an hour, they were unpalatable. Someone suggested there were lingering traces of the rock's volcanic origin...

William Kitching, son of Thomas and Jane Kitching, of Measand Farm, died in 1901. Both father and son, described as boatmen, were in Lonsdale's employ and were well-known to the trout fishers of the two counties [Westmorland and Cumberland].

Haweswater is not a quiet lake. The Canada geese sometimes give a round of raucous calls and there is a medley of seaside sounds from Wood Howe, where big gulls nest. A screeching, almost like someone tearing coarse fabric, may be heard in the woods near Burnbanks, where the bird life includes the jay, a jazzily-patterned member of the crow family.

Canada Geese.

33

From the painting "Drawing the Net at Haweswater", by Jacob Thompson (1867).

Farmers and Shepherds

When it is a bad year for the sheep, there are hard times in the dale.
                                                    Isaac Hinchliffe (1925).

As long as there are sheep on the fells, there'll be a Mardale Meet.
I'm good for a few more yet...
                            Isaac Cookson, on his 61st attendance (1952).

There's neah fooak nowadays to what they were: what, fooak used
to be a yerd atween t'shooders (shoulders) and a foot atween t'een
(eyes).
                            Rev Joseph Whiteside, of Mardale, 1902.

OLD Mardale reeked of sheep—Herdwick sheep, big of bone, thin
of flesh, coarse of wool, but perfectly tuned to the crags and ridges
of Lakeland. The farmers claimed for the Herdwick an extra rib.

An equally fanciful story tells that Herdwicks were descended
from a galleon of the Spanish Armada, wrecked on the Cumbrian
coast. Some sheep made it to the shore and bred on the craggy
fells. Others say the Herdwick was introduced by the Norsemen.

What we see is the indigenous sheep of the north-west mountains, much improved by selected breeding and "tidied up" last
century.

The Herdwick is a relatively small sheep with a frosty grey-white
face. The body is deep and round, with a coat dark in young stock
and becoming greyer with age, when it has a soft, creamy-white
undercoat.

The Lakeland system of sheep farming is to have a specified
number of Herdwicks as the property of the landlord, a number
which remains at the farm through changes of tenancy, to preserve
the heaf-going instinct by which sheep are attached to the tracts

of fell on which they were reared.

The Mardale farmer was only vaguely aware of the number of sheep he owned apart from when he conducted a census at the summer clipping and the autumn dipping. The sheep were counted and any stray animals returned to their rightful owners. What began as an informal group of friends and neighbours became formalised as the Mardale Shepherds' Meet.

The code of honour of the fells decrees that strays be brought down to the Meet to be identified by reference to their ear and wool markings (lug marks, wool stripes and pops!), any sheep remaining unclaimed at the local Meet being sent to other Meets and, if still not identified, being kept for a year before they might be sold to defray the expense of their "keep".

Sheep marks take on several forms which can be bewildering to the layman. Punching, cropping, key-bitting, fold-bitting, ritting, upper and under halving and forking are some of the more common methods of "lug" marking, which may be on one or both ears. A veteran farmer told the *Cumberland and Westmorland Herald* representative at the Meet in 1952: "T'combinations are like t'perms in t'football pools."

The wool markings, renewed annually after clipping, are generally strokes of red, blue or black, or perhaps they take the form of the initials of the owner. Horn markings are a further aid to identity.

Nowadays, the Herdwick is frequently crossed with the Sward'l (Swaledale)—and then crossed back again when a particularly hard winter thins out the breeding flock. Beatrix Potter, who became Mrs Heelis, wife of a Lakeland solicitor, was a champion of the Herdwick breed of sheep and, leaving many farms in central Lakeland to The National Trust in her will, decreed that a stock of Herdwicks should remain on each of them.

Sheep farming is possible because those unsung heroes, the

sheepdogs—often cur dogs, later good quality collies—made it possible for the flocks to be gathered from the fells in quick time.

It is relatively easy to farm in Lakeland in summer; it's the winter—the long, hard winter—that tests the stuff a farmer is made of.

In the little farmhouses of Old Mardale, on winter neets, when friends called in for a crack [gossip], it was almost entirely sheep talk which engaged them. If any other topic intruded, it would be fox-hunting. Isaac Greenhow, of Goosemire, was able to talk a little about gardening. Isaac had a rose-bush on which the flowers were white. They were said to bloom at Christmas. 'Appen!

The Mardale obsession with sheep is summed up by a report in the *Cumberland and Westmorland Herald* in the 1880s—an account of a boon clip, when neighbours and friends gathered at a farm, in this case that of Hugh P Holme, to clip the fleeces from the fell-going flock and then to enjoy themselves with feasting and song.

"The morning opened beautifully fine. As early as three o'clock a large number of Mr Holme's friends assembled at Mardale. An early start was made in the collection and the clipping of some 700 sheep. The animals were in grand condition and the clipping progressed expeditiously, refreshments consisting of bread, cheese and nut-brown ale, being served without stint.

"The clipping was completed about three o'clock in the afternoon and the workers adjourned to arrange their toilets. Later, about 120 sat down to an excellent dinner, Mr Holme occupying the chair and Mr W R Mounsey the vice-chair.

"Dinner over, the company adjourned to a field overlooking Haweswater, where a series of sports took place. Amongst the prizes were two fleeces of wool offered by Mr Holme for wrestling. Later an adjournment was made to the dining room where in toast and song a very enjoyable evening was spent."

At times, red deer from Martindale joined the sheep on the vast sheep range of the fells. Noble Ewbank used to relate that in hard winters, the deer appeared in search of food. He added, with twinkling eyes: "A lot more comes ower nor goes back." One determined stag reached Bampton, where it was stalked by two men who shot it in the river.

Sheep Clipping.

A herd of red deer, of Exmoor origin, is said to have been introduced to Naddle Forest by Lord Lonsdale. "These are the stags mostly responsible for the predatory raids on Mardale's meagre fields."

Most of the farms of Old Mardale were tenanted. Miss Noble, in her Bampton history, quotes an indenture of 1660 relating to an arbitration between the Lord of the Manor of Thornthwaite and his tenants, thirteen of whom lived in Mardale. Six were named

Holme, two Haton, and the others Strickland, Jackson, Bowman, Dennison and Browne.

In Measand, by the west shore of Haweswater, there were eight tenants—three Wrights, three Hodgsons, a Noble and an Aray. (By 1925, the number of tenants had shrunk to three in Mardale and one in Measand).

Isaac Hinchliffe, in *A Backwater of Lakeland,* quotes from "an old account" written about 1825, with its evocative account of life in the dale before that date: "The chimneys of the houses were formerly of the most capacious extent and served not only as larders, wherein joints of meat were suspended to dry for winter use, but also as the favourite gathering places for the inmates of the dwellings.

"Under the smoky dome sat the women knitting, or spinning wool and flax, the men carding the wool, and the schoolboy conning the barbarous Latinity of Lilly; while the grandsire of the house amused the party with tales of Border strife and superstitious legends."

The writer referred to the wooden chest which served as "the common depository or strong room of the house." Wool from the backs of the native sheep was home-spun and woven into clothing. "The furniture of the house consisted of a long oaken table, with a bench on each side, where the whole family including servants ate together. Chairs of heavy wainscot work with high arms were in use, but the usual movable seats were three-footed stools.

"On winter evenings, lighting was provided by candles made of peeled rushes, dipped in the hot fat of fried bacon. The candlestick was a light upright pole, fixed in a log of wood, and furnished with pincers for holding the rushes.

"Hinchliffe noted that the usual food consisted of leavened bread (made of a kind of black oats), boiled animal food, the produce of the dairy, and a limited supply of vegetables."

Within living memory, the Mardale community had shrunk to nine inhabited houses and about forty residents. It was predominantly a farming community and the four principal farms were Chapel Hill, Goosemire, Grove Brae and Flake How, occupied by the Hudsons, Greenhows, Watsons and Edmondsons respectively. The Kitchings were associated with Chapel Hill and Measand. In later times, the Daffurns of the *Dun Bull,* at the head of the dale, combined farming with inn-keeping.

There were comings and goings. For example, the Edmondsons farmed both Flake How and Whelter, though the latter farmhouse was not permanently occupied. Hannah Edmondson, who became a Newton and left the dale for a farm at Knipe on her marriage in 1915, returned to Flake How to visit her parents, who remained here until, in the 1920s, they were succeeded by one of their daughters, Maggie, who had married Jack Lancaster. When the dam was built, the Lancasters moved to Hesket-new-Market.

A typical farmhouse, of seventeenth century date, was unpretentiously made of local stone and slate. A substantial porch had a pitched roof. Lime-washing the front of a building reflected pride of possession and gave the dale a pleasant appearance. Mardale had a futuristic pattern of drystone walls, many miles of walls, bordering meadow and pasture and extending up the fellsides to take in some of the rough grazings.

Now a Lakeland wall is really two walls in one, standing side by side, tapering with height, bound together by large stones known as "throughs" and capped by a row of stones. The most difficult material for walling is the beck-bottom stuff, which is smooth and rounded. One old waller said, with a smile: "You needed to sandpaper 'em before you put 'em in place."

A typical family had a few acres of meadowland for making hay, which was harvested by horse and simple machines. Oats were grown for porridge or to feed to the poultry. Grain was taken to a local mill, such as Bampton or Widewath at Butterwick, to be ground.

Ethel Taylor who, as a small child, visited her grandparents' house, Flake How, says: "It was a special treat to go to Mardale for a holiday. They would grow what they wanted. They were pretty self-supporting."

Whatever happened, they always had plenty of mutton. A popular pudding at the mid-day meal was "clootie", a suet pastry with layers of fruit of various kinds, rolled up like a Swiss roll and boiled in a cloth for several hours. Once a month, groceries were ordered from a representative of a firm at Penrith for later delivery.

Grandfather, Thomas Edmondson, was a typical dale farmer who, when he went to the fell to "leuk" sheep, generally rode a fell pony and had one or two dogs in train. Grandmother was called Isabella, and they had a moderately large family—Tom, John, Maggie, Annie, Hannah, Polly Ada.

Another child, Isaac, died in boyhood, having been kicked while playing football. He "took bad" at a time when "they couldn't do much for such complaints." (Isaac was buried at Mardale and, in the 1930s, re-interred at Shap).

Ethel was at Flake How when the hay crop was being taken in. Much of the work in a meadow was performed by hand, using rakes and forks. There was little machinery and horse-and-sled were a common sight, being also used on the edge of the fells in autumn, when bracken was gathered as bedding for the young stock over the winter.

A regular visitor at Flake How was Mr Barham, the last vicar of Mardale, a somewhat eccentric man who, it was said, slept in a bed which was surrounded by fencing. It was even whispered that he had a gun. "He was frightened that someone would break in." The vicar had many of his meals with the Edmondsons of Flake How.

And Grandma regularly sent baskets full of newly-baked food—scones, currant and apple pasties—to the vicarage.

The Penrith shops bought Mardale butter. Mrs Taylor recalls watching cows being hand-milked, and the milk being placed in a shallow container and left until the cream had settled, when the "blue" milk was drawn off and the cream stored in a crock. Once a week, it was churned to make butter, a somewhat tricky process which might take twenty minutes or a couple of hours, depending on the weather. The cream was slow to turn during a warm spell in summer.

"Grandma kneaded the butter until all the butter-milk had drained away. The men liked a drink of butter-milk when they came in from the fields. Butter was patted into oblong blocks using Scotch Hands [made of wood]. Grannie usually stamped the Flake How butter with a distinctive pattern—a rose."

Towards the end of the year, the Edmondson's pig was killed by Mr Lowis, Herbert McCormick or Jack Ewbank. The man who did the work usually arrived on a Saturday and, when the deed was done, repaired to the *Dun Bull* for a hard-earned pint. Jack Taylor says: "He had maybe got 7s.6d for doing the job and he'd spent most of it at the inn."

The pig was slaughtered in a most primitive way. It had its throat cut. Ethel told me she used to run away on pig-killing day so that she did not hear the squeals. Only the squeal was wasted.

The blood was kept stirred as the basis of black puddings, the head used for making potted meat, the trotters cooked until they formed a type of jelly and meat was minced as sausage meat and stuffed into intestines which had been turned inside out and cleaned.

Much was given away to neighbours, but the major pieces of pork were cured in salt petre and brown sugar and hung up to dry, when they might keep for years. "That was real bacon."

Mrs Bell, of Shap, a niece of the Daffurns of the *Dun Bull,* told me much about the hard, unrelenting domestic life on the farm in Mardale. She was hired as a servant girl when she was fourteen years of age; she went to Chapel Hill, at the recommendation of the vicar, and thus managed to avoid having to attend the hirings.

Her mother accompanied her to the farm and all her possessions were in a "canvas trunk". During that first term of six months, she started work at 5 a.m. and finished between 10-30 and 11-00 at night; she went out of the dale only once and never spent a penny except for the collection at church on Sunday.

Monday was washing day, an operation performed manually and likely to reduce the women of the house to prostration. In Mardale "we went outside the house to the stick shed, where the set-pot stood. We got a dozen bucketfuls of water from a pump over the sink in the house. The fire was lit early. You were running late if you didn't have the clothes on the line before 8-30 in the summer."

Washing took place with the help of dolly tub, dolly legs, a mangle with wooden rollers—and dolly blue.

The cattle being kept by Mardale folk were of the Shorthorn type, providing milk which, as related, was used at the farm or converted into butter for sale in Penrith.

When T Barbour was the constable at Bampton, with oversight of Mardale, he was consulted about a matter in dispute between father and son. Should a new-calved heifer be kept or sold? After appearing to give the matter grave consideration, he advised the sale as advocated by the son.

The animal topped the market. As Mr Barbour told me: "I was pleasantly surprised at the publicity my decision received."

A Few Verses from the Mardale Meet Hunting-Song

(Not great words but containing some pawky humour and evocative of the spirit of the time—the hunt, booze-up at the *Dun Bull,* the church service, a drive to Lowther, then back to Mardale and a reflection on a hunting life after death. The chorus was sung after each verse, which must have made this old song inordinately long).

Now, listen, my lads, and let the roof ring,
For a song of the chase I'm going to sing,
To Joe Bowman, the huntsman, hearty and hale,
And his far famous pack—the Hounds of Mardale.

Chorus

Tally Ho! Tally Ho! Tally Ho! with a ding,
Let the wilds of old Mardale with "Tally Ho!" ring,
Tho' the flowers of the forest are withered and gone,
Old Joe's on the mountains, so, boys, follow on,
Tho' storms sweep the mountains and thunder resounds,
Joe Bowman, despite them, will follow the hounds.

Now we're on Reynard's track with the hounds in full cry,
O'er hill and down dale, and then up to the sky,
To the bold beetling crags of the mist and the storm,
Where Reynard seeks earth, Hark away! 'Tis the horn.
Joe Bowman is calling, draw deeper your breath,
And let every good hunter be in at the death.

Now list' to the wail of that wild "Tally Ho!"
Poor Reynard has given his brush to the foe.
No more he will roam these lone mountain glens,
Or steal off at night with the farmer's old hens.
The rover is dead, the chase now is o'er,
So let us return to the Dun Bull once more.

We return to the Inn as the shades of night fall,
The Landlord and Molly are there in the hall,
The rafters re-echo with wild hunting lays,
And Mardale's old Inn is all in a blaze.
Old farmers, young shepherds, keen hunters—drink deep!
For to-night we are met, Mardale's revels to keep.

Dark and wild grows the night, and louder the din,
'Till you'd think that the Devil had taken the Inn.
With laughter and song, and calling for more,
Confused and combined in one glorious uproar,
Each neighbour, a brother, companion and friend,
What a pity this jollification must end.

As the flush of the dawn illumines the sky,
The roar of the travellers is starting to die.
A dozen, contented, sleep under a table,
While a few go to bed—when they find they are able.
Old Joe ever talking, unsteady yet steadfast,
Plays cards with the heroes and sits up for breakfast.

T'Auld Church

Mardale has perhaps the smallest church in England. In the doorway hangs a plate testifying to the virtues of a past vicar who ministered to his lonely flock for fifty years.

The Manchester Guardian, 1918.

MARDALE Church, dedicated to the Holy Trinity, was indeed one of the smallest in Lakeland—comparable with Wastwater, Wythburn and Swindale. It had seating for fifty people and, towards the end of its life, served a local population of about seventy. Worshippers were summoned by the clanging of a bell which had been cast in 1825.

It is assumed that the church was built on the site of an oratory which stood on what became Chapel Hill—the "Chappell Hill" of the Shap registers. The first reference to Mardale, in 1670, is taken to prove the existence of a church at that time. At the dissolution of the monasteries, Mardale came into the extensive Shap parish.

Mardale Church, of seventeeth century date, with its walls over three feet thick, was typical of many another in the fell country, being low, broad and simply furnished. A special feature was the oaken gallery, dated 1737. It was installed at the time an oak screen and communion rails were fitted. Mardale's tower was somewhat younger than the church and larger than the average for a small dalehead community.

The Mardale registers began in 1684, the second name to be entered being that of Elizabeth Holme. A deed of consecration of the churchyard, dated 1728, over-stated the case by claiming that "this Church was erected and Divine Service performed in it

45

from time immemorial."

The first burial at Mardale, of John Turner, Mardale Green, took place in 1729, prior to which a dead person was conveyed, strapped to the back of a horse or pony, up the zig-zags of what became known as the Corpse Road, which at its highest point has an elevation of 1,656 ft and leads to Swindale and Shap.

Hall Caine, in his novel *The Shadow of a Crime,* told how some wicked man died in Mardale with an undivulged crime on his conscience. As his coffin, strapped to the back of a horse, was in transit to Shap for burial, a thunderstorm arose and the horse bolted. For three months it roamed Swindale Common—an area of many humps and hollows—and the coffin remained on its back. In due course, the horse was captured and the man buried at Shap.

The last to be borne over the fells to Shap was John Holme, of Brackenhowe, on June 7, 1736—some seven years after the first interment in Mardale churchyard.The chapel was granted its own burial ground when the Mardalians complained of the distance to the parish church causing "excessive expense for funerals," and declaring that "the souls as well as the bodies of infants taken to be baptised are endangered."

The mural tablet in the porch of old Mardale Church, to which reference has been made, relates to the Rev Richard Hebson, who for over fifty years was pastor of the chapelry and for a still longer period served as "a most diligent" Master of Measand School. Hebson died on September 25, 1799, aged 75.

A row of tombstones set against the east wall were of the Holme family, formerly known as the "Kings of Mardale" and represented at the dawn of this century by the benevolent Mrs Holme. Indeed, two Holme brothers—one of whom was vicar at the time—had the vicarage built and presented it to the living.

The *Ruridecanal Magazine* for the 1890s evokes the Victorian heyday of Mardale Church which, though tucked away at the head of a secluded dale, had a diverse social life. In some respects, it was primitive still. The path for those attending the evening service in winter was lit by an oil lamp. Inside the church, paraffin lights brought a responsive glow from items of brasswork. A harmonium wheezed an accompaniment to the hymn-singing.

The energetic vicar of the time was the Rev W Terry, who became known as "Terry of Mardale". He was here for sixteen years and then moved on to the parish of Waventon and Dundraw, where he served for another twenty-four years before retiring to Ulverston to live with his eldest daughter. She was at that time headmistress of the Grammar School.

The Rev J Whiteside, vicar of Shap, wrote of Terry that "he remains a model to the fellside clergy whose lot is cast in very lonely and difficult surroundings". He introduced slide shows on topics as diverse as "Paying Poultry" and "Mission Work in Japan". So the Mardalians, though hemmed in by high fells, were not left in ignorance about the big world beyond. People were attracted to Mardale, as for the annual Mardale tea and concert, when wagonettes brought people from the surrounding parishes.

Not only was it the heyday of the "magic lantern". Another ingenious device, the phonograph, brought tinny recorded music into the dale. People responded generously, one of them meeting the cost of restoring the rails outside the church. Small boys were told not to mis-use them by swinging on them!

The numbers attending Mardale church climbed until, on a single day in March, 1894, three baptisms were recorded. These were of the son and daughter of William and Eliza Kitching, of Measand and for Joan and Agnes Richardson Hudson, of the *Dun Bull Hotel,* the "precious gift" of a daughter, who was christened Agnes Ann.

When in 1898, seven-year-old Isaac Edmondson of Flake How, died, the verse selected by the Vicar reflected the staunch religious faith of that period:

> *Sleep on, beloved! Sleep and take thy rest,*
> *Lay down thy head upon thy Saviour's breast;*
> *We loved thee well, but Jesus loves thee best.*
> *Good-night.*

Mr J Hudson's witness was commended by the vicar for he was a long-serving churchwarden. Scarcely an issue of the magazine was free of a vote of thanks to Mrs Holme, the uncrowned Queen of Mardale, and its Lady Bountiful. On one occasion she subsidised a trip to Blackpool by meeting half the cost. In 1895, Mrs Holme gave the young people a pre-Christmas treat at her home. "As the weather was stormy, a conveyance was sent round to collect the younger ones." The treat included tea and games. "Fruit and sweets were lavished upon all..."

On Christmas morning, the Church choir sang the anthem: "I will lift up mine eyes unto the hills". When the Sunday School prizegiving took place (in the day school) a programme of sacred songs and solos, recitations and a reading, preceded the distribution of books—by Mrs Holmes, of course—and there follow a "magic lantern" show. Oranges and pieces of cake were distributed.

Mardale was placed on the list of parishes to which an annual grant of Bibles and Prayer Books was made by the Lord Wharton trustees, the books to be distributed among those children who memorised certain passages from the Bible.

Mrs Holme met the cost of fuel and light for Mardale Church and among her extra gifts in 1895 were a complete set of Psalters and a new length of matting for the aisle. Miss Barrow provided altar flowers and Mr Sowerby voluntarily rang the bell and was the verger.

Continued on page 57.

Above: A car is being driven along the dusty road lying west of Haweswater. A new road was blasted on the Naddle side of the valley.
Below: Mardale Church, demolished by the reservoir-builders. Much of the stonework was re-cycled, being used in the draw-off tower.

M. C. W. W.
← PUBLIC FOOTPATH
GATESCARTH PASS TO LONGSLEDDALE
NAN BIELD PASS TO KENTMERE
FELLSIDE TRACK TO BAMPTON VIA
NORTH WEST SHORE

Above, left: Mission Hall at Burnbanks.
Right: One of the cast iron Waterworks signposts.
Below: The Old School, re-built at Walmgate Head and now being restored.

Above: The canteens at Burnbanks, a shanty village where some 200 workmen were accommodated.
Below: Haweswater United, who played on a sloping field.

Top: Fell ponies grazing near Haweswater. *Above:* Signpost at the start of the Corpse Road. *Right:* The Haweswater Hotel, built by Manchester Waterworks.

Top: Bishop of Carlisle, the Archdeacon and Lord Mayor of Manchester at the last service held in Mardale Church. *Above:* Syd Wear. *Right:* Mrs Bell, of the Dun Bull inn.

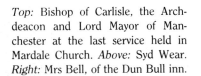

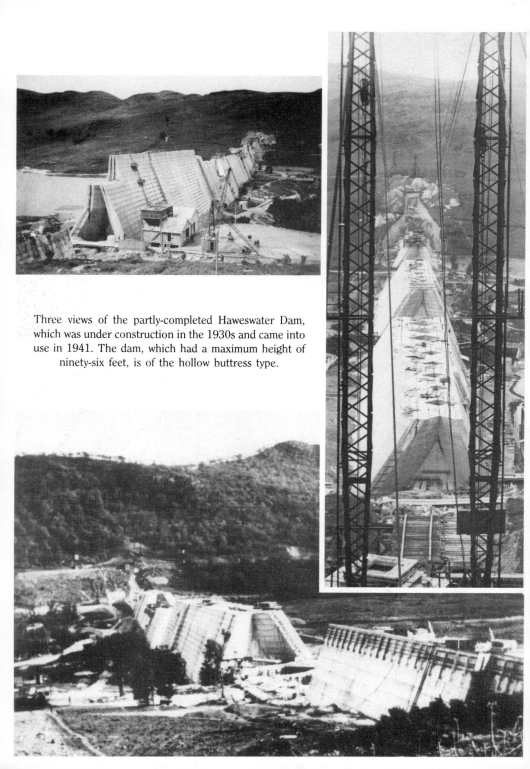

Three views of the partly-completed Haweswater Dam, which was under construction in the 1930s and came into use in 1941. The dam, which had a maximum height of ninety-six feet, is of the hollow buttress type.

Above: Constructing the new road up the dale. A crushing plant provides aggregate.
Heavy railborne equipment was in use.
Below: Tunnelling near Haweswater as part of the extensive system of aqueducts.

Haweswater in a Drought Year

Above: Canon Baily and Woode How.
Below: Mr Kitching, the shepherd, and one
of the 17th century bridges.

The Sunday School treat included races for special prizes—toys and sweets. After tea in the schoolroom there was a cruise in Mrs Holme's rowing boat—with Mr Veitch as skipper—to the shore near Naddle Forest, where two hours were spent in games and sports. "The return voyage was made at six and the rest of the evening taken up in watching local views projected by "magic lantern".

In autumn, the Shap Cyclists' Club visited Mardale one Sunday afternoon, attending a special service and having tea at the Vicarage. As winter set in, yet more boxes of lantern slides arrived at the Vicarage for special presentations, including "How we got our Bible" and Stanley's last journey across Africa. Another time, an overladen programme included tea, concert and a dance which ended at 12.30 a.m.

The Hudsons left the *Dun Bull* and their successors, the Baldrys, were given a special welcome, Walter Baldry offering to supply oil for the church lamp free of charge. Mardale Church now had a library, boys' club and science class. The Boys' Club funds benefited from the proceeds of a slide show by the Vicar dealing with "Our Mardale hills and how they were built" and "Our lake, how it was dug." The lantern was modified for working from acetylene gas. "The result is much brighter pictures, less trouble and no danger."

The Church Jubilee, on June 20, 1897, was marked by a weeknight of "merrymaking". This was a treat for the children, each of whom received a commemorative medal, tea, games in a field by Haweswater and, in the evening, supper at the *Dun Bull* for the adults. "At ten o'clock a huge bonfire, laid ready on High Moor, was kindled by Miss Barrow, and it soon brought a crowd of young people to the spot. Fireworks were "let off" and when "Auld Lang Syne" had been sung, "the party made their way, in the darkness, down the hill."

In the summer of 1898, the Church interior was improved by the provision of rug seating in every pew and the appearance of a brass pulpit desk. A fund to provide a new organ was launched to replace the harmonium which had "done duty" for over three decades. "The tone has become harsh and reedy with constant use." The new organ, purchased in 1899, was an American type, giving "a vast improvement in tone and greater power of expression." Mrs Holme gave the first public performance on the new organ, having (typically) paid off the balance outstanding in the organ account.

That year, the annual Choir and Sunday School treats took the form of an excursion to Blackpool, the company of ten Mardalians being augmented by twenty Bamptonians, each of whom had paid the travelling expenses (about 4s.6d in all). This included the fare by horse and brake from Bampton to Shap and back, together with railway fare to and from Blackpool.

The return journey began at 8 p.m. and it was long past midnight before the last lamp in Mardale was extinguished. For the Mardale folk, Mrs Holme covered half the cost of the trip.

In September, 1899, the Choir trip was to Morecambe. Sixteen—repeat, sixteen—members of the Mardale choir had a day's excursion, leaving the dalehead by wagonette at 6 a.m. to meet the 7-30 a.m. train at Shap. "The party was safely landed in Morecambe by 9-30...They were all safely in their homes once more at 9 p.m."

The concert which should have been held in January, 1900, was postponed because of a flu epidemic. A humorous sketch entitled "Wanted—a Servant" was being rehearsed by local amateurs. Tickets for the concert would cost the usual sixpence, with sixpence extra for tea and another sixpence for the dance.

The Archbishop of York, staying in the parish with his family in Octoer, 1900, took an early celebration of holy communion, with the vicar assisting. The Measand Mission, very active at the turn of the century, held services on Wednesday evenings in the kitchen of the farmhouse.

The eighth annual tea and concert took place on January 17, 1902, a fine and moonlit night. So many visitors streamed in that "the small schoolroom was crowded to its utmost limits. Wagonettes ran from Askham, Bampton (2) and Shap and many came on foot from places over the fells."

On Whit Monday, the Girls' Friendly Society held a picnic at Riggside. "A tent, chairs, tables, hassocks, portable organ, &c., were taken up the hill, and at six o'clock all assembled in the tent." A hymn was sung and a prayer offered before a visiting lady outlined the aims of the Society. "Tea followed as a matter of course and the rest of the evening was spent in games and dancing."

An unusual sight in Mardale churchyard was that of a churchwarden, Mr Greenhow, supervising a "wood-cutting day" in January, 1901. With help afforded by Messrs Greenhow, Watson, Mounsey, Edmondson, Hudson and Baldry, a fallen yew tree was safely removed—from the church roof.

The Mardalians were reminded of warfare in distant places [the Boer War] when Lt H Little of Hutton Hall, Penrith, handed over for the use of the Mardale Rifle Club the service rifle he had used in that conflict. In 1907, Mr Terry was thanking "Mr A Pearson (Pearson's Weekly, &c)" for 1,000 rounds of ammunition.

The benevolent Mrs Holme lived until 1915, celebrating her ninetieth birthday. Her later days were spent away from Mardale, but such was her love for the place that in summer she spent a week or two at the *Dun Bull*. Her friends kept her in touch with the affairs of the valley.

Towards the end of the Mardale story, the Rev F H J Barham had spiritual oversight of the parish. A harmonium was used to accompany the singing and, in emergency, the vicar provided a gramophone with records of the set music for the service.

Miss Maggie Edmondson, of Flake How, normally played the harmonium. In due course, she and her young man announced they were to be married and the banns were read—twice—without a hitch. At the third time of asking, only two people were present, the prospective bride and the vicar, whereas according to law the publication of banns is not legal unless the congregation consists of not less than three persons.

At the proper time, the vicar explained the state of the law. The bride-to-be recalled the incident for Nigel Holmes of Radio Cumbria. "The vicar said he would have to leave the church and find someone else. I thought: 'Oh, dear'. But anyhow, he went across to Chapel Hill Farm and got two people in. So that was all right."

She became Maggie Lancaster and lived at Flake How. When she was expecting a baby, she mentioned to the vicar that she would have to give up her job as organist for a while. So he bought a gramophone.

She had twins. The vicar, a bachelor, fussed over the babies and volunteered to look after them when mother and father were busy with farm work, such as at haytime. "He used to feed them with chocolate. I should think they liked to see him. When my girls were two or three years old, he said they were old enough to attend church. I said they would not keep quiet. He said I should bring them and see what happened. I took them to church. They each had a new outfit, including coats and hats. When I went to the organ, they followed.

"The vicar left the reading desk, got hold of them by the hand and took them to a seat, where he gave them a little lecture and a piece of chocolate each. You can imagine what their new rig-outs were like when they'd finished eating it. They were never any bother after that..."

Mrs Hannah Newton (nee Edmondson), who died in 1984, aged 96, was brought up at Flake How, Mardale, and regularly attended the Church, sometimes playing the organ and sometimes occupying a choir stall. She remembered when Mr Barham played gramophone records. Once a mischief-maker took the record of a hymn tune from the turntable and replaced it with "Stop your Tickling, Jock".

Mrs Newton's brother practised fly-casting from the church balcony and (said Hannah) he was so good at this he could pluck feathers from the ornate hats of ladies in the pews below.

In 1927, the large vicarage, behind its screen of trees and bushes, had a padlocked gate and looked neglected. In the days when a cleric lived here, groceries and mail were left on the wall bordering the road. Visiting Mardale for the Shepherds' Meet, T Barbour, who was then a police officer, saw an elderly man walking towards the church.

This was the Rev Barham, the last vicar of Mardale. The policeman's training enabled him to recall some fine points of dress and manner—the long-faded black coat and an equally faded wide-brimmed Quaker style hat and field boots which were tied up with string. The figure was stooped, the gait slow, aided by a stick. The vicar showed signs of neglect. His shirt cuffs were fastened with large safety pins.

"He lived alone—a gentle, solitary, pathetic eccentric. I never knew anyone who had been within the vicarage."

Mardale Tittle-Tattle

(culled from the Ruridecanal Magazine, 1895-1902)

1895

Arrangements are being made for our next Concert and Coffee Supper. It will be held in Easter week to purchase a substantial curtain for the inner door of the Church and so, if possible, to keep the west end of the Church warmer during the winter season.

The Sunday School library is at last in full working order, and the books are in great demand. The Religious Tract Society treated us in a most generous spirit, not only supplying the books at half price, but also adding ten volumes as a free gift.

For the Harvest Festival, a large hamper of most beautiful flowers, with others of fruit and vegetables, were sent by Mrs Holme and further gifts of corn, plants, or flowers were sent by Mr Kitching, Measand Farm; Mr Mounsey, Whelter; Mr Edmondson, Flake How; Mr and Mrs Hawell, Riggindale; Mrs Greenhow, Chapel Hill; Mr and Mrs Hudson, *Dun Bull* Hotel; Mr N Ubank, and Mrs Wilson, Bampton.

A Service of Song, entitled "Little Dot", was given by the Sunday School children on November 18. Miss Forster read the story and Miss Terry presided at the harmonium.

1896

The School Inspector writes: "This School is conducted in a quiet, steady and unassuming though thoroughly efficient manner, and the scholars are progressing satisfactorily."

The Schoolroom will be opened from 6 to 9 p.m. every Friday

evening this winter for the boys and young men of this parish. Reading and games from 6 to 7; an elementary science class in magnetism and electricity from 7 to 8; a class in wood-carving from 8 to 9.

The Christmas treat for day school children was a tea provided by Mr and Mrs Baldry, of the *Dun Bull* Hotel. A large party assembled and spent a very merry evening. Hearty cheers were given to their kind hosts by the children on leaving.

For the Advent week-day services, satisfactory congregations were present in spite of the stormy weather on most of the evenings...A watchnight service was held on New Year's Eve but on account of the stormy night only few were present.

1897

With regard to Emigration to Canada, the High Commissioner (Sir Charles Tupper) has promised us the use of 100 lantern slides to illustrate a lecture on "Farms and Farming in Canada". This will be given in the School on March 14th and in other places during the same week. Mr Edmondson, of Flake How, will take the chair...

It is important that all Library books be sent in...so that they can be returned to Leeds. A new supply will then be sent for use in the winter months.

At the annual tea and concert, the Vicar accompanied the various performers on the piano. The following was the programme: Glee, "O'er the waves we go", Choir; songs, "Bailiff's daughter of Islington", "Mr Pittman"; "Another Day", Miss Forster; "The lighthouse", Mr H Baldry; "Where is my wandering boy?" Miss Wilson...

At the annual Flower Service, the offertory, in the form of eggs, amounting to 103, was sent to Shap Workhouse for the use of the sick and infirm.

The Vicar has received admission tickets for Carlisle Infirmary and Silloth Convalescent Home. These are for the use of any parishioner who should unfortunately need them.

Mr Christopher Wilson, Barrister, Walmgate Head, Bampton, has most kindly presented to the parish a copy of the original deed constituting Measand Grammar School.

A Guild or Club for girls and young women [meets] each alternate Monday at the Parsonage throughout the winter months, commencing each evening at 7. Games, magazines, picture books, &c., are provided in abundance, and Miss Forster has most kindly commenced a series of short lectures on Domestic Economy. Mrs Terry and Mrs Hudson will superintend the sewing and the Vicar will give some elementary lessons in music.

The Church was prettily decorated for Christmas...Mr Isaac Greenhow kindly sent a a large supply of holly covered with berries.

1898

A new and beautiful supply of large coloured pictures on "The Early Ministry of Our Lord" has been purchased for use at our children's Monthly Services. They are printed in America and are certainly a great improvement on anything we have had before.

The collection at the Flower Service amounted to 134 eggs, which were afterwards sent for the use of the inmates of the Shap Workhouse.

We are always wanting, but this month only small matters. We want a set of bookmarkers for the Church Bible and a smaller and more portable copy of the Prayer Book for use at the Communion Table.

We hope to open the Men's Reading Room early in November. It will be furnished with a bagatelle board, chess, draughts, &c., and a supply of daily, weekly and monthly papers and magazines

We hope to open the Men's Reading Room early in November. It will be furnished with a bagatelle board, chess, draughts, &c., and a supply of daily, weekly and monthly papers and magazines will be on the tables. Smoking will be allowed and every effort made to render the room as attractive as possible.

A new lamp (central draught) has been provided for use at the choir and other practices, and a small pitch-pine lectern has been purchased for use at the Measand Mission Services.

Carols were sung at the Evening Service on Christmas Day and a Watch-night Service took place on New Year's Eve.

1899

The Fifth Annual Tea and Concert was followed by a dance, which was under the able management of Mr Wm Kitching and Mr Mounsey, the former acting as M.C., while Mr F Rowlandson, Drybarrows, supplied the music. About 40 couples were present. . . We again wish to express our obligations to all who assisted in making the festival such a success, including Mr Hudson and Mr Mounsey for the loan of horses, carts, &c.

At a Vestry Meeting, the Churchwarden called attention to the strange custom of not having any offertory at the evening service on the first Sunday in the month. It was resolved to revert to the old custom, and have an offertory at each service on that day.

The great feature of a Social Evening for the Reading Room was a bagatelle match between Measand and Mardale, in which the former won.

For the Harvest Festival, a model Dutch barn was made and sent by Mr Wm Greenhow, Riggindale. Gifts of corn and fruit were sent by the farmers, and a liberal supply of flowers came from Bampton and Lowther.

1900

The children attending the Sunday School had their annual Christmas treat on Friday, January 7th. A phonograph, kindly lent to the Vicar, proved a great treat for all present.

The offering of eggs taken at the Flower Service amounted to 78. Of these, 50 were sent to the Penrith Cottage Hospital and the rest were given to our own sick. The congregations at present are exceedingly good on account, partly because of the large number of strangers staying in the neighbourhood.

The whole cost of the Children's Treat was most generously borne by Mrs Holme, who sent a large supply of provisions and a liberal donation to pay for the toys, sweets, &c. Mrs Edmondson, Flake How, and Mrs Mounsey, Whelter, also most kindly sent a large supply of milk and cream.

1901

The sad news of the Queen's death was announced to the parish by the tolling of the church bell. The flag on the tower was placed at half-mast and remained so for some days.

The annual Flower Service for children and young people was held in the open-air, under the yew trees in the churchyard. The flowers were placed in the Church and afterwards laid on the graves in the churchyard.

1902

At the Band of Hope monthly entertainment, in February, the sketch by Miss A Edmondson, Miss E Coulson and Mr W Wilson, entitled "Wise Just in Time", was full of suggestive teaching to those wise to learn.

Some further improvements have recently been made to the Reading Room, viz., additional seats covered with felt matting, the illustrated weekly *Black and White* placed on the table, and a complete set of ping-pong, with tables and trestles, provided for the use of the members.

Off to School!

THE old school, as founded in 1713 by Richard Wright, was diminutive, scarcely able to accommodate more than a dozen children.

The founder's impulse was towards the instruction of children at Measand and surrounding townships in "the English and Latin tongue, and other good literature." When he died, his property came to a nephew, Richard Law, whose name also appeared on the tablet placed on the porch of the school.

On the Old School, at Measand.

The Law family included Edmund Law, Bishop of Carlisle. He had thirteen children, three sons—John, Edward and George—becoming Classical Medallists at Cambridge and, respectively, Bishop of Clonfert in Ireland, Chief Justice of the King's Bench and Bishop of Bath and Wells.

Mardale School concentrated on the Four R's—the fourth being Religious Instruction—and was closed now and again when there

68

was an epidemic of measles. During the summer holiday, 1895, the Schoolroom was improved by colouring the walls, though the effect was subsequently offset by the hanging of "a large number of pictures and diagrams". The Governors provided a harmonium. The schoolmistress was congratulated "upon her cheerful surroundings."

The children did not lack visitors. Apart from seeing the Governors and school inspectors they were visited by distinguished folk, such as Sir Joseph and Lady Savory, Miss Markham and Captain Markham. At the annual Sunday School treat in 1899, Miss Wingfield-Digby, of Bournemouth, while staying in the parish, presented each child with a copy of the "Marked Testament".

In the summer of 1898, the west end of Mardale School was panelled, the tender of Wilson Ewbank of Bampton, to do the work, being accepted. "It was also decided to do something definite to cure the smoke nuisance in the schoolhouse kitchen. Mr Christopher Wilson and the Vicar were appointed a committee (of two) to have the work done. As this latter work promises to be of a costly nature, a hope was expressed that the farmers in the district who had children attending the school would do the carting of material free."

By 1901, the number of children of school age in the parish was steadily decreasing, so the teacher was paid a fixed salary of £70 per annum, instead of, as at present, making the salary dependent on the governmental grant.

By 1918, merry voices were reported from the infant school, where about a dozen youngsters were being taught. In 1927, seven scholars remained. Their headmistress, Miss Foster, who had been in charge of them for seventeen years, was sad. The construction of the dam would compel her to leave Mardale. And this she did not want to do.

Life at the Dun Bull

So enclosed is this part of the dale that from Martinmas to Candlemas no gleam of sunshine reaches the Dun Bull, but in the days to come the sun will shine on the waters above where the Dun Bull used to be.

Isaac Hinchliffe (1925).

It was a real old place.

James Taylor, 1993.

THE *Dun Bull*—an inn cum farmhouse—stood where the road up the dale gave way to a walled track leading to the high passes of Nan Bield (for Kentmere) or Gatesgarth (into Longsleddale).

Just when it was distinguished by a name and a sign is not known. For many years, most farms in the district brewed their own ale and, such was Lakeland hospitality, no traveller would be turned away thirsty or hungry. Mardale Head had an inn when a traveller/writer called Edward Baines called here on his tour of 1834. He referred to the place as the *White Bull.*

It was left to Jonathan Otley, an early guide book writer (1837), to first publicise the *Dun Bull.* Those with experience of it tended to hurry on so as to be at one of the Bampton inns by dusk.

The *Dun Bull* came into its own as an inn at the end of the road which was a meeting place of shepherds and huntsmen. In 1840, when a party was held chaired by Bowstead of Measand, the throats of those who attended were lubricated by punch ordered by John Holme, the current "King of Mardale". There was much toasting, one toast wishing good health to Lord Lonsdale, and songs galore, including a popular item entitled The Blind Fiddler.

Harriet Martineau (c1865) reported that the Mardale Green Inn had a hostess and that she made her guests comfortable. She

Smoke Room of the "Dun Bull", 1917.

found the food was "homely", and the bed clean. The host would, if necessary, act as guide to the passes.

Harriet also mentioned Mardale's trade with Manchester. Each week, 30 cwt of butter was collected from the scattered farms by the carrier's wagon. The butter was taken to Shap, the nearest railway station, for rapid transportion to the city.

As an inn, the *Dun Bull* became renowned for the Mardale Shepherds' Meet, to which stray sheep were brought, to be claimed by their rightful owners. One of its supporters recalled it principally as a boozing event.

The inn also catered for anglers tempting trout in the becks and tarns or larger fish in Haweswater. Climbers and fell-walkers, wearing tweedy outer clothes, with knicker-bocker trousers and boots, also stayed at the *Dun Bull*, sleeping within easy distance of the riggs and crags.

Thomas Lamley, an eccentric Victorian landlord of the *Dun Bull*, built a tower on Wood Howe and anyone using it could see all the paths which converged on Mardale and also the approach road as far down as Measand. The tower was called Lamley's Folly.

Lamley was responsible for adding a wing to the *Dun Bull*, an engraved stone giving his initials and the date 1827. Lamley kept the local tongues wagging, especially when he transported goods from Penrith Market in a cart which was a hollowed-out tree trunk on wheels.

It is related of one couple who presided over the *Dun Bull* that each would diddle the customers if they could get away with it. Some lads grabbed a Herdwick tup and put it into the cellar. When the hostess went to draw some more beer, she saw gleaming eyes and tossing horns. Presuming it to be Old Nick himself, she yelled at her husband: "Eh Billy, he's cumt for us at last; me for me froth pints and thee for thy double chalk marks."

The Daffurns are well remembered. For the Shepherds' Meet at the *Dun Bull* in 1921, a record crowd gathered. Mrs Daffurn had provided seventy large loaves of bread, which quickly disappeared. The staff had to set to work on the Saturday evening and bake more bread.

In the winter of 1934, Frank Alcock and a rambler friend spent the night at the *Dun Bull*. The Daffurns had moved to the *Greyhound* at Shap, leaving Mr and Mrs Bell in charge. Frank retained the bill: "2 High Teas—5 shillings, 2 Beds—6 shillings, 2 breakfasts—5 shillings; total—16 shillings."

During the following summer, Frank took a photograph of the now famous hostelry, which would soon be demolished. He wrote about this last visit before the Flood in the *Cumberland and Westmorland Herald*. "My old mountaineering friend Ron and I had walked over from Windermere, via Garburn Pass, Kentmere, Nan Bield and Small Water. After a good dinner at the 'Dunny' we were accompanied by a lively foxhound puppy on a post-prandial amble to the top of Chapel Hill [now an islet called Wood Howe]."

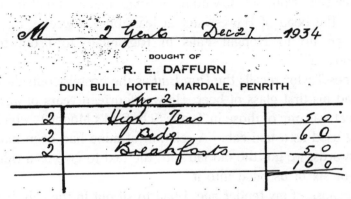

Expenses incurred by Frank Alcock and his friend Ron in 1934.

Frank recalled that on that last evening at the *Dun Bull* a cheery little Irishman, who was employed as a labourer on the dam, tramped into the bar, downed eight pints in about a quarter of an hour, bade the others a polite farewell—and tramped back to Burnbanks. Mrs Bell said the Irishman had been visiting the inn every day except Saturday for many weeks. She added: "On Saturdays, he goes with his pals into Penrith for some REAL drinking."

T'auld place was pulled down. Its successor as a hostelry, the grandly appointed and grandly named Haweswater Hotel, complete with walled and terraced gardens, was sited on a ledge of rock between the new road and Guerness Woods. Anyone staying here would at least have a bonny view of the fells soaring beyond the water.

It is not an eyesore, and indeed is not noticed by the majority of motorists, who are concentrating on the winding road. In the 1930s, the Council for the Preservation of Rural England observed: "Instead of a long, low, two-storeyed building in local whitewash...this casino-like structure will dominate the landscape, a lasting disgrace to its perpetrators."

Lucy Bell, from her new home at Shap, made a point of returning to the head of Haweswater at least once a week. "In spring we'd go up to Hopgill Falls in Riggindale to listen to the cuckoo..."

James Taylor recalls the *Dun Bull* as the hostelry outside which he had his first glass of beer. He was fourteen years of age, and his seat was one of those in Teddy Schofield's Model T, which was being used as a taxi cab. "A relation of mine had been married. Afterwards, we got the old lad with the taxi to give us a ride out. Five or six of us piled into it.

"Because of my tender age, I had to sit out in the cab, but one or two of them kept coming out with glasses of beer for me. I got quite a few."

Teddy Schofield lived at Clifton. On Keswick Gala Day, "which was held on August Monday—the old August Monday, the first of the month—cycling was a premier sport. We used to get off in the morning from Great Strickland, travelling in the old taxi cab. The bike riders said: 'Away you go.' They used to overtake us at Threlkeld. It took us hours to get to Keswick. We used to stop at 'Clickam', on the Greystoke road, for a drink..."

Mardale Shepherds' Meet

IT WAS said that the Mardale Shepherds met on High Street and that after the serious business of re-claiming sheep, horse racing took place along the line of the old Roman road. There was also wrestling, Cumberland and Westmorland style, a style of such antiquity that "they" claimed it was used by Jacob when he wrestled with the Angel.

Shepherds and farmers followed the fell tracks "ower t'tops" to attend the meet. Walking was a universal occupation in those days. Tommy Fishwick was once heard to say to a friend: "Yan wants nowt wi' riding as lang as yan legs 'ell carry yan."

According to W C Skelton, the number of sheep which changed hands at this annual November gathering averaged between one and two hundred, mostly "mountain herdwicks" which were easily identified by their distinctive markings "and generally restored to their rightful owners by Messrs T Edmondson and R Ebdell, who have discharged this duty for many years."

Mardale Shepherds' Meet was an event which made a strong appeal to "real hardy fellsman hunters". At various times, there was a hound trail, clay-pigeon shooting and even sheepdog trials. One year, the organisers were at the point of looking for candles before the final trial was "shot off".

In the evening, a smoking concert took place. Mr Skelton recorded that the "main portion of the pack" cast off in the large dining room "and every room in the house filled with overflow meetings—or rather concerts."

The big room was the focal point. "A tray is sent round, money is subscribed for the evening's refreshment. Each individual orders what he has a mind to drink and it is paid for out of the general pool by the chairman. Toast and song follow in quick succession."

The chief toast was that of the shepherds, coupled with the name of the oldest, and was honoured with a verse of "While Shepherds watch their Flocks by night", reverently and tunefully sung.

The Mardale Meet's popularity depended for years on the fox-hunting reputation of Joe Bowman (Hunty or Auld Joe), who had charge of the Ullswater pack. Eventually, visitors rolled up from all parts in all manner of ways—"Rolls-Royces, expensive furs, patent-leather boots, silk hats, white waistcoats, kid gloves and silver-mounted walking sticks."

Joe retired in 1924, when there was a splendid "do" at the *Dun Bull* and presentations were made. New songs were launched, including a rather tedious "Oh, Ho, Ho." Here is a verse:

> *There's varra few like Joe in heaven;*
> *Oh, ho, ho!*
> *They've mappen gitten six er seben*
> *Oh, ho, ho!*
> *Gay sports who gev Auld Nick the slip,*
> *Oh, ho, ho!*
> *An kap 'im aff wid hounds an' whip*
> *Oh, ho, ho!*

Joe was presented with a silver horn, inscribed
THE HORN OF MARDALE
> *May he who windes this silver horn*
> *Aye wake the echoes of the morn*
> *And heavenwards where e'er he wend*
> *The spirit of Auld Joe attend.*

That Sunday night, Mardale Church was packed for a harvest festival celebration. The vicar (Rev H J Barham) arranged it to coincide with the Meet. According to local custom, the hymn "Crown Him with Many Crowns" brought the service to an end.

Mardale folk, and those of the surrounding dales, might be dead but they were not forgotten, being recalled in song and story. The history of the Meet was apt to be vague. Isaac Hinchliffe quoted an old account that after a good day's sport, huntsmen, shepherds, visitors, sheep-dogs and terriers (hounds are not admitted) all turn into the *Dun Bull* for a hearty meal.

Most people agree there was a smoking concert, held in the dining room. Hinchliffe records that a long table on trestles stood in the middle of the room, and around it sat all those who had

"gathered" during the day. "A chairman is appointed and sits at the head of the table, while under the table are sheep-dogs and terriers galore. Toasts are proposed in the usual way; then the chairman calls for a song, and if there is a chorus, so much the better. Everyone is supposed to sing at least one song.

"Sometimes, if a song has a good swing, the men get particularly enthusiastic, the shepherds beat on the tables with their sticks, and the sheep-dogs and terriers join the chorus with enthusiasm or execration, no man knows which."

Jossie Green, of Naddle, was recalled for his especially fine rendering of "Tarry Woo'," though it took time, and much ale, to work him up to the stage where he sang at the right pitch:

Tarry Woo'! Tarry Woo'! Tarry Woo' is ill to spin;
Card it weel! Card it well! Card it weel ere you begin;
When it's carded, rolled and spun, then your work is
*   but half done;*
But when woven, dressed and clean, it be clothing
*   for a queen.*

Isaac Hinchliffe heard Joe Bowman sing a hunting song after two o'clock in the morning "and be out with his hounds, fresh as paint, before nine." No one worried too much about having a bed; after a day's hunting and night's drinking and sinking, some slept on chairs, some in the barns.

At one hunt recorded by Cornelius Nicholson, of Kendal, "a man named Dixon fell from Blea Water crag, an overhanging precipice which was estimated at three hundred feet in height; and though terribly bruised and almost scalped, he broke no bones and recovered from the shock.

In falling, he struck against the rock several times without afterwards remembering that he did so, and on coming to the ground he sprang instantly to his knees, and cried out: "Lads, t'fox is gane oot at t'hee end; lig t'dogs on, and I'll come syun." He then fell down, insensible. The part of the crag where this incident happened became known as Dixon's Three Jumps.

In 1927, the Meet (held at the *Dun Bull*) was attended by over seven hundred people. Robert Daffurn now presided over the *Dun Bull* and also ran a sheep farm with nine hundred sheep "heafed" on the fells.

T Barbour, visiting the event in his role of policeman, recalled that Daffurn spoke with a South Country accent. "I understood he had graduated to the Dun Bull by way of Lowther Castle, having been in the employ of Lord Lonsdale."

The policeman had been here before. "An item in the entrance hall which never failed to arouse attention was a large basket containing Blue Persian kittens (for sale at ten shillings each). "I was curious to know how the continuity of supply was maintained because the basket was seldom without those attractive creatures. One day, Daffurn took me to a large loft, which was divided into breeding pens for a number of captive Blue Persian cats."

The policeman mentioned to Mr Daffurn how much better trade seemed to be now that news of the drowning of Mardale was generally known. Daffurn took his visitor to the front door and pointed to those sitting outside the inn, announcing in a loud voice: "Look at them! They come in here and buy a penny postcard, use the toilets, then sit on my seats eating their sandwiches."

Lucy Bell, at her cafe in Shap, told me about the *Dun Bull* of those days. Robert Daffurn, who was her stepfather, had previously had experience at the *Mitre* in Penrith and, as related, he also acquired the licence of the *Greyhound* at Shap. The Mardale business extended with the acquisition of the large house which had been the residence of the Holme family and stood adjacent to the inn. Guests at the enlarged *Dun Bull* were attended by a moderately large staff—two waitresses, a cook, two housemaids and a handyman, plus the family.

Robert Daffurn, in 1932, asked Mr and Mrs Bell to supervise the Dun Bull in its closing phase. This they did for four busy years. She recalled a gusty day when a car belonging to the hotel was being driven by the lake when the car hood was plucked off and blown into the water.

For the annual Shepherds' Meet, everything in the main rooms had to be hidden, except for the chairs. Beer was distributed in buckets. People came for the day, but it might be ten days before the last of them had sobered up and departed. Tom Edmondson, of Penrith, played cards or dominoes at the *Dun Bull* until closing time. Then the games were continued in a stable, using a kist (wooden chest) as a table.

One hunt supporter, returning to the hotel on Sunday morning, said: "I've been sleeping with Mother Green." He had, in fact, spent the night on the hotel lawn.

Jack Taylor heard that a Kentmere man walked over the pass to play the piano for the celebrations following each Shepherds' Meet. The pianist had a fancy waistcoat with pockets. "He played the piano for about two days and two nights. On the third morning, he'd run out of the money he earned by his efforts and set off to walk home again.

"When he reached the summit of Nan Bield pass, he sat on a stone to have a smoke, felt in a waistcoat pocket to get a bit of tobacco and found half a sovereign. So he went back to the *Dun Bull* and spent another two days there..."

When Manchester took over the inn, a manager was installed until the opening of the new hotel. "We were up there when the new road was made," said Mrs Bell. "It was always the 'new' road to us."

The last of the Shepherds' Meets took place in 1935, after which the event was transferred to Bampton. It was still known as the Mardale Meet. And familiar faces assembled from the Mardale fells, from Martindale, Patterdale, Troutbeck, Kentmere, Longsleddale, Shap, Helton and, of course, from Bampton.

The *Dun Bull* survives only in photographs and the tales of a rapidly declining number of those who patronised it.

Manchester in Lakeland

As yet, no sign appears of the threatened invaders except a couple of men wandering about taking levels.
The Manchester Guardian, October 1, 1918.

I think there will be no more charming spot in the country than Haweswater when we have finished with it. . . It is our intention to improve the appearance of the whole surroundings because we shall do as we have done at Thirlmere.
Sir Edward Holt, Manchester Waterworks Committee Chairman, at a dinner in Penrith (1925).

The water will rise to the steeper slopes and substitute for a typical English declension of hills to the water's edge the more melodramatic abruptness of a Norwegian fjord. . .
The Manchester Guardian, April 28, 1927.

The dam at Haweswater, though by no means nearing completion, is already a bulky white wedge on the landscape.
Cumberland and Westmorland Herald, June, 1937.

MANCHESTER, with its Haweswater Act, 1919, acquired the lake and an extensive catchment area for the construction of a reservoir which would raise the lake 29 m (96 feet). The former lake would almost double its length and cover almost three times the original area.

Manchester was given the authority to build subsidiary reservoirs in Swindale and Wet Sleddale, water from which would be directed into Haweswater. And an aqueduct 73¼ miles long would be built to connect the area with the taps of thirsty Manchester.

That was the idea announced at the end of the Great War. Not until the early stages of World War Two would the main reservoir be brought into use.

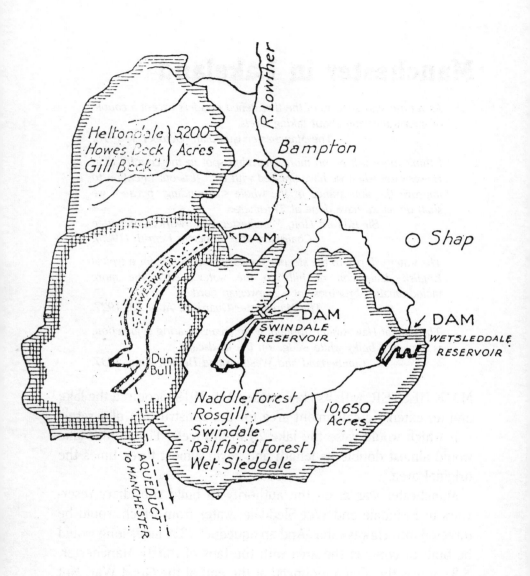

An Old Plan of the Drainage Area.

Scale: 1 inch = 2 miles.

You must grant the water engineers verve and imagination. They devised many schemes for the Lake District, most of which were not carried out in their original form. In 1866, there was an idea to supply London by raising the levels of Thirlmere and Haweswater and conveying water from these lakes through tunnels to Ullswater, the level of which was to be raised by four feet. The water would be sent South by aqueduct.

In 1894, it was proposed that both Liverpool and Manchester should draw water from Ullswater and Haweswater, but in the event Liverpool used Wales as its cistern and it was left to Manchester alone to stake a claim in Lakeland's ample rainfall.

At the close of the 1914-18 war, a newspaper correspondent wrote: "As Mardale has a census population of under a hundred, the human displacement will not be great."

The Manchester Guardian described the area as "perhaps the least visited of the lakes. . . but in missing Haweswater people miss one of the most lovely of the lakes. . . There is something primitive in it, a native wildness as of a scene untouched by man's aid, for afforestation has wrought big changes round other lakes."

In 1923, when rambling was becoming a popular pastime with urban folk, news about the transformation of Haweswater generated concern about the effect of the new works on the ancient passes and footpaths. Most people knew the *Dun Bull* would have to be demolished and its site would be covered with water. There was some talk of a new inn being built on Chapel Hill.

The Longsleddale track, dropping down Gatescarth Pass, would turn west and skirt an arm of the new lake. The Nan Bield route would not come far down the upper dale.

In July, 1925, a large official party arrived at Penrith by special train had lunch at the George Hotel. Motor cars and small charabancs were available for the journey to Haweswater. A large part of the watershed was viewed from above Rosgill Wood.

Bampton had not previously seen such a spectacle as this cavalcade of assorted vehicles which stopped for a while, with engines switched off, one of the party having recalled staying at Bampton and of having his sleep disturbed by bells. Now, "as it was but five minutes to the half-hour," a halt was made "in order that the Manchester Corporation might gain some impression of chimes as they are heard in rural England."

A line of vehicles halted near the church. "During the interval to the half-hour, a member of the City Council, whose knowledge of Latin came as a great surprise to his fellows, walked about the churchyard, reeling off translations of the inscriptions on the ancient tombstones."

For a few moments before the pointer of the clock arrived at the half-hour, a deadly silence fell on the party. "Then it appeared to dawn on some that a practical joke was toward. Out of the stunted steeple issued a sound which, to be appreciated at its full worth, ought to be heard at midnight, when the snow is falling and the wind is howling in the valley.

"Manchester, famous for its musical sense, stood aghast as the chimes ding-donged, in amazing disonance, the half-hour. The party moved on, sobered by the experience, and it was not until Haweswater came into view that the majority of the members...recovered their wonted high spirits."

The position of the dam was indicated by posts and flags. It was a period of drought; the lake level was low and hardly any of the becks had flowing water.

The visitors were given technical information by the City Engineer, L. Holme-Lewis, who mentioned that Haweswater lies about eighty miles from Manchester and one of the large engineering tasks was the construction of an aqueduct, connecting the lake with Heaton Park reservoir. The aqueduct would pass via Gatescarth Pass and Longsleddale. It would consist of thirty miles of tunnel, eleven miles of covered channel and thirty-three and one third miles of pipes.

Mr Holme-Lewis warmed to his task of describing the consequence of Manchester's large-scale tinkering with Lakeland plumbing. The dam would raise the overflow level 95 feet and increase the surface area to 970 acres. "The present length of the lake is two and a-half miles. When the water level is raised, it will be extended to four miles," he announced.

He mentioned the eminent suitability of the watershed "on account of its being sparsely populated and the fact that the rainfall is substantially higher than the average for the whole of the country, though the rainfall at Haweswater itself is rather less than at Thirlmere, which also is the property of the Manchester Corporation."

Reeling from a statistical battering, the party were driven along the dale road to the *Dun Bull,* where afternoon tea was served. Back at Penrith, dinner was consumed at the *George.* Alderman Sir Edward Holt, Chairman of the Waterworks Committee, respond to a platitudinous speech by the Lord Mayor (Alderman West), broached the matter of paying for the multi-million pound scheme. "Some of you don't know how hardly the Waterworks Committee were hit through the [1914-18] war. Everything we touched, including labour, cost more . . ."

Sir Edward commended the officials who were concerned with the new reservoir, including Mr Holme-Lewis and Mr C E Stracy, the secretary. He ended a speech, which his listeners punctuated with spirited "hear, hears", by asserting there was no intention to spoil the Haweswater area; the Manchester Corporation would actually improve on nature. "In my opinion, at the present moment, Haweswater is very much over-rated as a beauty spot . . ."

In the spring of 1927, workmen were busy clearing timber from the site of the dam. A year later, even more small white flags dotted the hillsides on each side of the lake to indicate the new water level. The British Waterworks Association, visiting Haweswater, were told that the town of Bolton had once set one eye on Mardale but found the place too large.

In May, 1929, Manchester Waterworks Committee were ready to outline their plans. The Haweswater scheme would cost £10 million. The initial stages would involve making new roads from Shap. A writer in the *Daily Mail* wrote: "The whole scheme, which has been discussed in detail since 1925, is to be thrown across the Mardale Valley and a tunnel stretching from the south side of the lake to a point north of Kendal will be bored."

Work on the dam—the first hollow buttress dam in the world—began at the northern end of Haweswater in 1930, only to be suspended for a few years because of the Depression. A reporter for the *Sunday Graphic* wrote (February, 1935) about the impending flood. His piece appeared under the heading: "Water Shroud for Lake Beauty Spot: Dynamite Battle with Nature".

He observed: "This is the last year when the shrill, not unmelodious whistles of the farmer beckoning his dogs to the sheep will be heard in the doomed valley leading to Mardale. Manchester Waterworks Committee are raising the level of Haweswater and, like thousands of other pilgrims, I climbed down from mist-crowned Kidsty Pike into this silent, magnetic gem of Lakeland and dwelt upon the pity of it all."

He saw the "horrifying contrast between the old road twisting on the opposite shore of the lake and the new road swaggering along past the Naddle Forest." Further up the valley, the local Territorials were being allowed to practise their warlike skills by blowing up some of the buildings.

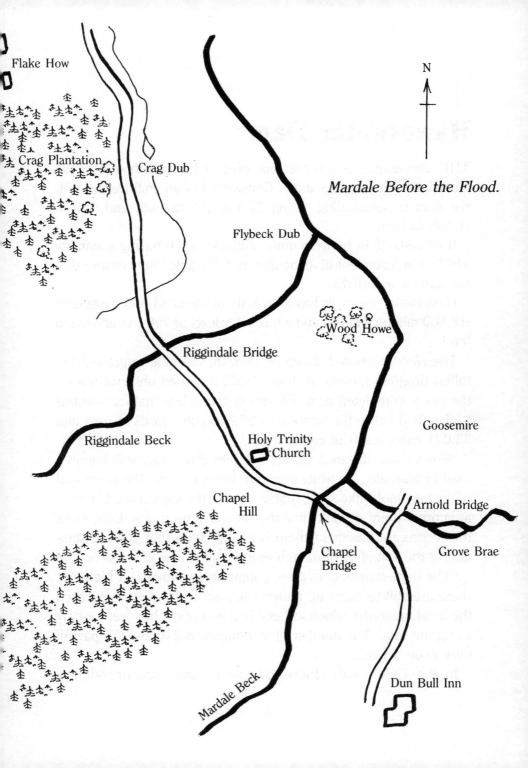

Flake How

Crag Plantation

Crag Dub

Flybeck Dub

N

Mardale Before the Flood.

Wood Howe

Riggindale Bridge

Goosemire

Riggindale Beck

Holy Trinity
Church

Chapel
Hill

Arnold Bridge

Chapel
Bridge

Grove Brae

Dun Bull Inn

Mardale Beck

Haweswater Dam

THE appearance of a monstrous plug at the mouth of Mardale moved many a writer to anger. Considered as an engineering feat, the dam is outstanding, being 27.5 m (90 ft) high and 470 m (1,150 ft) long.

It consists of 44 buttress units of blocks, each having a stability which is independent of its neighbours. Flexible joints ensure that the dam is watertight.

Haweswater reservoir has a capacity of about 84,500 megalitres (18,600 million gallons) and a top water level of 790 feet above sea level.

The *Herald,* printed at nearby Penrith, was able to present the fullest progress reports. In June, 1937, it carried observations on the partly completed dam, informing its readers that excavations to date had led to the removal of 27,640 cubic yards of rock and 33,021 cubic yards of earth.

"From some distance up the old fern-clad, cranesbill-haunted road to Mardale, the white concrete barrier across the lower end of the lake looks like some titanic ship on the slips of the builders; at another point, it looks like the Assuan Dam in dry dock; close to the massive basement there is a suggestion that you are standing at the foot of the Pyramids of Egypt in course of construction.

"The huge segments that are completed are forty feet high, but these are still to taper up another fifty-six feet before they reach the height planned, which will end in a four and a-half feet footway along the top." The number of workmen was 210 and the payroll over £600 a week.

In the 1930s, with Hollywood-type cinema films providing a

cultural bombshell, the reporter—given a tour of the basement of the dam, a series of chambers—recalled the closing scenes of the film of H G Wells's *The Shape of Things to Come*. "You enter the dam on the Bampton side through concrete arched doorways which look as though they might lead you into King Solomon's mines. Inside, you are in the huge octagonal chamber, gleaming white as the concrete catches the light from the still open groined roof.

"You see the arched doorways leading to still further mysteries, get a vision of white bays and dazzling bastions, and expect Mr Jameson, the resident engineer, who is leading you through these mysteries, to be changed into Mr Raymond Massey (a popular film star) at least. . .It is the hugeness of the conception which rather astonishes you when you get into its innards."

The outflow from Haweswater was by now passing through the pipes provided for conducting the compensation water under the dam. "Here again, you enter a hall of machinery—or what will eventually be a hall when it is roofed in—and you see a couple of enormous iron pipes snaking through the dam, each pipe fitted with big control wheels, like the steering wheel of a titanic motor car, to regulate the pressure of the storm water.

Our reporter gets high marks for imagination and style. "This is a cribb'd, cabin'd and confined phase in the history of the prattling Haweswater beck, which emerges from the imprisoning shades to sleep in green pools, to shimmer over pebbly shallows and babble into bluebell-haunted bays."

In this strange mini-world, unlike anything else in Lakeland—a chamber cut off from sunlight—"the beck looks greenly sinister" being "a miniature Panama Canal masquerading among dark locks and lapping round queer machinery and grim pipes and the turbines and the dynamics of the Electric Age. . ."

New Roads

THE new road from Naddle to the dalehead, east of t'watter, was made by direct labour in the period from 1929 to 1931. It was no easy task, for the ground was rocky and thickly wooded.

This road was planned to be twenty feet wide, the retaining wall to be of immense size and strength but constructed of "dry" stones, concrete being laid as the foundation where the wall was highest. Mortar was used only at the level of the pitching and surfacing. Three bridges were made of reinforced concrete arch slabs, faced with local stone. The longest bridge, spanning Haweswater Beck, has two spans and totals sixty feet.

Another new road, dating back to 1930, extends for almost six miles, being originally intended to connect the site of the dam with the rail sidings at Shap. The road is twelve feet wide, composed of reinforced concrete slabs. Local people travelled for miles to see one of the seven sets of cattle grids, then a novelty. (The original idea had been to fit "automatic gates" which would be operated by the weight of a vehicle passing over a treadle in the roadway).

The Aqueducts

A NINE-MILE aqueduct (including five miles of tunnel) had been made by the 1940s. The aqueduct ended north of Kendal, where another pipeline joined it to the existing Thirlmere aqueduct just over two miles away. This link was used to deliver the first supplies from Haweswater to Manchester in October, 1941, although completion of the entire scheme took a further thirty years.

A second aqueduct, constructed between 1948 and 1955, linked the initial nine miles of Haweswater aqueduct to the storage reservoir at Heaton Park. The new 71-mile aqueduct included thirty-one miles of concrete-lined tunnels, the longest, which passes under Bowland Forest, having a length of ten miles.

A later development enabled Haweswater to receive water from the adjoining valleys of Swindale, Naddle, Heltondale and Wet Sleddale. Ullswater has been used since 1971 to "top up" Haweswater by an average of up to 114 megalitres (25 million gallons) a day, water being pumped from Ullswater into a tunnel under Tarn Moor, flowing by gravity to Heltondale.

The water supply from Haweswater was improved by the Shap aqueduct—12 miles of pipes and tunnelling below Shap Fell, created at a cost of about £9 million. This came into service in May, 1978.

A New Hotel

OUR MAN from The *Herald* described [June, 1937] the new *Haweswater Hotel* as "the far-from-dun successor to the *Dun Bull* at the head of the Mardale valley". The old inn had closed its doors on the previous Saturday following a surge of motorist visitors who were anxious to take a final farewell and collect souvenirs.

The new hotel, designed by Mr W Ellerton, a Manchester architect, and built by Messrs P A Baines and Sons, of Kendal, was officially opened by Alderman Walker. Who else? He presided over the Manchester Waterworks Committee and could be forgiven for looking pleased with himself when he saw his name, inscribed in stone, at the front of the hotel.

The *Herald's* article was illustrated by a three column-wide photograph by F Kenyon, Penrith, and the feature bore an eye-catching heading : "Haweswater's 'Castle of Chillon'." Another deck of the heading echoed the Wellsian theme with "The Shape of Things to Come in Mardale."

The *Herald* was granted a private view of the new hotel before the opening ceremony and breathlessly reported that this "is the last word in modernity, for it is practically an all-electric hotel and the furnishings and fitments are in keeping with the modern note."

The approach to the hotel was stated to be "Borrowdale-like in its appearance." The site, "on a plateau-like spur beyond Walla Crag, backing on to the 'bluebell-filled and fern-clad' Guerness Wood, has been blasted out of the solid rock." This was being turned into a natural rock garden by the Penrith firm of Herd Bros., who were decking the crevices and ledges with appropriate plants.

The *Herald* man noted: "Above the outcrop is a sloping mat of bleaberry and heathery turfs cut from the lower slopes of the Mardale fells and replanted in much the same way as Silloth turf is turned into bowling greens." The hotel grounds were, indeed, a natural rock-garden and the views from the windows were classified as "superb".

In 1937, with the dam not yet complete, the hotel's elevated position looked distinctly odd. And so it would remain until the level of the lake had risen ninety feet. Then "the burnished birches, stunted oaks and fern-entangled scrub immediately below the hotel will be submerged. The water will be lapping the rock bastion on which the hotel is built, leaving but a fringe of tree and fern below the new road, which passes immediately beneath the castellated garden frontage of the hotel."

The blue waters of Haweswater would then be so close it would almost be possible to drop a fishing line out of the bedroom windows or from the ornamental terraces in front of them...

Needless to say, the views were "magnificent". The official

description is well fitted for organ accompaniment. Looking to the head of Mardale valley, a visitor could see the blue bastions of High Street and Harter Fell with their "shadowy ravines and twilit passes." Opposite them were the "sun-kissed" slopes of Bason Crag and, to the right, "the mellow massif of Measand, yellow with broom, its falls cascading in silver pencils down the brant fellside."

Hotel visitors were spared the sight of the dam, which was round the corner. "Everywhere on this side are hanging woods, just now fresh and fragrant in their May-time vestments. . ."

It was time to enter the new hotel, this "last word in modernity", where a welcome was provided by the host and hostel, Mr and Mrs Harold Hazlehurst. She had a Haweswater connection, being a daughter of Mrs Bellas, of the *Crown and Mitre Hotel* at Bampton Grange.

The ground floor had its entrance hall, dining hall, writing room, drawing room, smoking room, terrace lounge, an ordinary lounge and a solarium or sun room, mostly with French windows opening on to the terraces "and all furnished in tasteful keeping. . . Synchronised electric clocks are let into the walls."

The fourteen guest bedrooms, which were mostly double, were fitted with electric fires in chromium-plated panels in the walls. Hot and cold water was laid on to each room. "The woodwork is very beautiful and highly polished, and this is seen to great advantage in the well which rises from the entrance hall to the roof, so that the visitor when he steps out of his bedroom on to the landing may look down the well into the entrance hall. A modern illusion gives the appearance of spaciousness.

"All inside doors in the entrance hall are fitted with glass, with a border in chess-board pattern, with one square of glass clear and the alternate square opaque. Standing in the hall, instead of inhospitably closed doors, you see through the clear glass the brightly furnished and sunny rooms beyond."

Burnbanks

Aquaville is possibly the name to be given to the temporary town shortly to spring up in the wilds of Westmorland. The town will be built a few miles from the hamlet of Brampton to house 700 navvies...
                                            Daily Mail, May 29, 1929.

...a new village for waterworks men is growing up among spruce trees; they have a village hall and other amenities, and the whole will tone down into quite a pleasant village. I do regret the spruces.
                                            Doreen Wallace (1940).

WHEN Manchester Waterworks Committee announced their £10m Haweswater scheme, newspaper writers responded excitedly. A shanty town would appear in a Lakeland wilderness. Thousands of men would be imposed on a sparsely populated area. The place would be like one of the mid-West frontier towns. It was named after the location—Burnbanks.

Aquaville, as the *Daily Mail* called the Burnbanks scheme, was to have its own cinema, chapel, hospital, police station, recreation hall, canteen (wet and dry), school and sports ground. "The houses will be wooden huts accommodating up to fifteen persons in some and six in others."

Syd Wear arrived here in 1929 and lives in the section known as Naddle Gate, where the dwellings were intended for office workers—timekeepers, cashiers, and their dependants. At Naddle Gate, redwood was used for building. The houses are as sound today as when they were erected. "I've a spare bit of redwood; it's as dry as tinder and yet you can hardly lift it."

In Burnbanks itself, just round the corner, were 62 huts of four different types, the largest having accommodation for a "hut keeper", his wife and family, thirteen cubicles for the accommodation of lodgers, a large common living room, washing and drying rooms. The smaller huts were of the three, two or one-bedroom type.

Syd Wear says of the Burnbanks accommodation: "The buildings went up like mushrooms. They were very warm in summer and very cold in winter."

In the early days, some workmen lodged at the farms, but after two years or so, when Manchester was encouraging the farmfolk to look for a living elsewhere, this type of lodging became scarce. Family by family, the Mardalians found farms to rent or to buy.

Burnbanks was regarded as something special for workmen. They had a recreation hall, which had a "proper" stage, curtains and lights. The maple dance floor was reported to be "hanging on chains". Apart from local talent, The Askham Players occasionally performed here. Women met once a week and there was a girls' club. Sixpence gained admission to one of the Friday night "hops" which had a habit of extending into Saturday morning. A ham sandwich supper cost a shilling.

Burnbanks had a dispensary, attended several times a week by Dr Prentice of Shap. A nurse was available for minor afflictions. The Burnbanks mission hall was used by all religious denominations. And all were illuminated and heated by electricity, generated by water power and three sets of Ryston and Hornsby Diesel engines which, coupled to dynamos, had a capacity of 850 horse-power.

T Barbour, stationed at Bampton as a constable in 1927, was provided with a bicycle for mobility. The navvies were men who tramped from job to job, and most of the men he knew arrived from Halifax, where there had been some public work. "A navvy was invariably alone, recognisable by his heavy jacket and moleskin trousers tied at the knee. Heavy boots clad their feet. All their possessions were in a small bundle, usually enfolded by a large red handkerchief.

Navvies were seldom in fights or brawls, yet at week-ends they tended to drink until they had spent up. "Some navvies stayed for weeks, some for months. They left, nearly always singly. I have walked alongside navvies. Their gait never varied, either uphill or downhill."

Horace Horrox, a Bolton man, began work for Manchester Waterworks at Haweswater in September, 1929. He was only 22 years of age and at first was very lonely. Horace told Nigel Holmes of Radio Cumbria: "Coming up here to work nearly broke my heart. I thought it was very quiet after living what you might call a hectic life in a Lancashire town, where I could go to the pictures and football matches.

"There was nothing up here at that time. I just made the best of it. I went to the pictures in Penrith, went to church regularly on Sunday evening, went to bed early—and that was that!"

Mr Horrox drove the lorry and cars for the engineers. He was also, when needed, at the wheel of an ambulance, taking an injured workman to the doctor.

"They brought a lot of people in from West Cumberland and one or two from Manchester. The Manchester men didn't seem to like it much and some of them went back. The West Cumberland people could only get a job if they had a green card through the Labour Exchange. Some of the men were nearly thirty years of age and had never done a day's work on account of the Depression. Now they had to work or they would not have got any dole. If you didn't work in those days, you didn't get anything."

W C Cannon, who I met at the *Crown and Mitre* in Bampton, many years ago, told me of the time he was in charge of a club at Burnbanks—a wooden structure which catered for the leisure needs of the two hundred workmen enrolled as members. Between the wars, the beer came by rail to Shap and was conveyed to Burn-banks on a motor lorry driven by a Mr McCormick, of Brampton. A pint of beer cost fivepence, with Guinness retailing at sixpence.

Many of the men were "football daft", the team using the playing field beside the river. A writer in the magazine *Cumbria* in 1988 recalled some of the players—the Thompson brothers, the Redheads, "Dic" Cook, Bobbie Eastham, the Sullivans and Jewells, Big Billy Toon, Little Billy Toon and the Crabtree brothers.

Eric Jewell was to recall (*Cumbria,* 1978) the Bedford motor coaches which connected Burnbanks with Penrith. Sometimes, in those straitened times, a schoolchild who normally had to walk to and from school, a round trip of about seven miles, would plead with his eyes to be given a free ride by bus. "One or two of the drivers usually obliged."

The highlight of the month for the Jewell children—and the others at Burnbanks—was a Saturday bus excursion with their parents to the market town of Penrith. It invariably included a visit to the cinema.

The first shop at Burnbanks was run by the daughter of a man injured in a tunnel explosion in 1929; she kept newspapers, tobacco and sweets. Harry Scott, of Hartlepool, in a letter published in *Cumbria* (June, 1989) recalled life at Burnbanks and especially the recreation hall, where he appeared as the wicked uncle in a children's version of *Babes in the Wood.* He recalled the tennis court and sports field. He won prizes in the children's sports.

Before leaving school, Harry worked as an errand boy in the grocery shop. The draper's shop, a branch of Leightons of Shap, was open on only a few days in the month. An "electrical building" was the place to which the Burnbankers took the batteries from their wireless sets to be recharged.

Among the characters of Burnbanks was Gobby, a woman prone

to gossip about her neighbours, and The Aspidistra, who spent much of her time at the window, behind the lace curtains, watching all that happened outside. She could see out clearly but the lacework made it difficult for anyone to see her. There was just a vague form—or perhaps a twitch of the curtain—to suggest someone was present.

The source of water for Burnbanks, which stands almost in the shadow of Haweswater dam, is Blea Water, in a pocket of High Street, which has a small, inconspicuous weir.

The Little Dales

Riggindale

RIGGINDALE, between High Street and Kidsty Pike, is rarely mentioned in print. Little of human consequence seems to have happened here. With a length of about one and a-half miles, it is more of a recess than a dale.

At the head of Riggindale is a cragscape, with corries, but nowhere near as imposing as the corrie which holds Blea Tarn, just over the rigg. Riggindale has an abrupt ending on the shore of Haweswater.

Yet this little valley has grandeur, and the charm of the place is in its clean simple lines. There is a feeling of loneliness. Its southern crags bear a stubble of rowan and birch. To the north, an upsweeping fellside does not seem to have recovered from the shock of being over-run and scoured by glacial ice. Here are screes, with coarse grasses, and a few diminutive trees, mainly rowans.

Riggindale beck, fed by water draining from the dalehead crags, and by a number of springs, flows in a leisurely fashion, with ox-bows. Walkers near the river may find themselves on a quaking landscape.

Manchester Corporation demolished the old farmstead in Riggindale, a dwelling which in latter days had served as a holiday home. An outbuilding remains. The drystone walls are now much gapped. An ancient trod between two lines of upended stones leads to the beck and offers a choice for walkers between the reservoir shore or upbank to Kidsty.

In October, when the red deer of Martindale are rutting, the wind carries the sound of their roaring far across the fells. Outside the rut, hinds and young stags find their way into Riggindale as springtime greens up the bottom land. The deer graze near black or brown ponies.

The fell pony was for long used for farm work, either in shafts (for carting hay or peat) or ridden by a shepherd. Fell ponies helped to sustain the packhorse trade, which carried fuel, slate, wool and general goods. Kendal, a terminus for packhorses, despatched loads on over 300 ponies each working day. Some trains operated as far as Yorkshire; yet others went on to London.

The croak of a raven is heard—a sound which would have been familiar to the Norsefolk, to whom the raven was a sacred bird. Wheatears "chack" and the meadow pipit descends, in shuttlecock flight, its wing and tail feathers stiffly extended and with a continuous outburst of song. Canada geese float on the reservoir like two-tone buoys.

Where, today, people look out for golden eagles, the white-tailed eagle was part of the local fauna. White-tails nested on Walla Crag in 1787, assembling at their eyrie "35 fish beside 7 lambs and other provisions for the young one." Eighteenth century writers tended to exaggerate, but at least a pair of eagles must have been present—among the last of their tribe to nest in Lakeland.

Swindale

Swindale is (to quote the farmer I met) "a pleasant little valley in good weather. It can be very nice if you don't have to make a living here."

Swindale (referred to as Swithindale in a document of 1679) is some two and a-half miles long, ending in a formidable range of crags known as Black Bells.

The dale is approached by public road from Bampton Grange or Rosgill. The best general views are from the fells or the (private) concrete road dating from the inter-war period. Swindale is seen as a dale hemmed in by crags which have a thin coverlet of trees.

Surprisingly, the dalehead fields are large, flat and reasonably fertile. The meadows have not been sprinkled with modern fertilisers and produce a range of wild flowers as well as grasses.

Swindale consists of just one farm, though previously there were three: Swindale Head, Truss Gap and Swindale Foot, where the old farmhouse was demolished years ago and a new house constructed. In 1977, I chatted with Thomas Whitfield, the farmer, who though born in Bretherdale near Tebay had a term of work at Swindale Head in his young days.

He recalled with affection the help he received from that great authority on sheep, William Wilson, who was known throughout the Lake District as "Herdwick Billy". Later, Thomas Whitfield farmed in Wet Sleddale, the next valley—also owned by the water authority. He was there for twenty-two years.

At the time I met Thomas, Swindale Farm had 650 fenced acres, with extensive fell rights. The Swaledale stock numbered 1,100 ewes and 300 hoggs (young sheep). The weather had been running against the Whitfields for two years and they were considering reducing the size of the flock. In drought, the hillsides brown up, the soil forming a thin skin over the rock.

Winter covers with snow the soft hollows, where the best grazing is to be found. The bare hill-ends are eaten away at the approach of spring. In late May, the grass may have just begun to grow.

The Rev J Whiteside, in a paper on Swindale, told of the Rev Stephen Walker, who became curate in 1816 and vicar in 1833. The parsonage was so decrepit, he stayed with his parishioners in turn, keeping his sermons in a box and taking one from the top of the pile each Sunday. He was staying with Mrs Sewell of

Swindale Head when that outspoken lady told him to "stir up that box; they's beginning to come verra' thick."

When Bishop Villiers of Carlisle asked the parson, in the vestry, why he had not answered a letter sent three weeks earlier, he was told that "it will be coming to me someday."

Sometimes, the local people were vague about which day it was. When an argument broke out in church as to whether it was really Sunday, John Fell remarked: "T'parson's reet; gang on."

Swindale school was founded in 1703. The chapel was built in 1749, to replace one of grass sods with a straw-thatch roof which is said to have been consumed by sheep.

Thomas Fishwick, of Swindale Head, attended the Mardale Shepherds' Meet for 66 years.

Wet Sleddale

Wet Sleddale, an open and shallow valley, lies just inside the Lake District National Park.

As Sleddale Beck, the river Lowther rises at Brown How, some 1,866 ft above sea level. After flowing northwards for a while, the beck takes a sudden turn and loses over three hundred feet in height when descending a staircase of black rock in the shadow of scars around which the ravens bark. For a few hundred yards the beck swirls and tumbles in a gorge whose banks are lined by rowans.

Seen on the map, the stream system resembles the veins on the back of a leaf. There is a reference to the Lowther as a river in a document of the 12th century.

The area is criss-crossed by sheep trods and deer tracks. Between Steps Hall and Wet Sleddale lay the ancient "assize road" between Kendal and Appleby. The Judges came this way long before the coach road over Shap Fells began to be used early in the eighteenth century.

The dam in Wet Sleddale is seen by anyone travelling by road or rail. Manchester poured 125,200 cubic yards of concrete into the mouth of the valley, creating a wall 2,000 feet long and 70 feet high. Sensitive by now to public opinion—for it was one of the later works—Manchester arranged for the concrete on the downstream side to be faced with an exposed Shap Blue aggregate. Excavated material was used for landscaping and trees were planted as a screen.

Water from Wet Sleddale flows into Haweswater through an aqueduct, consisting of tunnel, pipeline and cut-and-cover. The impounded water threatened to inundate a seventeenth century packhouse bridge, so it was dismantled and re-erected higher up the dale.

The farms of Wet Sleddale are of the period 1690 to 1703. New Ing was built about the later date, and here for many years lived the Noble family. A hoary tale relates that Lancelot Noble, sent with a message to the vicarage, later reported to his mother that "t'priest's rang in his heed. He said: 'Where have you got your cap?' An', mudder, it was on my heed aw t'time." Another early eighteenth century structure is believed to have been a school.

The dalesfolk, fiercely independent and self-reliant, came from a spirited stock. In 1360, some men from this area violently entered the house and grange of the Abbot of Shap, whereupon the bishop commanded the rural dean and the vicars of the local churches to excommunicate them. The process was solemnly carried out with bell, book and candle.

A track, rutted and littered with big stones, like a beck bottom, leads into the upper reaches of the valley. Drystone walls and buildings crumble at the end of a sheep farming tradition which began over a thousand years ago.

Wet Sleddale was anciently known as Bannisdale; why it should have the prefix "Wet" is not known, and as the most easterly of a clutch of little dales it is drier than its neighbours. There is moisture enough, judging by the profusion of ferns, especially parsley fern.

Botanists with the patience to examine a large tract of countryside also find sweet mountain fern, mountain pansy, primula farinosa, yellow pimpernel and tormentil, one of my favourite plants, the yellow flowers of which spangle the moist ground for months at a time.

In one of the drier areas of the valley is a reminder of medieval life in Wet Sleddale—two enclosures and sections of the boundary walls standing twelve feet high. The late W T Palmer wrote of a "deer park" above Sleddale Hall, the stock from which was removed to Maulds Meaburn.

A friend, Peter Delap, of Appleby, long since formed the opinion that it was something far more interesting—a medieval deer trap, providing its owner with a supply of venison during grim winter days when most of the human population lived on animal flesh which had been salted down.

The two enclosures stand in a part of the valley on which deer, if rounded up, would naturally converge. Animals which followed the wall would keep close to it and be easily deflected by an ingenious baffle (somewhat obscured by a later wall) into the first of the big enclosures. A second enclosure might have been used as a killing area. A magnificent oak tree may have developed from an acorn which had been among the food provided for the deer.

Last Days of Mardale

Tolling the church bell for the last time was more than a farewell to the old church; to the dalesfolk it meant total obliteration of the centuries-old associations of their families with this remote corner of Lakeland.

The Newcastle Chronicle (August 19, 1935).

Everyone felt it when they closed the church. There was an idea they should consecrate a piece of ground higher up on the hillside. Then one of the villagers said: "Who'se going to go there?"

A Mardale farmer's wife.

IN THE LATE 1930s, visitors came to lament the passing of Mardale. Baddeley, the guide book writer, spoke of a countryside "terribly disfigured by the progress of the Manchester waterworks" and commented that "the defacement arising from chimneys and spoil heaps...and the smoke nuisance...would certainly not be excused in Manchester itself."

The church was to go and also the old *Dun Bull.* A newspaper writer with the initials C.N. commented that Manchester was irrevocably changing the look of Mardale with its hard, flinty road and concrete works. "The water meadows under a rainy spring sky will be at the bottom of the reservoir...Climbers on Kidsty will be told yarns of Mardale as the legends grow about Lyonesse and the sunken continents. But for years yet, a few will remain who hold the truth about this drowned jewel of England."

Mardale was in terminal decline in the late 1930s. C Geoff Bailey wrote to *Cumbria* magazine as follows: "In early autumn, 1936, I came down from Mardale Ill Bell past Small Water to a village of silence. The farms and buildings were roofless and deserted, the animals were gone and it seemed that even the birds had sensed what was afoot and had departed.

Grief needs a focal point. In the case of Mardale, this was the church. To the native born, it was a changeless aspect of a fast-changing world—a symbol of the continuance of life in the dale. Its demise seemed to snuff out a thousand years of history.

When it was announced that on August 18, 1935, the Bishop of Carlisle would preach at the last service, he commented: "I count the unavoidable destruction of this typical church of the Lake Country a loss which will touch the hearts of all who know and love it."

For the last service, several thousand visitors converged on Mardale. They were described by the *Newcastle Chronicle* as "Lakeland lovers who made this last pilgrimage on foot, in motor coaches and in the long line of private cars which choked the one narrow lane which winds in and out up the valley for ten miles."

A correspondent of *The Daily Mail* who drove along the narrow winding track up the valley, long before the service began, found it filled from end to end with traffic, "and I was told that every conveyance for miles around had been chartered for the journey."

People came mainly out of curiosity, only to be overwhelmed by the sadness of the occasion as they filed through the church and (to quote again from the *Newcastle Chronicle*) "amateur photographers 'shot' to their hearts' content, capturing pictorial records of the old place".

The saddest man in a huge assembly was said to be the Rev Frederick H J Barham, of Newark, well remembered as Vicar of Mardale. He donned his clerical garb and wandered about in the crowd, talking to his former parishioners.

He had not been invited to take part in the service. A farmer's wife commented: "We thought it was wrong. He'd been at Mardale such a long time. He didn't really want to leave. He was so sorry

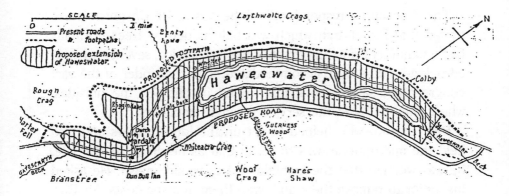

Proposals by Manchester Corporation, as published in 1927.

about it. So I said: 'Well—if you don't want to go just yet, I can keep you a little bit—perhaps a fortnight'. He said: 'Oh, that would be nice.' So I had him a fortnight. And every day he went across to the vicarage, to have another look round."

There was room in the church for only seventy-five people and so tickets were issued. (A correspondent of *The Yorkshire Post* reported that eighty-one, including the Bishop and clergy, had been crammed into the building).

It was a day to inspire journalists; they used their very best cliches to accentuate the poignancy of the situation. The reports filed by emissaries from *Manchester Guardian, Daily Mail, Yorkshire Post, Newcastle Chronicle, Cumberland and Westmorland Herald* and *Westmorland Gazette* were well-suited to be read to an organ accompaniment.

Wrote the special correspondent of *The Daily Mail:* "The mourners of Mardale have gone. The pigmy church cradled in the green basin of this isolated mountain valley—thronged this afternoon by greater crowds than ever before in its centuries-old history—is silent and deserted. The last service has been held, the last sermon preached and the last Blessing pronounced."

The "special correspondent" of the *Newcastle Chronicle* mentioned that the church which was half hidden by trees normally had a handful of worshippers. For the last service, seventy privileged ticket-holders were accommodated. The remainder of the vast congregation sat in the fields around or climbed the hillsides, where they followed the service through amplifiers.

Billy Barton, who helped to set up the loudspeakers and also held the microphone, was to recall that as he drove to Mardale, he was worried that the amplifier valves would smash. He asked his junior to remove them and wrap them in some coats. Mr Barton travelled at low speed while this was being done, much to the annoyance of other drivers on the tortuous road beside Haweswater.

The reporter for the *Newcastle Chronicle* had paid a lone pilgrimage to the church in a downpour of rain shortly after breakfast and, writing about it movingly, with a somewhat casual approach to history, he found "something symbolic of Mardale's future in this relentless downpour." He mentioned "the mist-wreathed hills and the rainwater dripping cheerlessly from the branches of yew trees which men once planted to provide bows for the Kendal Archers in the days of the Scottish raiders."

The wet, misty morning was attuned to the mood of the villagers he met as they prepared the church for its last service. "In the churchyard, an old man, oblivious of the rain, was carefully trimming a hedge. Probably that was the easiest way he knew of shutting out of his mind the fact that the hedge—an old friend—would be but a memory in the future."

Ernest Simpson, a young man, had "the historic task" in the afternoon of climbing up the narrow stairway into the belfry and tolling the bell which called Mardale to worship for the last time.

Thomas Rutherford, describing the last service for newspaper readers, mentioned "a strange peace" in the valley that day. "The folded hills like ruffled velvet, the lake gleaming blue in the sun-shine, a burning sun beating down on the meadows, the sound of a bell breaking through the stillness..."

The service, conducted by the Bishop of Carlisle, Dr H H Williams, was attended by the Lord Mayor of Manchester, Alder-man S Woollam, who represented (wrote *The Daily Mail,* bitingly) "the multitude for whose good Mardale is doomed." Also present were the Rev W H Cormack, Vicar of Shap, and the Rev F S Sinker, who read the lesson.

The assembly sang an appropriate psalm: "I will Lift up Mine Eyes to the hills". The selected hymns were "O God Our Help in Ages Past", "The Church's One Foundation" and "Bright the Vision that Delighted".

Among the congregation was the oldest inhabitant of the dale Miss Kitching (aged 75) who, though "sternly conscious of the occasion", could say little except: "I never thought I should see the old church closed."

The Bishop, well tuned to the concerns of the day, did not weep nor wail for Mardale, saying: "We must take for granted the fact that great urban populations need pure water, and the presence of the chief magistrate of Manchester here to-day is proof that the city is well aware of the sacrifice the valley is making and feels genuine sympathy for you in your great loss."

The Bishop did not favour the erection of a new church elsewhere which would merely be a museum of old Lakeland ecclesiastical relics. He stressed the more urgent need of new churches for housing estates.

The Daily Mail's man-on-the-spot strummed the heart-strings of his readers. "Now the last car has gone... As the mists drift closer and closer with their damp, chill touch, a tiny figure high on a dis-tant bluff marks the last dalesman homeward trudging his lonely way. The mourning of Mardale is completed... In the gloom, the mammoth peaks crouch low and protecting over the Lost Church...In the calm quiet of evening there comes wind-borne the slow plash of waves on the waiting lake..."

The latter-day visitors to Mardale saw Mardale Church as a ruin. There was talk that explosives might be used on the church, but the vicar of Bampton contacted a church dignitary who insisted to the contractors that it should be taken down, stone by stone. (Windows and much stone was re-cycled, forming part of the new draw-off tower by the reservoir).

The register of Mardale Church had been closed on July 28, 1935, when George Ernest Crabtree was baptised there. The record of human comings and goings was only half full, though the first entry was in 1813. Black oak pews, beetle-free, were fashioned into seats for the new *Haweswater Hotel,* which took shape eighty feet above the revised water level. The bell went to a new church, St Barnabas, on a housing estate at the edge of Carlisle.

Towards the end of 1935, the bodies in Mardale churchyard were exhumed and most of them re-interred in a corner of the cemetery at Shap, a corner which became known as "the Mardale portion".

It is a peaceful spot, well away from the village, in a truly rural setting, and on a clear day the Lakeland fells are visible to the west. The visitor to this cemetery enters the plot up several steps. Fourteen headstones arranged on the wallsides include some which had adorned the graves of the ubiquitous Holme family.

Five other bodies were re-interred elsewhere, at the request of the relatives. In the case of the Edmondson family, this was at Askham.

Horace Horrox, who helped with the work, recalls that the coffin of Hugh Parker Holme had been lined with lead and was of such a weight that it took five men to lift it on to the back of the lorry that transported it to a new resting place.

In the drought of 1984, those who negotiated the mud to reach the site of the church saw the stumps of the yew trees which had been sawn off and cleared away by Manchester Waterworks.

Some of those with long memories of Mardale hoped (in vain) that a new church would be built above high water mark, using perhaps some of the money (£2,405) which Manchester had paid in compensation for the loss of Church, vicarage and glebe land.

Most of the furnishings of Mardale Church were allocated to the new Church of St Barnabas at Carlisle. This was done despite objections by the Shap churchwardens and the lineal descendant of the Holme family, who were represented at a session of a Consistory Court (August, 1935) by Mr Q L W Little, a Penrith solicitor.

When the Court considered the future of Mardale's old font, the Vicar of Shap was asked if that parish really wanted it. He replied that Shap already had three fonts. The Court decided that the principal contents of Mardale Church should go to the new Church in Carlisle. In fact, the Jacobean oak pulpit was acquired by Rosthwaite, in Borrowdale.

On Wednesday, May 27, 1936, "the tiny mushroom village of Burnbanks", and the Haweswater district generally, entertained a large party of distinguished visitors when the Manchester Waterworks Committee arrived to inspect the city's latest water scheme. The party numbered 135, being headed by the Committee chairman, Alderman William Walker, and the Lord Mayor and Lady Mayoress, "both wearing their chains of office."

It had been a comfortable journey from Manchester to Shap. A correspondent of the Cumberland and Westmorland Herald said the train, made up of first-class restaurant cars, was treated by the L.M.S. Railway Company as though it was the Royal Train.

"It was a lovely day for such an excursion and the mountain urn which holds Haweswater never looked daintier or more delightful in its bright spring raiment. The garb was, however, slightly unusual for the Lake District." Silk hats, frock coats, striped trousers, spats and gold chains were not often to be seen at the base of the Haweswater dam, but they were all there...

An invitation had been extended to the Earl of Lonsdale. He humorously regretted the fact that the Corporation had chosen Derby Day for their outing. He was unable to arrange to be in two places at one and the same time.

Meanwhile, the old Measand school had been taken down, stone by stone, and rebuilt at Walmgate Head. It is now a private residence which, in the summer of 1993, was in the course of being extended and renovated. It was good to see the inscribed stone on the porch still in place and looking cleaner than I had ever seen it before.

Old Mardale perished, but the memory lingers on. A quarter of a century ago, the vicar of Bampton received two census forms: one for Bampton and one for Holy Trinity, Mardale. He did his best to complete them, but how can you estimate the number of fish which frequent the flattened ruins of a church beneath the waves?

Haweswater Today

You see below you a great mad road, wide enough for three cars, flatly running two miles further up the dale than the highest house, leading to nothing.
                                                Susan G Johnson (1958).

HAWESWATER has its busy side and its quiet side. When the summer sun brings a responsive gleam from a hundred cars parked at the end of the road, east of the water; when more cars arrive by the minute and there is a threat of chaos from one incautiously parked vehicle, it is pleasant to saunter along the footpath west of the water.

This is a pedestrian's route, and among the walkers are a scattering of determined people en route from St Bees Head to Robin Hood's Bay, on the now famous Wainwright Coast-to-Coast route.

A footpath for day-trippers begins at Burnbanks, where the direction signs are in the old style, headed by initials representing the archaic title of Manchester Waterworks. Someone has ensured there is a gap between trees in the vicinity of the dam to provide a clear view of it, a view framed by conifers.

The last time I went this way, in the summer of 1993, a buzzard was wheeling and mewing over the crags and an astonishingly fat stoat bounded from one patch of bracken to another.

The path broke from the cover of trees and now I had a stunning view of Naddle Forest, beyond the gleaming lake, and the fells huddled together around the head of the water—huddled as though for mutual comfort.

In pre-reservoir times, Measand Beck Hall presided over a delta which, at The Straits, gave Haweswater a waist like a wasp. Now there is little to see beyond a former outbuilding, within which grows a large tree; and the remains of walls and old pastures, cropped by Swaledale sheep, which stare at passers-by with eyes which have an ancient look about them, as though they are half as old as the rocks.

It was the presence of the beck which led to centuries of habitation in the Measand area. Walkers, crossing a wooden bridge, glance upwards to where cold fell water leaps from pool to pool—a series of waterfalls and gin-clear pools, shaded by gnarled trees and with plants growing from cracks and crannies. In summer, the flowering of bell heather provides some purple patches to relieve the light tones of rock plated with grey lichen and a hundred shades of green.

On my first visit to Haweswater, almost forty years ago, I met Mrs M Scott, wearing the uniform of postmistress and pushing a bicycle on the last stretch of her round, which went as far as the *Haweswater Hotel*. Shortly afterwards, I stepped to one side as a bus run by Messrs Hartness eased its way down the twisting road.

I met Syd Wear (brother of the huntsman, Joe Wear) and heard from him that three huge oil engines had generated electricity for the construction work and the concrete was conveyed to the dam by overhead buckets.

I chatted with the astonishing Sir William Walker, who had been a member of Manchester City Council since 1909 and who still attended meetings from his home at Naddle Gate, formerly one of the staff bungalows. He told me that he had lived here since his own home in Manchester was bombed. There was then no demand for the bungalows of Burnbanks and he had four from which to choose.

His first glimpse of Haweswater had been in the early 1890s, when he was cycling with a friend, making their way to Carlisle. They left their cycles at the top end of Longsleddale and walked over Gatescarth to see the lake.

Haweswater was converted into a reservoir—and Old Mardale died of drowning—at a time when the district needed employment and money. Farming was in the doldrums in the 1920s and 1930s.

A H Griffin described how for thirty years Mardale was a forgotten valley. "People don't come to see a dead lake and a lifeless dale, especially on the less popular eastern fringe of Lakeland." Griffin added that the valley was still a lovely place—"if you stand with your back to the dam."

What he foresaw were the profound changes brought about by the coming of the M.6 through Westmorland, leading to a tourist invasion from the Midlands, and the completion of Manchester's water treatment plant near Kendal, giving Manchester a more relaxed view of public admission to its catchment area.

At Mardale, the Flood of water has been followed by a torrent of tourists, especially in drought years, when there's romance in the air with the reappearance of parts of the "lost" village. In 1973, the water level sank to over fifty feet below the lip of the dam, which was a record low. It was possible once again to trudge through thick mud along the old road to the bridge and visit the old settlement of Mardale.

I visited Old Mardale with Canon T E H Baily, vicar of Shap, who had spent family holidays in Mardale before the Flood. I met him by chance. He told me that his father, the Rev G H J Baily, served for a time in Burneside and later, in the mid-1920s, he had a busy parish in Sunderland.

It was then that holidays were planned in Mardale. The *Dun Bull* accommodated visitors, but the Bailys were a large family and renting accommodation made their holidays possible "In those days, there was always a house which was temporarily empty."

The family travelled to Shap by train and used horse-drawn transport for the final stretch, into Mardale. Canon Bailey recalled that one journey was made in a milk float and that some time later the transport was a Ford car. There was no road on the Naddle side of the reservoir. Squirrel-haunted Naddle was little visited and there was a "feel" to the landscape which was quite distinctive.

The Canon and I located the remains of Mardale Church—now just a heap of stones, not far from where Chapel Hill Farm had stood. The focal point of our view was the old bridge across the main beck. The structure was complete though it had been under water for three decades.

"Down there" (and Canon Baily directed my attention to ruins around which the walls were still tall and firm) "was Goosemire, a small house." He identified the outbuildings, the sheepfold, dipping-trough and the small fields. The Bailys had stayed at

Goosemire during one of their holidays.

I commented on the good condition of the walls. Canon Baily recalled that when the reservoir was completed, the water came up gently. He plunged his stick into the mud and we estimated the depth of the mud at that spot as two feet. Streams were running in the old courses. "You can see why Goosemire was a damp house when we lived there!" Water was gurgling within a few yards of the old habitation.

We passed the stump of an ash tree which, I heard, had been felled for firewood in the 1920s. We crossed one of the seventeenth century packhorse-type bridges. The stones forming the arch were still firmly in place. Canon Baily located a small patch of red paint on one of the stones. At that point the local post-box was attached to the wall.

We passed near Dinah, the name of a field where clay-pigeon shoots had been held. The ground was still littered with pieces of baked clay from the shattered target "clays". Across the former road, still neatly squared up and smooth, was what had been a tennis court, close to the *Dun Bull*.

What would the old Mardalians have made of these high-tec days, such as is evidenced by a building of Burlington slate, with a slate roof, which stands among the trees near Haweswater dam and contains powerful electrical pumps, capable of moving fifty-six million gallons a day? The water engineers think twice about using this facility, for the pumps run on electricity, an expensive source of power.

In designing the building, care was taken to build-in sound retention materials so the whine of the pumps are not too conspicuous to passers-by.

In 1973, Manchester Corporation's water undertaking was transferred to the North West Water Authority and has subsequently been privatised. North West Water have co-operated in the establishment of the largest RSPB reserve in England—that centred around Haweswater, covering some 27,000 acres or about five per cent of the Lake District National Park. It is bounded by High Street and Harter Fell and includes some of the best heather moors in the country.

The spirit of Old Mardale is best evoked through its farming, for although the farms of Mardale went under water, Naddle Farm endures. The successors of the old Mardale farmers and shepherds have all-terrain vehicles and light alloy crooks, but their knowledge of the ways of sheep is just as intense.

The spirit of t'auld days is to be found at the Mardale Shepherds' Meet. In 1952, some twenty assorted Swaledales and Roughs, plus one solitary Herdwick—all strays—were penned in Sargent Noble's yard at Bampton Hall. All the sheep were claimed by the evening.

A special item of conversation was the sole representative of the Herdwick breed among the strays. The older men recalled when there would be thirty or more Herdwicks on view. Other breeds had taken the place of what had been Lakeland's distinctive sheep breed.

"It's a great pity," said one shepherd. "T'Herdwick maybe doesn't carry as much meat as some other breeds, but thoo can't beat it for King's Mutton. A four-year-old wether [young male]— my, t'mutton's grand!"

Jack Harrison, of Sleddale Hall, had attended his first Mardale Meet in 1906, and before leaving the district he farmed at Swindale Foot. The proud boast of Henry Metcalfe, then living at Butterwick after many years spent farming at Dale Foot, Helton, was that he had attended the Meet for sixty years "without a miss". He remembered when there was more ale spilt on the floor than is supped in the average Lakeland pub today.

Fifty years to the day after the last service took place in the old Mardale Church, an open air service was held at the foot of

117

Haweswater Dam, by permission of North-West Water. Over four hundred people, most of them wearing raincoats and carrying umbrellas as the rain sheeted down, formed a semi-circle near a large oak tree on a rise where an altar had been set up, arrayed with the original cross and candlesticks from the old church.

The form of service, that of fifty years before, was conducted by the Rev Wilfrid Braithwaite, who was present in 1936. The Rural Dean, the Rev John Mellish, spoke about the relevance and recognition of sacrifice. It should not be forgotten that the Mardalians, a small, close-knit community, gave up their homes and their livelihood to provide water for big industrial areas further south. Their sacrifice had resulted in inestimable benefit to thousands through the much-needed provision of water.

I do not think the Mardale folk, who were as heafed to their valley as the Herdwick sheep they tended, saw the Manchester invasion in quite those terms.

Maggie Lancaster told listeners to Radio Cumbria: "I dream of Mardale lots of times. I can see my father or see me taking tea into the hayfield. Sometimes I even see t'auld vicar. Everything is just as clear as it was fifty years ago. When I dream, of Mardale, I think: 'Oh, I wish it was like it used to be in the days gone by'. It's just a sheet of water now..."

Appendices

1. Of Harter Fell
(Anon)

Who leaps outright from Walla Crag
Leaps bold enough—leaps bold enough;
Who sleeps all night on Harter Fell
Sleeps cold enough—sleeps cold enough.

2. The Vicars of Mardale, 1703-1934

Michael Sommers (1703-1721)
William Lanehorn (1721-1722)
Jonathan Tinclair (1722-1725)
William Robinson (1725-1726)
Thomas Baxter (1726-1731)
Richard Holme (1731-1734)
William Collinson (1734-1739)
John Watson (1739-1741)
Bartholomew Hayes (1741-1749)
Richard Hebson (1749-1799)
John Bowstead (1800-1842)
John Rowlandson (1842-1858)
Thomas Holme (1858-1880)
Henry Wilkinson (1880-1882)
Charles Henry Scaife Hatfield (1882)
Arthur Anderson Williams (1882-1885)
Charles Newton Greenwood (1885-1890)
Hugh Charles Baldwin (1891-1894)
William Terry (1894-1910)
Frederick H J Barham (1910-1934)

3. Christian Names of the Family of William Kitching, Boatman on Haweswater

He married a Bousfield from Brough or Kirkby Stephen, on or about February 17, 1873.

1. Ada Jane Marie
2. Janet Augusta Louisa
3. Tom Harrison Bousfield
4. Gladys Waistell Lennex
5. Florence Winifred Hunter
6. Hugh Harvey Hayton
7. Brunskill Hayes Bland
8. Arthur Hazel Duncan
9. Albert Ashenden Donald Sykes
10. Selina Rose Parker
11. Lowther Lonsdale Liddell
12. Noble Boustead Holmes
13. William Theodore Barron
14. Mabel Gertrude Constance Fothergill May

Hugh and William emigrated to Canada (c1904); William returned to Cumbria. Hugh settled in Montreal and has six sons. Arthur, Albert, Selina Rose and Noble went to Canada c1910. Noble returned to the home acres.

Arthur died in Toronto, Albert was killed on the Somme and Lowther at the Dardenelles. Tom, wounded on Army service about 1917, nonetheless lived until 1966 and died a month short of his ninetieth birthday.

A Seeker's

Past Lives

Paul Williamson

www.capallbann.co.uk

Paul Williamson
32 Coniston Road
Lancaster.
01524 61035

A Seeker's Guide To Past Lives

ISBN 186163 272X

Cover design by Paul Mason

Published by:

Capall Bann Publishing
Auton Farm
Milverton
Somerset
TA4 1NE

Acknowledgements

I would like to thank Eleyna, Kate and Jane, whose vital contributions were necessary to improve the text of this work. To all those who have been willing to bear their souls and share their accounts of past life regression experiences that they have had, I would like to extend my heart felt gratitude and appreciation. Finally, I would like to acknowledge those Spiritual influences that have guided and inspired me and helped to sustain my interest to complete this project.

Other books by Paul Williamson, also published by Capall Ban:

Atlantis The Dark Continent

Soul Pathways

Healing Journeys

Contents

Introduction

I have given talks on past life regression on numerous occasions, to large and diverse groups. Many people seem open to believing in reincarnation, and in the possibility that we have within us the memories of past lives, that we can bring to the surface of our consciousness. Obviously it is a topic that fascinates; when conducting these presentations, I usually have no difficulty in finding volunteers for taster regression sessions to show others how the process works. Yet when it comes to people actually daring to undergo a full individual regression session, far fewer are willing to commit.

There are many reasons for this: fear of the unknown; a suspicion that regression can risk one's mental health; lack of willingness to make the financial investment required; self-consciousness about what family and friends will think; personal or religious belief of what is right and wrong.

When people come for talks, they can safely allow their curiosity to flow and their interest to be awakened. In this context, past life regression can be like entertainment - an audience does not need to feel too committed to it. Most of us need to feel that what we do has relevance to our everyday life - many people look at past life regression using this criterion before being prepared to take it seriously. I feel that this is where there is a lot of misconception surrounding past life regression because I believe that it can be very relevant to the life we are living now.

Over the sixteen years or more that I have been a practising past life regression therapist, I have become a strong advocate of its use as a transformational therapeutic tool to help people. It is not my wish that such a powerful and effective form of therapy remains on the fringes of our society.

Hence the main impulse that has driven me to write this book is the desire to make past life regression more accessible to those who are interested in it. I have attempted to share openly about the many aspects of what may be involved for those who want to explore inner experiences through regression. It has not been my intention to convey the impression that past life regression is cosy and nice. Past life regression can be hard work, challenging and potentially life-changing. But in an age when people want to improve themselves, achieve their capabilities and liberate themselves from inner fears and barriers, past life therapy is an ideal process that could enable people to do that.

I believe that there are boundless possibilities for personal healing and inner spiritual growth that can be achieved through this medium. It may not be appropriate for everybody, but for those to whom it does appeal, I want to offer my encouragement and enthusiasm as an advocate of its use.

I would like to invite seekers to enter into the inner voyage of discovery that may be possible through past life regression. It is my wish that this book can serve as a map to help people's orientation as to what they may expect from such explorations, how they can get the most out of it and feel safe within the process. In the following chapters, I hope that from my knowledge and experience, I can offer some signposts and foundations to help those who want to learn more about this subject.

Case Studies

In addition to my own thoughts, I would like to share the experiences that some of my clients have had when undergoing past life regression. The people concerned were invited to write a little about their background beliefs and how they felt about actually engaging in a past life regression session beforehand. I then asked them to give expression to their experience of the regression, and the outcome of how it impacted upon their lives afterwards. Most of these accounts have required little editing, and where this was needed, I have tried to remain faithful to the authenticity of their experience. I would like to express my gratitude to all the people who have contributed their inner stories to this book. They have shown a lot of trust in me, and have been willing to expose their vulnerability regarding themes and inner issues that have, in the main, been deeply personal in nature. They have enabled me to illustrate many of the points that I have raised with actual experiences – and it is to willing, brave and courageous seekers like these that I wish to dedicate this book.

Chapter 1

The Soul and Reincarnation

In this chapter I would like to outline my understanding of the main concepts referred to in this book. These definitions are intended to enable you, the reader, to comprehend the major themes that follow. To consider subjects such as the nature of our soul, or the purpose of our incarnations here on earth, is quite a profound undertaking. Moreover, this book aims to offer pragmatic suggestions, for helping people in their quest to explore their inner selves, rather than to be a work of philosophical importance. But it is essential that the meaning ascribed to terms like 'soul' and 'karma' can be properly conveyed.

My study of the subject of reincarnation has been proceeding for well over the last twenty-five years. During this time my own cosmology about how the universe operates on a human level has been developing. My attitude is that it is healthy for all of us not to take any teachings given to us for granted, but to test them within us using our own inner sense of truth. There are those that may be wiser and know more than we do, but it is essential that we feel empowered to make our own decisions - and that we do not let someone else do this for us.

For the purposes of this book, the main sources for my understandings have come through my observation of past life regression sessions, my own inner guidance and teachings from other spiritual sources that have felt appropriate to me. From this basis I will define the main terms used in this book.

As human beings, I believe that essentially we are beings of light and energy. At some point in our evolution, we attain the gift of individual consciousness. This marks a separation and differentiation from the oneness or consciousness that is 'God'. I believe that a spark of this 'God' consciousness remains within us and, with it, a longing to return to that source from whence we have come. Therefore, within our individual consciousness, there is the urge for us to gain maturity and experience so that we can become as 'God' ourselves. The totality of our individual consciousness is what I would call our soul.

There are many ways that the soul can learn so that it will evolve and grow more God-like. Like all physical life around us, each soul is unique. Unlike other forms of life, as human souls we are given the faculty of free will. This faculty gives us responsibility for our own path of learning and how we grow. Therefore we choose our own way forward. We are not alone and there may be many other spiritual beings of all descriptions with which we are connected. But the relationship that we form with another being is up to us, and forms an aspect of our learning.

One path that we can choose is to have physical incarnations upon the earth. This is just one of many options available to us as a soul to take our learning process forward. When we decide to do this for the first time, it may mark the beginning of a cycle of experiences in the physical world that lasts for many, many lifetimes.

The procedure involved in entering into physical incarnation is quite complex. As souls we need to choose a purpose about which we want to learn through this experience, for every lifetime. This means that while we are still preparing ourselves in the spiritual realm we, as souls, consciously choose our parents, the kind of circumstances in which we grow up, our disposition, the significant people and challenges that we want to meet, and the goals we want to achieve.

Descending into our earthly body involves our consciousness becoming much more restricted than the expansive state to which our soul is accustomed. The vibrations of the physical world are much denser than that of the spiritual realm our soul usually inhabits. This means that only part of our soul is able to engross itself in physical matter to live as a human being on earth. The part of us that remains in spirit is called our Higher Self. Within our Higher Self is contained the memory of all the experience that we have gathered through previous lifetimes and other experience, plus the knowledge of our life purpose for our present incarnation.

When we are born, there is much that we have to learn about the physical world. We have to adjust to our physical bodies, our desires and appetites, our thoughts and feelings. Soon layers of consciousness form, meaning that our knowledge of our higher self, and the realm of spirit, is largely hidden from us. During those moments when we are still, we may be dimly aware, with the wonder of life, of that longing to be connected with 'God' and the rest of our soul. But it will be up to us whether we follow that inclination and seek contact with the spiritual aspect of life or not.

Once we start to incarnate as human beings we are likely to become involved energetically with interactions and relationships that we are not able to complete. When we desire something and we do not get what we want in the way that we want it, then we feel frustrated and unfulfilled. After we have passed through our physical deaths, we will be aware of what we have not completed, and we will want to do so. This will almost certainly necessitate the need for us to return for further incarnations. As we enlarge the scope of our activity, the level of our frustrations and desires will probably increase. Yet, through every experience, we learn and gain maturity as a soul. After each incarnation we absorb the experience of the previous life into our soul. Once started, our yearning is to gain the soul skills necessary to cope with all manner of experience on earth. In some lives we may be more successful in gaining these skills than in others.

In the spiritual realm, it comes naturally and easily for us to be loving and respectful towards all other beings. We are much more consciously aware of the natural order of things. This is not so straightforward for us to always accomplish when we are living lives on earth. With our free wills, we are likely to greatly disturb any natural harmony that exists.

6

But we will also feel it deep inside us when our actions are discordant with what may be a spiritual need.

For instance, people have a deep inner need to be shown respect and kindness. If we are not loving and respectful to others in a particular incarnation then, at the end of that life, we will know what we have done; we will feel the need to do better so that we can be more sensitive to those other souls' needs.

Fundamentally, I believe that the main lesson that we have to learn on earth is about love - learning to love in all its facets. We also need to gain wisdom in numerous situations so that we can use our free will appropriately.

At the end of each lifetime, the experience gained from that part of us that was in physical incarnation is integrated into our greater soul, so that our soul becomes united again. As we mature as souls, we gain talents and abilities, strengths and weaknesses. It is necessary for us to overcome our weaknesses to a considerable degree before we can become free from the need for physical incarnation. Our weaknesses consist of limiting patterns of behaviour, whereby we continue to act in ways that are not in harmony with our inner need. An example of this could be where a soul feels that he has to be in control and is afraid of trusting in others. Another instance may be when a soul continues to go into isolation and close his heart rather than face up to immediate challenges. There are many subtle variations as to how we can keep ourselves stuck by repeating limiting patterns of behaviour.

Before each lifetime, we meet with our higher teachers and helpers in the Spirit realm to form an agenda of what we aspire as souls to experience and learn in the coming incarnation. When we return to Spirit after our sojourn on Earth, we might have managed to fulfill some parts of what we intended to achieve, while with other aspects, we could have fallen short and not done what we set out to do. Those tasks that we do not complete are carried forward so that we can attempt them again in another lifetime.

While we are in physical incarnation, we need to try to abide by the universal laws of cause and effect. These are called the Laws of Karma. To remain in balance as a soul, as has been stated, we need to aspire to treat all other living beings with respect and love, and to be true to our path. When we deviate from this, it causes a reaction. This reaction can necessitate that we change our behaviour so those things are in balance again. If we cannot make the adjustments that are needed, by following our inner urges to make things right, then the need for redress may extend into further lifetimes if it is not fully resolved within the lifetime where the mistake occurs. How we act will be mirrored back to us in some shape or form, sooner or later. All that we do has consequences in terms of effects.

By using the gift of free will it is common for us, while in physical incarnation, to become very self-absorbed. In this state we may not recognise immediately when we cause hurt to another. For our soul, it is paramount that we learn to respect the needs of others, so that we do not cause unnecessary hurt. The needs of the soul and the desires of our free will can drift quite far apart if, with our free will, we decide not to listen to the urges of our soul.

Sometimes our souls choose lifetime after lifetime with a similar theme, because with our free will we refuse to listen to what our higher self is urging us to do. We repeatedly hurt others or avoid some situation that we need to confront. We do this because we do not want to listen, or because of fear or some other emotion that we find difficult to manage, such as guilt, anger or loss. It is quite a task for us as souls to learn to manage all the various emotions, thoughts and physical situations in which we might find ourselves while on earth.

I'll give an example to try to make this clearer. As a soul we may choose a life with a parent who has a very bitter and angry attitude towards life. The influence of that parent may be very strong and make us inclined to adopt a very similar attitude in our own life when we get older. If we can listen to guidance from within, we may be able to withstand this influence and transmute the energies of it into something else. We could forgive our parent and use that hurt that we have suffered as compassion to help others who have suffered similarly. But if we react negatively to the influence of this parent, we might as adults cause a lot of hurt to others. Then we may need to go into a similar life again, until we can learn how to withstand this kind of influence.

There are many facets of human experience that we need to learn about. As we gain maturity as souls, the kind of tests and challenges that we give ourselves will tend to become more difficult.

During our evolution, we may even choose some experiences where we are almost bound to hurt and cause harm to others. These will be our darker lives. I believe that every soul, once they start physical incarnations, will, at some point in their evolution, seek these kinds of experiences. We do this so that we can experience what it is like not to love and then to have to embrace the darkness that this type of experience brings. When a soul chooses to live out a darker life, it will face an even greater restriction of consciousness than on other occasions. I know from some of my regressions that these lives are very unpleasant to endure. By going through this type of experience, we learn to value love and recognise how important it is. It feels absolutely appalling to be without love. Once we have chosen some darker lives, our drive to seek love will be greater, and this helps the soul to mature.

Within our consciousness in a particular lifetime, we build up a bank of experiences that lie within us. These exist largely within our subconscious mind. With our normal ego consciousness, we are aware of only a small portion of these experiences. Our usual consciousness is quite limited in terms of what we can perceive.

People are often very selective about what they wish to know concerning the experiences of their subconscious mind. Anything uncomfortable or fearful they may be inclined to avoid. Therefore, people who do not want to know anything about their inner life, live completely according to the desires of their free will. Fears operating from inside restrict the scope of their activities. Occasionally, the prompting of their higher self can make itself known, but more often not. When they don't listen to their inner guidance, I believe that people are far more likely to make a mess of their lives and do things that they will later regret. People then reach a point in their lives where they are challenged to look more deeply at what they are doing. If they do this, and seek help, it may be the case of trying to pick up the pieces. Otherwise things tend to get worse before they get better.

When people choose to live a spiritual path, they want to listen and learn what their higher self has to tell them, and choose, as much as possible, experiences in harmony with the needs of their soul. Following a spiritual path, we need to learn how we can connect with our higher self. In addition, we need considerable courage to do what our higher self suggests to us. Fear often causes our free will to vary our actions from the needs of our soul. Therefore, when we choose to listen to our higher self, we are also tested to overcome our fears.

There are various layers within our subconscious mind. Through meditation and listening to our conscience, we encourage elements of our deeper mind to reveal themselves. By wanting to know the truth of our inner being, we attract that awareness to us. When we start to connect with our higher self, we begin to have memories of our past lives and other experiences normally forgotten. By reaching for the knowledge that our higher self wants to impart to us, we raise our vibrations. This enables past life memory and other inner knowledge to be more easily transferred to us. When we meditate, we still our minds so that we are no longer occupied with the chatter of our usual preoccupations. Again, this helps us to become more sensitive so that we can listen within.

Our souls need help so that we can progress wisely. There are beings wiser than we are who help us. These may be called our guardian angels or spiritual guides. They are our inner friends. When we choose our life purpose, one of these beings is assigned to us as our personal guide for that lifetime. This guide is there to assist as much as possible with our higher self so that we are true to our purpose. Our guide also ensures that our higher self is kept safe. When we choose to live a spiritual path, we might be able to learn to make contact with our spiritual guides and angelic helpers. We may benefit from the teachings that they can impart. Connecting with our guides helps us to acquire experience of a deeper form of unconditional love, which in turn helps us to live out our life purpose. For all of us, gaining direct knowledge of the spiritual realms helps us to learn about love, and to bring spiritual love into the physical plane. Such action is spiritual service, something that our soul will find deeply satisfying.

Whatever our purpose is, it is likely that by accessing past life memory it will become clearer to us. What we do with that knowledge is then up to us.

Chapter 2

Frequently Asked Questions

On first encountering past life regression, many questions can arise. In this chapter, I have assembled the most frequently asked questions with the answers that I give in response.

Question: *Does everyone have a past life?*

Paul: It is hard for me to be definitive about this. Although I have been working professionally as a past life therapist for many years, the number of people that I have regressed is tiny in relation to the overall population of the Earth. Even regarding those whom I have not been able to regress, it would be foolish of me on that basis to conclude that these people do not have past lives. They may still have memories of past lives in their consciousness but not be open with my methods to accessing these at this time.

There are a small number of people with whom I have attempted regression for whom, even though they were quite open subjects, the experience of a past life was not forthcoming. With one man in particular, in response to the suggestion asking him to recall what he was doing before this life, he felt that he had some perception, but it was not as a physical body. In the way that he related to living on our physical plane he was quite clumsy. I suspect in his case that he could very well be experiencing his first incarnation on Earth.

My hunch is that there are many such people incarnating for their initial experience on our Earth. With our world population being as vast as it is at the moment, I am sure that there are a lot of young souls amongst us tasting physical life for the first time.

Question: *How many past lives do we have?*

Paul: This appears to vary enormously from person to person. We each have a unique soul with our own individual history and patterns as to how our existences have unfolded. For some people with whom I have worked. there are strong indications that they have lived only a very small number of lives prior to this one. With others, there have been signs that they carry the memory of hundreds if not thousands of previous incarnations.

Sometimes people's belief systems can affect their perception about how many past lives exist for them. At the outset of therapy they may believe that they only have a very limited number of lives. However, as their outlook becomes more open, they become aware of many further lives that initially they were not ready to acknowledge. Certainly I have been surprised at how much my own boundaries have been extended over the years. When I first started I believed that I had only a quite limited number of previous lifetimes. Now I feel that I have had many, many past lives and the list of personal incarnations of which I am aware is growing all the time.

Question: *How far back can past lives go?*

Paul: This depends very much upon the individual. Some people have memories of lifetimes that appear to stem back to extremely ancient times, many, many thousands of years ago. Past life regression recall would suggest that the history of human civilisation on our planet is far more extensive, and reaches much further back in time, than is assumed with the prevailing scientific thoughts of our time.

Of course, people access lifetimes of incarnations as Stone Age hunters and gatherers. This is to be expected. But some of the past life memories that people bring forward, concerning places of very ancient origins, appear much more tantalising and depict civilisations that are little known of by people today. Regressions to societies such as those that I identify as the legendary continents of Atlantis, Mu and Lemuria come forward quite regularly. These are just three of the very ancient civilisations. I know that there are many more. Not every experience is familiar to me in terms of its location, and the practice of dating these lifetimes can be very speculative.

Some souls take much longer to learn their lessons than others, and if they keep making mistakes that they do not rectify, then going to the source of particular problems can lead to incarnations that date a long way back into history. Also there are people whose souls are very sensitive and carry the memory of very ancient events quite close to the surface of their consciousness.

Question: Is our most recent past life the most important one for us to access?

Paul: For some souls, this can certainly be the case. There could be issues and unfinished business from our most recent life that have led precisely to the conditions that we have chosen for our present incarnation. Where this is evident, the experience of this regression can be very intense because the resonance from that lifetime to this will be very raw, with no other experiences in between to modify it.

Traumatic elements from this past life can remain hidden until the soul is ready to face up to it in its life now. There may then be other past lives that will emerge first. These regressions could also be dealing with similar themes, and provide a preparation to help the person be ready and stronger to access the memory of this most recent past lifetime.

At times, the most recent past life may not be relevant or important at all. It could have simply been a lifetime where a cycle of learning was completed, allowing the soul to move on to themes very different from that incarnation. The inner challenges confronting the soul in the present life could link much more with other past lives, where these challenges have been previously attempted. It could also be planned on a soul level for any unfinished business, from the most recent life, to be worked out

14

in a lifetime several hundred years further along that soul's path, rather than in the present life. There are many possible patterns that can come into play.

In approaching regression, we need to use our intuition and trust that we will be guided to explore the most pertinent past life experience for us, whether that is our most recent past life or one much further back.

Question: *What does it mean if I can't get into a past life?*

Paul: This can mean various things. To be able to open our inner minds and let the memories from a past life impress themselves upon our consciousness is quite a big step to manage. Some of us have conditioned ourselves with our thoughts to only be open to 'rational' ideas, not accepting anything that we cannot verify. Such an outlook acts as a barrier, inhibiting regression from working. People can also carry fears on a subconscious level - they feel unsafe to open their minds to this type of experience, and have insufficient trust in a therapist to surrender their minds into his or her care. Letting go of control could be an inhibition that is very difficult for that person to overcome.

Sometimes it may not be right for a person to access a past life at that moment. It could be more important for them to sort out problems from their childhood first. They may not actually have an agenda relating to past lives that needs exploring. Yet if a soul feels drawn to knowing about its past lives, then I feel that this will be for a reason.

Opening the inner faculties to access a past life memory is like getting a muscle to work. This muscle may have not been used for a long time, if at all. With other people it can be a faculty that is frequently being utilised for inner exploration of various kinds. With practice this muscle will be able to be employed. When people are determined enough, even if they can't succeed at accessing a past life straight away, with perseverance and continued practice they are very likely to make progress eventually.

Question: *Will I be able to drive after my session?*

Paul: It is a good idea to allow ourselves to return from a past life regression session slowly. There will be much for us to absorb. It is quite likely that we will have been aware of our present life body throughout the session. But our focus will have been upon the other world of the past life that we have been exploring. Consequently, in returning to normal consciousness, we have to release ourselves from the past life so that we can focus once again on the concerns of everyday life that we are living now. I feel that it is appropriate for us to give ourselves time to make this transition.

We need to gather the experience of the past life into our normal memory and to come to some degree of acceptance relating to it. We also have to adjust to our present life's physical body with its needs, so that we can move our body and do normal things.

As long as we do not try to force the pace, this process will occur naturally, typically taking five to ten minutes. We may be tired after the session and benefit from some rest. This can be our body's way of helping us to integrate the experience.

As we adjust to normal consciousness again, we can stretch, engage in conversation, move about, and ensure that we are able to relate about things concerning our everyday life. Again, I recommend that we do not schedule anything too strenuous, especially on an emotional or mental level for immediately after a session. If we plan a quiet time in the hours following a regression session, it will help us to integrate the experience properly. There should not be any problem with driving; we just need to give ourselves some time to make sure that we are ready. We are responsible for feeling safe enough to be able to focus on the task of driving, mentally and physically, before we get into our vehicle.

Question: *Is it OK for me to bring someone with me to the session?*

Paul: If you feel nervous about what could happen in your session, then it could be very supportive to have someone there that you trust. I generally encourage this if someone makes such a request. The only reservation that I have is when that person who is there with you is sceptical about past life regression or tends to react negatively to what they witness. This could have a detrimental effect upon your ability to accept your own experience.

The person with you needs to be tolerant of the experience of past life regression, with a heart open to listening to you to affirm what you go through. At best, having someone else there as a witness can be very validating, and will help you to gain faith in your own inner abilities.

If you feel that you need this kind of support at first, you could find after one or two regressions that you then prefer to undertake the regressions alone with your therapist. By doing this, you may feel freer to judge your experience, and more able to stand on your own two feet when exploring your inner worlds.

Question: *My teenage daughter is interested in past life regression. Is it suitable for children?*

Paul: Children can be very open and receptive to past life exploration. Especially when they are young and less conditioned by the demands of our modern society and education system, spontaneous memories of past lives can come to children readily. I have come across many accounts of children doing this. I suppose that, while young, the barrier that exists in our memory separating the experience we have of our current incarnation from previous ones is less firmly formed.

Generally I would be inclined to trust a child's instinct about this. If a child is open and eager to explore a past life, then it could be entirely appropriate. I would not in any way try to force a child in this direction. It would need to be explained to them what such a process involves, so that they can understand it in their own way. But in my experience it is not something that children find difficult to comprehend. Parental support would be needed, of course, especially with younger children.

I have worked with a number of children of varying ages with past life regression. They tend to be able to access the memories very well. Usually the types of lives they access are not too demanding, emotionally or mentally, and this is important so that what they experience is something that they can digest.

When they are supported positively by those close to them, I feel that having a past life regression can be a precious experience for a child.

Question: *What is the difference between past life regression and past life therapy?*

Paul: Past life regression invokes memories of previous lives that we have lived and brings these experiences to the surface of our consciousness. This can be approached through meditation, hypnosis, and other methods that induce an altered state of consciousness where the subject can become receptive for these memories to come forth.

People can explore their past life memories to gain self-knowledge and self-awareness. For others it may be more relevant as a curiosity, and to gather specific information about the past.

Past life therapy is about utilising past life regression to learn more deeply about ourselves through the patterns of our past lives. There can be investigations about how these patterns link with the structure of our lives today. We might want to use past life regression to resolve inner conflicts or to understand more fully the nature of life, death and spiritual realities. There are many potential avenues of exploration with past life regression. When these explorations help us on an inner personal level, this can be termed past life therapy.

Someone could be interested in pursuing past life regression to gather information about what clothes a particular past life character wore, or what dates he died, or what historical events he witnessed. Seeking these details could appear, from a therapeutic angle, rather superficial. However, for the individual concerned finding out this information could have a profound effect.

Almost any past life regression work has the potential of being therapeutically useful. It depends upon the subject and what that person needs in heart and mind. When people feel authentically drawn to past life regression, wanting to discover some truth, then the work they do will be past life therapy.

Question: *I don't seem to be able to talk with anyone in my family about my past life experiences – they think I am mad. Who can I talk to?*

Paul: It can be very difficult if you feel that you cannot share with your family what is meaningful to you, especially if you rely upon them and are dependant on them in certain ways. However, an interest in past lives can be like a very fragile plant that needs love and nurturing if it is to survive and flourish. Therefore, ideally, we do need people who will understand what we believe in.

It may be helpful to join a meditation group, a healing circle or some self-help class to meet with some like-minded people. If you open yourself up, there could well be someone with whom you will feel an inner bond waiting to meet you.

Sometimes, it will not feel sufficient just to relate to your therapist about these things. It is unlikely that your therapist will have any connection with you in your everyday life, and that is where you will need the support.

Question: *I have encountered people in my past life experiences that I am sure that I know in this life but, if I talk to them about it, they totally block me. What can I do about that?*

Paul: We cannot force other people to acknowledge what may be for us, an incontrovertible reality. In our own lives we need space to decide for ourselves what is true and what beliefs we want to adopt. We need to give other people that right as well.

In identifying souls from our regressions to previous lifetimes, we need to be careful that we don't draw a conclusion about the identity of some character, because we want or expect that person to fit a particular role. It is important for us to have a very open perception about this. Souls that we know now might appear in all kinds of shades in relation to us within past life experiences. Some of these may be sympathetic to us and some not. We also need to acknowledge our own shadow and the capacity in us to have expressed darker qualities, as well as those that we may consider more positive.

It is possible to identify past soul links in regression sessions, but we might not always get it right. In my own experience there have been many occasions where such identifications could be verified and affirmed by the other person. When this happens, it can be very helpful and instructive in the relationship.

On a personal note, I have had situations in my life where somebody kept on identifying me in past lives as a negative character in relationship to them. From my own investigations I felt that their identifications were accurate, but that this was only one part of the story. From my side I sensed that this person's soul had far more often been cruel towards me. Again, I feel that the discoveries that we make can be coloured by what we are seeking to find. I do not consider it appropriate to use past life regression as a means to condemn someone else and make them look bad. In a relationship, there is always learning that is needed on both sides. Otherwise there would be no need to meet.

Question: *Why do sessions with you last for at least one hour and a half?*

Paul: Occasionally my sessions are shorter than that. However, I feel that I generally need time with people to explore all the subtleties that can exist within the memories of a given lifetime. To condense an experience of many years into an hour or two of recall already seems like quite a daunting task. But on the other hand, I suppose we don't really need to know every small detail like what we have eaten for breakfast on each day of our past incarnation!

To go into the memory of a past life is, in the way that I work, a deeply meditative experience. People need space and silence to allow the various strands of thought and feeling related to the past life to be drawn out of them. There is also a need, once any catharsis has taken place, for digestion so that things can settle and realisations can be assimilated. From the depths of the experience, people also need time to return and relate the regression to their everyday life now.

Some people typically need two or three hours to navigate themselves through a past life session. Others have a temperament where they can cover the ground more quickly. Once I had a marathon session with a client that lasted seven hours.

After about three hours I am usually at a point where I need a break. In regression sessions I need to concentrate intensely upon what is happening. I also try to be sensitive to my clients so that I will not overload them. It is a matter of getting the balance right. If there is too much time taken the client may become over exhausted, but if there is too little time taken the session may lack depth and miss out important aspects of the process.

At Mind Body Spirit shows I offer past life taster sessions that last 15-20 minutes.

Question: *Will past life regression help me to understand why my life is in such a mess?*

Paul: I believe that before we are born we, as souls, decide upon challenges that we want to meet in our lifetime so that we can grow. We might choose very difficult and substantial challenges that will test us severely, or we may be gentle with ourselves so that our life purpose will be quite straight forward to achieve.

Once we are in physical incarnation, in the midst of confronting a challenge, we tend to struggle and feel confused. This confusion will be part of the test for us to find a course of action that meets our challenge rather than avoiding it. When we meet our challenge, we will be acting true to ourselves and this will give us a feeling of strength inside.

If we fail to meet our challenge we could feel lost and that our lives are in a mess, but as human beings we all make mistakes. If we do not meet a challenge at an initial attempt, it is very likely that we will be given further opportunities to redeem ourselves later on so that we can get back on track. So, if we have taken some wrong turnings in our lives, there is every chance that we can pick up the pieces and find our way again when we are ready. This process is quite independent of any past life experience that we have had.

We may come across a past life where, as a soul, we gave ourselves similar challenges to those we are setting ourselves today. Perhaps then we made errors and didn't succeed in our purpose, and consequently we have had to test ourselves with those same challenges again. Going through that past life and experiencing where we went wrong could galvanise us with understanding and insight, so that we can step out of any difficult spaces we are in, to make better and more constructive choices now.

Past life regression shows us what is in our past that we no longer need. Therefore, it can help illuminate what is worthwhile in our lives today and what is not, and thereby help us to perceive a pathway forward from any mess that we may find ourselves in.

Question: *Why do lives from so long ago still affect us today?*

Paul: If we examine the single life that is our present incarnation, and how this lifetime has moulded us to be who we are today, it is not only the events from the last days and weeks that affect us, but often experiences from much further back as well. Even incidents from our childhood that we no longer remember can have an impact upon our lives. An example of this is sexual abuse. People can suppress the memories of this having happened. But whether the person consciously remembers what took place or not, the damage to that person's sense of trust and openness is just as likely to be evident.

People who have been adopted can carry the wound of abandonment concerning their natural mother even though they may not be conscious of where these feelings stem from. Such a separation could have taken place in the first weeks of life, while the infant is still adjusting to life outside the womb.

Within us I believe that we carry the memory of everything that we have experienced. This all contributes to building the person who we are today. It is clear then that even the earliest memories will have an affect upon who we are now.

At a deeper level, the soul experiences of our past lives will also have been important elements in the development of our character and the person that we are today. Inclinations, strengths and weaknesses will have been carried forward and will shape how our being expresses itself. Gaining self-knowledge so that we are more aware of the building blocks that make up who we are can help us to make informed choices about how that building needs to proceed. Some frames may require strengthening; others might need to be replaced. The building could also be fine just the way it is, and therefore the main work needed could be in making additions so that the building can be more complete, rather than taking any remedial action.

Our inner beliefs and the patterns of our thoughts and emotions all go into creating our soul building blocks. None of this is fixed and all can embrace change. We cannot change the memories of what we have experienced. What we can do is to alter our attitudes and relationship to this past and what we believe now. As we do so, we free ourselves to make new choices about what our soul building will be like. We are both the architects and the builders of our soul being, and as such we have the power to contribute greatly to the creation of our own being.

Memories from our far distant past can have a strong affect upon us, especially if they need attention. We can only discover what we have to learn from these experiences by investigating them. From our past there may be things we need to remember so that we can operate more fully towards our potential. There can also be patterns from our past that we need to release.

Question: *Do we have lives of the opposite sex?*

Paul: In the course of our evolution I believe that we as souls want to experience all aspects of life, so that we can accept it and cope with it. Therefore we choose male bodies in some incarnations and female lives in others. Sometimes being in the body of one sex can help us learn a particular lesson that we need. With another lesson we may feel that to be in the body of the other sex would be more suitable.

It is not necessarily the case that we will end up having the same number of lives of one sex as the other.

For instance, I am aware that in my evolution I have chosen many lives as a leader and someone in charge. Sometimes I have utilised these energies well and at others I have not. I have had to learn to use the energies of power and control appropriately. Souls each have their own issue, but for me this has been an issue that I have struggled with over many lifetimes, so that I could find a balance. Consequently, from my own investigations, I believe that I have lived a greater number of male lives than female ones, especially in more recent times. In most periods in history, males have been in positions of power more than females. Choosing strong male personalities on a number of occasions has enabled me to test, from a position where I could be very dominant, whether I would be oppressive to other people or treat them with compassion.

We all have our own path of learning. Another soul may need more sensitive female lives to provide tests about learning to overcome a pattern of over-passivity or to embrace motherhood in all its aspects.

As souls we try to balance out our deficiencies and habitual patterns to remove distortions in the way that we relate to others. Sometimes having the same number of male lives as female ones would not enable us to achieve that.

Question: *How will I cope if I find out that I have done something horrible in one of my past lives?*

Paul: I suppose that the simple answer to this is to urge you to trust in the process.

In my experience nearly all of us have had instances - if not in our present life, then in our past lives - where we have been horrible to others and possibly hurt them very much. This is life as a human being. We do make mistakes, and do not always keep our hearts open so that we are kind and loving.

When we discover our fallibility in this way, it just puts us on a par with the rest of humanity - we are no better or no worse than everyone else. To become aware of this can be quite an enriching and humbling experience.

If we find out, for example, that in a past life we murdered someone who is very dear to us now, we might feel very bad about this. However, at the same time, such a discovery will prompt us to question our motives and our intentions in that relationship, and perhaps in general. When we love someone, we do not want to hurt that person. To really feel what it is like to have hurt someone we love cannot help but open our hearts, making us much more determined not to do such a thing again. Exposing our vulnerability to this possibility nourishes our souls, because it propels us to seek more deeply into our inner self for answers and guidance.

We can easily feel guilt and regrets about our mistakes and shortcomings. Dwelling on these things can have a freezing effect upon our actions and restrict opportunities for growth. Once we have acted in a hurtful manner, it cannot be undone. We can try to make amends if we wish, but basically we need to learn from how we have acted and move on. When we experience our mistakes in past lives through regression, we can, if we are open to it, learn about these patterns from some very deep perspectives. When there are resonances from those past life events with our present experience, we can gain a lot from exploring them. For many people, guilt and regret are two factors that hold them back from fulfilling their potential. We need to leave our actions in the hands of 'God' or 'Spirit' rather than punishing ourselves unnecessarily. The negative judgements we make of ourselves are likely not to be very balanced or helpful.

We need to understand the factors at work in what we do, especially our more negative actions. The more insight we gain, the freer we become from patterns that prompt us to be self-destructive or destructive towards others.

Anxiety or fear that we might have done something horrible in a past life could indicate the existence of such an experience in our consciousness. What we do with it is up to us. We never have to go into a past life where we have hurt others unless we choose to do so with our wills. If we do decide to explore it, it may be hard and bring up many difficult feelings from inside us. As we digest it, it could help us to be a better, more sensitive and well-rounded person. If we don't feel ready to face it, it is probably prudent for us to leave it alone. Our fears will always direct us to put things off, so we may need to meditate to find a quiet place within us where we can ask ourselves if it is the right thing for us to do or not.

Question: *Do we have to be born again?*

Paul: Many people have expressed to me that they don't want to be born again, or even that they feel that this is going to be their last lifetime. I feel that the vast majority of us will need to return for further incarnations, whether we wish to or not. What we desire on a personality level will not necessarily reflect the needs of our soul.

Living in the physical plane can be very hard and people naturally, at various points, will want to give up or end it all. The challenge of 'choosing to be here' is quite tough for many souls and there can easily be the tendency to opt out and resist being in physical incarnation. Of course, that attitude will not help us to learn our soul lessons or achieve the life purposes that we set ourselves.

In our development as a soul, when we learn sufficient lessons and gain enough balanced maturity, we can reach a point where do not need to physically incarnate anymore. Generally I feel that such an achievement can only be reached after hundreds if not thousands of incarnations, and is an individual process for each soul.

I do not know what it is like to achieve this because I do not believe that I have reached that point myself, but I imagine that it is a great cause for celebration, possibly relief, and a feeling of success. From what I gather, even though it must be an immensely important point of transition, reaching this level of transcendence only marks the beginning of yet another journey of growth and learning that is needed.

Such advanced souls can still choose to incarnate physically although they will not be obliged to do so anymore. Souls that do this will not necessarily be Spiritual teachers but are more likely to be living ordinary, quite inconspicuous lives. They might choose to return for a particular physical experience, to help a fellow soul, or to serve in some other way. I imagine that they could be people that on a deeper level don't seem to be ruffled by life's dramas. They will probably not be interested in past life regression, because there will be no need for them to explore this.

With our egos, we may like to believe that we are very advanced as souls, and that we are near to the point of transcendence. But I don't really feel that we know this whilst we are in physical incarnation. The final tests to be completed as souls in preparation for transcendence would not be true tests for us if we were fully aware of their significance. We might think that we are doing very well and meeting every challenge that comes our way, but there could still be a great many soul challenges that we have not faced. Also, our judgement of how well we are managing a given situation may not correspond with the truth, on a deeper soul level, of how much we have accomplished. With our surface consciousness we can easily miss aspects of particular situations that are very important for us to grasp on a soul level. Our beliefs and attitudes can prejudice our outlook.

I feel that the best we can do is accept that we are ordinary fallible human beings who make mistakes but do our best, and then let life take its course.

Question: *Do we always advance as a soul from one life to the next?*

Paul: Once we have gained some experience and learned a particular soul lesson, I feel that this will be etched upon our soul and remain there. As such, I do not believe that any advance that we have made as a soul is ever lost.

However, if we make a mistake that gets repeated in further lives we create a distortion in our soul that needs to be balanced. Until we remedy this problem, it will inhibit our soul growth in the area of our soul in which the mistake was made. The more often that we continue to make that mistake in further lives, the more work may be needed to rectify the problem. In a particular lifetime we could have a realisation that enables us to break the restrictive pattern in which we have been operating. From this moment this specific distortion in our soul can then rapidly diminish, depending upon how complex the problem has grown to be. It might still be necessary for us to live through several lives where there is the potential to make the same mistake, with the intention that we can demonstrate our capacity to cope as a soul with that type of situation. Of course, we might step into the same pitfall and have even more experiences to face before we are able to resolve this. Ultimately we need to eliminate this pattern as a weakness in our soul being so that we can advance further in this direction.

Because we have such a lot of facets to our nature we could grow in wisdom and maturity in some aspects of our soul being while other areas remain more stunted and undeveloped. We will make the choices from one life to the next about which facet of our being we want to focus upon and try to make progress.

I do not believe that we will necessarily advance as a soul in a lifetime where we repeat mistakes that we have made previously. However, I do not feel that we will be going backwards either. What we will be doing in these situations is to create a need to rebalance a distortion in our being. This then could lengthen the number of lifetimes and experiences that we need to meet gracefully before we can reach that point of transcendence into Spirit.

If, during the course of a given lifetime, we make some mistake (we hurt others or are cruel to them) or even omit to carry out some responsibility that on a soul level we have agreed to do, we will generate personal Karma. As well as learning the soul lesson inherent in the experience where we have made our mistakes, we will also need to balance our relationship with those we have hurt. Every hurt or wound that we engender in others also produces a distortion in our being. Again, although these distortions result do not result in us going backwards as souls, they do create darkness in us that we need to release. We will need to manifest opportunities during our physical incarnations to do this, and serve those other souls appropriately. Somehow we need to learn to love other souls whatever they do to us.

When we study our own past lives through regression, we can learn where we have made mistakes and created distortions for ourselves previously. Once we acknowledge these weaknesses, we can open up to experiences that might help us to advance as a soul in our present incarnation.

Question: *Why do we 'forget' our lessons from previous lives, and our plan for this life when we are incarnated? Wouldn't it be much easier if we knew clearly what we were meant to be learning?*

Paul: With the way that our minds are constructed, we might find it to be very confusing if we were knowledgeable about our past lives. So many patterns and experiences would be before us, some of which would surely be irrelevant to us today. I do not believe that having this knowledge at our disposal could help us to focus upon our inner tasks relating to now. Even with regression, we can be given little windows of memories from our past lives, experiences that are usually very pertinent to our learning in present time. But these past life memories need considerable energy on our part to be digested and for us to assimilate them into our being. We couldn't cope with having them all there at once.

When we are a child, we cannot be mindful of what it is like to be an adult. We have to allow our development to unfold one step at a time. Likewise we cannot appreciate all the elements of our life purpose, and the plan we made as a soul before we were born, until we are ready to face up to them. We do this through gathering experiences, acquiring beliefs, making decisions, and stepping into action. When we digest one experience, we are ready to face the next one. We could not deal with them all at once; it would be a complete overload.

Part of our life plan might be about what sort of decision we would make when under a particular type of challenge, and whether we could handle the situation wisely. If we knew the plan and how we needed to act in advance, this would not be a test for us and we could not therefore learn anything as a soul through it. When we step into the unknown and dare to advance in a way that we have never done before, without knowing what the outcome will be, we gain the life experience that enables us to mature as a soul.

Perhaps at some point in our evolution as human beings we will, as a race, be able to cope with the knowledge of consciously being aware of all our past lives and our inner life plan. I do not believe that we are there yet.

Question: *Can other Spirits take over our body when we do past life regression?*

Paul: For some people, the aura of past life regression is bound up with 'the occult' and things that are dangerous and best left alone. These attitudes can stem from religious intolerance and also a fear of the unknown. Coupled with such suspicions is the fear that, if we engage in past life regression, we could be attacked by evil Spirits and left psychologically damaged.

Many people are superstitious and can become very fixed upon how they go about their daily lives. They try to ensure, by doing things in a specific manner, that they will protect themselves from negative influences and keep themselves safe. When people restrict themselves like this, it tends to be something in their own minds that formulates the decision about what is safe and what is not. From an outside perspective, for someone who does not share the same prejudices, this kind of limiting behaviour can be regarded as unreasonable. Even a person affected by their fears in this way may be able to acknowledge the ridiculousness of what they do. However, once an idea is established in the mind, it can be very difficult to shift.

Having said all this, I do believe that Spiritual beings exist: our Spiritual guides are close by us, trying to guide us to be true to ourselves. Also, I feel that there are negative Spiritual entities that can potentially affect us.

There are people who deliberately invoke demonic entities to help them to raise power for themselves at others' expense. This is something that can create a lot of problems. Such entities will come close when called and can help people, at least in the short term, to gain what they want. Demonic beings can only operate when a person's heart closes down. If these energies are used to affect or hurt others eventually they will return, and the person that sent out the energies will suffer similar hurt or worse.

30

It is not our right to interfere in the lives of others, and if we listen to our conscience, then we will know this to be true.

Negative entities are only able to come near us if we reach out for them or close our hearts. Life operates on the principle of 'like attracts like'. Therefore, if we seek for truth, and reach out for the loving help of our Spiritual guides, I feel that we will be protected. In these circumstances I believe that past life regression can be undertaken safely, without any negative entity being able to influence what happens.

I feel that the occurrence of Spirit possession by negative entities is actually very rare. Sometimes people imagine that they might be possessed or have some external voice from within them, telling them what to do. But I believe that these experiences are frequently creations of fear within the mind. These can stem from negativity arising from experiences that have not been integrated relating to the person's past, rather than being the influence of demons.

Occasionally, people can be affected by negative entities that have attached themselves to us to some extent. Past life regression can often help this problem to be released. The key to this appears to me to be about us learning to be able to take responsibility for our own actions, past and present. Once we admit our own mistakes and wrongdoing and open our hearts to this, these beings will have no hold over us any more. While we blame others and external influences for all our woes, we will feel powerless to do anything about it. Fear engenders feelings of powerlessness and easily distorts our behaviour so that we deviate from being true to ourselves.

At times we all suffer from fear, and I feel that the best thing we can do then is to reach out and reach within for help. If we feel afraid of past life regression, it is probably best not to approach it until we have worked through those fears. I feel that past life regression is one of the best tools I know to help us release fear and negativity from a very deep level within. But I feel that it will only work if we believe that it can help us.

Question: *Can we have a past life as an animal?*

Paul: Although I have come across clients that have experienced themselves living a past life as an animal, I have not been convinced that this is a literal memory. All of us have within us an animal nature, and for us to experience that directly can teach us much. We also have guides that can appear in the form of an animal. These animal guides are able to help us to explore the more instinctive sides of our nature. This may be a very helpful avenue for inner exploration for those that are interested.

There are many, many fields of enquiry that can open up through an interest in past life regression.

Chapter 3

What is Past Life Regression?

Past life regression is a process through which, by going into an altered state of consciousness, one can experience personal memories of lifetimes lived in the past. Usually these memories are of lifetimes set in historical cultures on Earth. Depending upon how well people are able to access them, these memories can be an all-engrossing experience or like memory flashes: for some it will be as if they are in a living dream, for others it can be less distinct - the person doing the regression might only have a general sense of what is happening, without being aware of the details.

Our normal analytical thinking mind acts like a screen that prevents us from having much knowledge of what is within our being. The next layer of consciousness within our normal everyday awareness is generally called our subconscious mind. The perception of our subconscious minds has a quality of innocence that is similar to the consciousness that we experience as children. Within our subconscious minds we hold our memories and beliefs and much of our feeling life. This is also the place from which our past life memories will emerge.

Meditation and hypnosis are two means with which we can learn to explore our subconscious minds. Both of these tools involve cultivating an ability to listen inwardly and to be still. Meditation is often described as the art of 'just being', while hypnosis involves manipulating the analytical mind so that it is not longer in control, but more an observer. From here people can be receptive to the processes of their subconscious minds and let them be expressed.

Using the techniques of hypnosis, or also through spiritual healing or meditation, we become able to consciously access memories from infanthood, life in the womb or even earlier. When people start to investigate memories, they usually find that there are memories of former existences and lives that they have lived, prior to their present incarnation.

Memories of past lives can also come forward spontaneously, without being called, and independent of people's belief systems. There have been many people with whom I have worked who, by opening their minds, have accessed memories of former lives on Earth, although they have not believed in reincarnation. From my investigations as a therapist, some people do not appear to have past life memories within them, but I am inclined to feel that this is the exception rather than the rule. A considerable number of my clients have had past lives revealed to them in their sessions without having had any previous inkling that they were there.

Within our subconscious minds I feel that past lives are living experiences that have influence, and are intertwined in the fabric of every other experience that we have ever had. These experiences are unique to each person and contribute intimately to our identity.

The question that we all must ask ourselves concerns the nature of the reality of past life regression memories. Some people are content to regard them as symbolic metaphors while others believe them to be, as they appear to be, lives that have actually been lived in the past. It is up to us to draw our own conclusions about this mystery. What I do know is that they are real and true within the mind of the person concerned and may take on many shapes and forms.

People regress to lifetimes dating from all kinds of different cultures and times. They may be aware of memories as personalities living out involvements with well-known historical events or (more likely) situations that have a localised content with little relevance to the world stage. Lifetimes can even come from prehistory, from cultures that little or nothing is known about from other studies. People can perceive themselves in these memories as male or female, living short lives or longer ones. The main thing, I feel, is for people to try and accept the lives that are revealed to them and open themselves to learn from them.

The experiences people have of past lives will be distinct memories of whole lives, from being in the womb, being born, growing up in particular circumstances, facing challenges and making mistakes. When we explore those memories thoroughly, as that past life personality, we will re-experience various emotions - the pain and suffering, the love and joy. We can even experience death and what it is like to survive as a soul to be in a realm of spirit that follows death. Our past life personality will have lived in a different time and have had different life experiences, but it will still feel as though it is us. We will know in the core of our being that we have lived those experiences.

Past life regression memories express themselves mentally, emotionally and very much energetically, through our present life being. Once we allow these memories to come forward, we have then the challenge of how we are going to relate to them. We may be able to accept the experiences and embrace them into our being, or we could try to block them and dismiss them. I believe that, once they have come forward, they will have an influence upon us whatever our attitude towards them.

I do not feel that past life regression experiences can be attributed to genetic memory because past lives often come up from a totally different culture to our present life heritage. Nor do I feel that such experiences are assembled purely from influences in our present lives such as what we have read or seen in films, and therefore illusory. Often past life memories have many surprising and unexpected elements about them, and have a very deep meaning for the person concerned. Likewise, I do not believe that past life experience can be explained as some wandering spirit wanting somebody's consciousness to express its story. The past lives that people access are far too personal for that, and generally have a direct bearing upon that person's present life problems and inclinations. Past lives that people access in regression cannot be easily dismissed as fantasy.

Such work is often fascinating and can challenge our basic conceptions of life. There is a lot to learn about how past life memories can be activated and what to do with them. I do not believe that it is something for people to undertake lightly. If we consider all the challenges and struggles that most of us have just to cope with our present existence, it can feel daunting to add the memories of another life to our normal consciousness. We may wonder how we might cope with whatever issues exist within that as well. But this is where we need to trust. Our present life is actually what is important to us. Past life exploration is helpful to us in as much as it can enable us to live our present lives more richly and fully.

In the forthcoming chapters, I wish to outline many of the facets involved with past life regression work. These include both the challenging aspects as well as that which could be regarded as rich and compelling. It is my hope that the information that I impart provides a useful foundation for anyone genuinely wanting to undertake this work.

Chapter 4

Approaching Past Life Regression

Seekers feel attracted to gather knowledge of their past lives for all kinds of different reasons. Some people have inexplicable images from the past flash into their consciousness quite spontaneously and feel the need to investigate these. It is quite common for young children to have glimpses of their past lives, either through dreams or even in the course of their everyday life.

When he was little my eldest son Julian had a very clear dream in which he felt himself to be a Native American leading a group of braves into an attack against the white people. At one point in the dream he turned around and got shot in the back. In the morning Julian could sense exactly the place in his back where he had been shot. When we examined him we found a small patch of eczema in precisely that same place.

People can have strong bodily and emotional reactions when they visit particular places. When these experiences defy normal explanations, they may lead those people to consider the possibility of past life memory.

A former client of mine had felt very attracted to visit southern France for a holiday. When she came to a particular house and opened the door she suddenly felt stricken with a wave of fear, even though there was nothing in the appearance of this house that seemed to be the slightest bit threatening. When my client was working with me later she regressed to a past life where she had been a Cathar living in southern France, at the time when Cathars were being hounded by the church and killed for being heretics. My client felt herself to be one of those who were persecuted. She knew instinctively that traumatic experiences within this past life contained the root of her fear surrounding that house.

Fears and phobias can indicate a past life memory that is near to the surface, especially when these fears and phobias cannot be linked to any earlier childhood incidents.

One of my friends has suffered from an instinctive fear of the sea. Whenever she used to go near the ocean she became very panicky and could not approach it. Nothing in her present life suggests that anything difficult has happened in connection with the sea. Since starting regression work with me, she has encountered a number of past lives where she drowned at sea, sometimes in quite shocking circumstances. In one particular life she was tied to a stake while the tide came in. Eventually she was submerged beneath the water. Her fears have eased significantly since doing these regressions. In fact I recently observed her paddling in the sea without any trace of fear or anxiety.

Another trigger for past life memory can be through meeting with specific people. We can encounter people who we instantly recognise, either feeling an attraction or repulsion, or perhaps having strong conflicting reactions that are hard to explain.

In my own life I have met many people whom I feel I already know. I am convinced that they come into my life for a reason and that I need to uncover that reason.

Many years ago my partner Eleyna saw me in a field amongst a group of people. At that stage she was barely acquainted with me, our only contact having been when she had a few sessions of therapy with me the previous year to help her with the birth of her fourth child. Suddenly she felt the overwhelming urge to run over and embrace me. There was no reason that she could tell for her to feel that way. She didn't act on her feelings but the experience touched her very deeply. Much later, when we had done a lot of inner work together, Eleyna and I discovered that we had been very close as lovers, partners and friends in many of our past lives.

Glimpses of past lives emerge spontaneously when triggered by specific events, or in dreams and meditation. However, a fuller experience of these memories for most people will only be revealed when working with a healer or therapist who can guide us through the experience of regression.

By allowing someone to guide us, we are able to surrender to the experience of past life memory without feeling that we have to control what we are doing at the same time. For our normal personality self there may be, at the very least, some hesitancy about accessing past life memory, for the simple reason that it seems to be part of ourselves that is unknown and therefore possibly threatening. When we operate with our normal self in the world, we like to know what we can expect, and we feel most comfortable when we can predict outcomes to our behaviour. Our personality self does not like to give up that sense of control. But too much control can make our life lack adventure. We can become victims of our habits and inner rigidity. As we allow space for new impulses to come into our lives, then the sparks of our inspiration and creativity can flow.

The other problem for our personality self is to do with trusting the faculty of imagination. Past life memories are revealed to people through the use of their imagination. It is easy for the personality self to conclude that any past life experiences amount to fantasy.

I believe that memories of past lives are 'channelled' for people to experience a source beyond the three dimensional reality of our personality self. Sometimes, when we encounter conditions in our present life that have a resonance with experiences from a past life, I feel that this past life memory may be drawn closer to our everyday consciousness through the vehicle of our subconscious minds. When we enter into an altered state of consciousness, opening ourselves for help with whatever problem we may be facing, then the past life memory concerned can quite easily come to the surface.

From the perspective of our normal consciousness it can represent a considerable challenge to be able to tell the difference between a profoundly true experience of genuine past life memory, and one which may have been created fictitiously by our sub-conscious mind. During regression therapy people may attempt, on a sub-conscious level, to either please the therapist or perhaps decide that they cannot accept a memory that may want to present itself. Therefore it might be possible for them to generate some form of fictional experience without even knowing consciously that they have done it. Generally when this happens, the person will feel uneasy about it. When challenged, if the person has integrity, then the truth will start to seep out.

More commonly I find that people feel they are making up a fantasy when in fact, to my instincts, they are tapping into an authentic memory. People need to build confidence in their own ability to access true memory. It is very easy for us to doubt ourselves.

Another element is that I feel that people sometimes censor their memories in regression and are aware only of what they want to experience. By doing this they may omit important pieces of information avoiding unpalatable truths in an effort to feel comfortable. This may happen at a subconscious level so that the surface consciousness is totally unaware of it happening.

I once had a client who accessed a memory of a past life where she was a young girl with her family having a picnic at the river. She kept lingering at this scene without anything of interest happening. The whole tone of the experience was quite flat. It was only in a follow-up session that she was able to admit to her consciousness that, during this picnic, one of her brothers from that experience drowned. The trauma of this event unlocked floods of tears and other emotions that this woman needed to release. It is quite often the case that people will conceal from themselves the very experience that they most need to bring out. Usually this is because at some level they are afraid.

People do need considerable dedication to persevere with regression experiences, especially when they sense something disturbing that could be incomplete. I believe that the best way forward to overcome this problem is to have faith, to inwardly pray, or ask for help and courage to face what wants to emerge from within.

Not all experiences from within are going to be difficult. Our inner worlds are continually in motion and experiences from there may fill us with wonder and great fascination. Past lives can also be positive as well as traumatic.

Eleyna's teenage daughter Amy was once going through a difficult phase in her life. Her relationships with various people close to her were not working and she doubted her self-worth and her ability to find happiness. It quite surprised me when she expressed interest in having a past life session. The lifetime that she accessed was one where she was a strong woman who brought up children and experienced a great deal of contentment and fulfilment in her life. This woman's life was simple but very stable. This experience served as an affirmation to Amy, helping her to feel better in herself.

Our inner consciousness tries to respond to our wishes and desires. Therefore, if we ask questions of it and are open enough inside, then our inner consciousness will answer our requests. Consequently, if we ask our inner consciousness or if our therapist asks on our behalf, to begin to recall a past life, this process is likely to happen. A past life will probably begin to reveal itself. This outcome depends upon our readiness to open to such an experience and also on there being a memory that is ready to come forward. However, if we feel drawn to seeking the memory of a past life, it is likely that somewhere inside us we know that there is something waiting to be discovered.

On occasions I have had people come to me wanting to explore their past lives but they have not immediately been able to do this. One reason for this can be to do with inner conflicts and fears needing resolution, from the childhood consciousness of the seeker, before memories of past lives will be able to come forward. People need to be emotionally equipped to cope with the experiences that past life memories may elicit, and can instinctively shield themselves subconsciously from opening up to such memories until they are ready.

What we think is important may not be what really matters from the soul perspective. We may desire to explore our past lives. But it could be the inner child work connected to our more recent experiences from our present incarnation that needs to be sorted out first. The desire for us to know our past lives will serve as our way to get there.

From another angle we might also stumble into an exploration of our past lives without consciously choosing to do so. People may suffer a tragedy in their lives and feel compelled to search within themselves for answers to make sense of it all. In a therapy situation people can go into an altered state of consciousness through meditation or hypnosis. Focussing on the problem that is there, and asking to go to the root of it, may lead to an experience where the memory of a past life is accessed. It could be that, from the perspective of the soul, the tragedy encountered by this person was intended at a deeper level as a test for the soul. The outcome of that person then making contact with his or her past lives could also be meant as a step on that person's Spiritual path.

The value of past life regression is that it gives an experience of something that would otherwise remain hypothetical. For people who have an intellectual belief in reincarnation this is not commensurate with gaining an actual experience of the memory of a past life.

Some years ago one of my colleagues asked me if he could undergo a session of past life regression. He was a powerful healer with a strong contact with his Spiritual guide. Yet he had never accessed a memory of any of his past lives even though he believed in the reality of reincarnation. It took some inner manoeuvring but, when he did finally access the memory that he sought, tears streamed down his cheeks. As I witnessed the past life that he shared, its content seemed quite unspectacular to me. However for him it was a tremendous breakthrough and he now knew, at a much deeper level, that for him reincarnation was a reality.

When we engage in past life therapy it is important to trust ourselves. When doing regression work I feel that it is very important to ask for inner protection and help. As we ask, so we are given. Most of us need all the help we can get to discover essentially what we need to learn about our inner worlds. Whether we ask for help from 'God', our 'guardian angel', or 'spiritual guide', I believe that any sincere request for help will gain a response and should help us to feel safe to surrender a little bit more. By introducing a Spiritual element into the inner searching in which we are engaged, we approach past life regression with reverence.

As a sacred process, past life regression involves learning about our soul. This is a task that cannot be undertaken frivolously. Seekers do better to approach what may be revealed to them during a past life regression with a positive and open outlook, rather than with scepticism. At the same time, we will not be able to force these experiences to manifest unless we are ready and the conditions feel safe enough. If we try to force such experiences to come to us with our will, we will only succeed in blocking both the channels to our inspiration and the openness that these experiences need.

As seekers we need to learn from within about how we can best perceive past life memory. Some people are more visually orientated and will see very clear images, and can connect then with other details of the experience like the thoughts, emotions and underlying sense of what is happening through this focus. Others sense and feel situations with the energies within their bodies. From listening and responding to this, allowing their bodies to physically move and their emotions to express themselves, images and an appreciation of a particular scene can follow. In other cases I have come across people for whom smell is the strongest leading sense. Whatever it is, seekers need to learn about their own strongest leading sense and let this be the means to take them into the past life experience.

By doing this we harmonise with our inner nature and are able to connect more thoroughly with whatever inner experience is necessary for us. Of course it is important for our therapist to also be attuned and learn about whatever is our leading sense as well. After doing this work for a while all our inner senses may become more finely tuned, so we can learn to access past lives and connect with them in depth through various means.

I remember when I was a university student I wanted to remember my dreams. When I awoke in the mornings I hardly knew anything about what had passed in the night. This had been going on for what seemed like years. Yet I was aware that as a child I had been conscious of vivid dreams. So in quite a determined fashion I started a journal: I had pen and paper by my bedside and in the morning I wrote down impressions even whilst still waking up. At first the images, thoughts and feelings were very vague. But there were impressions emerging. As I practised this each day the impressions grew stronger, and they became the outline of dreams. This process of strengthening continued until I began to experience vivid dreams during the night once again. Eventually I did not need to write down my dreams in the morning, each and every morning, for I felt that the faculty in me to remember my dreams had opened again.

In a similar way seekers can open their inner faculties to experience their past lives. It is a matter of honouring and acknowledging our inner experiences and giving them time and recognition in our lives. With the help of various people who have guided and supported me, this is how I have opened more and more fully to my own past life experiences. If you, as a seeker, have the sincere wish to explore your past lives, you need to trust that the right people will come along at the right time. It is a matter of believing that your own wishes are in harmony with what the universe wants to provide for you.

In my own practise my past life sessions with clients generally last at least one and a half hours. People need time for sharing before a session and time afterwards for assimilation. The session itself can typically, from my point of view as a therapist, be slow moving - but for my clients it can often seem as if hardly any time has gone by at all. I find it important to leave spaces of silence in the session. These are often the spaces when my clients learn most. At the right moment silence encourages my clients to develop their capacity to inwardly listen and let significant experiences unfold for them.

I use different methods to induce a state of being where a past life can be accessed. On some occasions I use a hypnosis induction. At other times I utilise a guided meditation approach. In further cases I might get the person to repeat a phrase or breathe into an energetic tension that they experience in their body. It depends upon my clients' needs as to which of these methods may be most successful and with what they feel comfortable.

44

After a session I encourage my clients to write notes about their session or even to draw pictures from it if they are artistically inclined. To keep a journal of their inner experiences can be helpful, as with my dream journal. Frequently people need rest after a past life session, so it is good not to plan anything too strenuous on any level in the hours immediately afterwards. There could be after ripples from the session and it is important for people to take care of themselves. I would also recommend strongly for people not to partake of drugs or alcohol in the time leading up to a session or immediately afterwards. Past life therapy is a sensitive and subtle process. It needs people to be as centred as possible, having all their faculties operating clearly with the least amount of distortion. After sessions I also advise my clients to be careful about rushing into any demanding activity straight away. During past life regression, people go into a very deep state of consciousness. It is not always obvious, when you are a client, how deeply you have been. It can take some time to fully return to normal consciousness. Therefore any and other tasks that require the full attention of your rational mind, should not be attempted until you are sure that you are ready.

When you have had a past life regression session you need to be careful about sharing your experience with others. To share an experience that feels very precious to you with someone who is sceptical, dismissive or even uninterested can hurt. Past life experiences are deeply personal, and deserve to be honoured and treated with respect.

Chapter 5

What Can Occur in a Past Life Regression Session

When you first begin accessing the memory of a past life in a regression process, you need help in focussing on any impressions you get so that you can begin to believe you are on the right track. Initially all kinds of scenes might flit through your consciousness, but this should settle and then hopefully you can let your awareness stay with one particular memory, in whatever way you perceive it. This memory may be a specific moment in that lifetime, from some highly charged significant event crucial to the unfolding of that life. It is also possible to access a life at a very safe and mundane moment. The main thing at the beginning is to focus upon what is there, and be patient about learning what it all means.

As your therapist asks questions, try to observe the impressions that come into your mind. Skillfully phrased questions will help draw out the experience that you need to go through. Initially, there is the need to become grounded in the experience of the past life, so that you can be focussed upon it and not distracted by other things.

Your inner consciousness will want to respond to the questions that your therapist puts to you. The questions asked of you will act as cues to draw out various layers of perception from within you. To help this process, the best thing that you can do is to become passive and allow whatever is there to be expressed. The more that you communicate, the easier it will be for your therapist to attune to your needs.

When I talk about becoming 'grounded in the experience', I mean that you need to reach a state of consciousness where you are as fully involved in the drama of the past life experience as possible. In this state, your body may react and experience various sensations. You will be aware of thoughts, feelings and perhaps imagery relating to the past life character that you have accessed. Helping you reach this point is probably your therapist's main challenge, especially if you are doing past life regression for the first time. If you don't get there immediately, your therapist may need to try various tacks until you are able to find a way in. It is important for you to vocalise your experience, no matter how obvious it may seem. By doing this, you acknowledge the reality of your inner experience, helping it to develop and move into focus. You may be asked to describe physical things, share your feelings or your thoughts. Through your expression of these experiences, even if it feels uncomfortable, you will be helping to open your inner channels of perception.

At first it is important, for your therapist to ask questions to help draw out as much information as possible about what is initially being presented. Introductory questions help clarify the sex of the person that you are experiencing yourself to be in the past life, the environment in which you are living, what is occupying you, and how you feel about what is happening.

Questions need to be asked that will put 'flesh and blood' onto the past life experience that you are going through. You need to feel that you are living there, and that an increasing number of impressions are coming to you. As you express these, letting your body react to what you are experiencing, the regression will move on further, with more information likely to be forthcoming. When your attention becomes absorbed in the details of the past life as a living experience, and you move beyond the initial stages, what you need to learn and access from it flows more easily.

When I am working with clients, I generally encourage them to become aware of their physical situation in the past life first, concentrating upon the mental and emotional dimensions afterwards. Occasionally, people enter a past life through some thought that, when expressed and repeated, causes a reaction linking to a past life. As people react emotionally to this thought, they are quickly absorbed by the relevant past life experience that is waiting. Similarly, some people find that a strong emotional and physical response leads to the experience of a past life. There are many possible pathways to open up to a past life memory. You just need to surrender to the approach that serves you best.

You will have a leading sense through which you can access the experience. So don't worry if you don't see clear visions, or cannot feel what is happening very precisely. If you can communicate what you sense and allow what you feel might be there, this can encourage your inner mind to help you involve yourself in the process more fully. In this kind of process, we need to activate the faculties of our imagination so that our perception of the past life experience comes alive. Therefore we need to honour what our inner consciousness presents to us, and even coax it into action.

Once you are in the experience of a past life, from the moment where you have entered into it, it can be suggested for you to move forward. Then the details of what happens next during various stages of that life can unfold like a dream.

When approaching regression for the first time, you could feel a little afraid or anxious about stepping into the unknown. Even with all the reassurance in the world, you may not feel certain about what you can expect or how you will deal with the experience. I feel that the best thing is to take one step at a time, and allow yourself to relax as much as you can. It is important that your therapist is steady and patient with you. As much as you can, allow your therapist to support you gently so that you can ease into the experience. People can become immersed in thoughts, feelings and memories arising from their subconscious mind without even realising that they are doing so. Don't be too hard on yourself or your therapist if you do not get spectacular results straight away. The key element is for you to learn to trust in your inner senses. But then, on the other hand, the experience that comes may completely astound you.

48

Some people, when they enter into regression find themselves caught up with all sorts of strange thoughts, feelings, body sensations and movements before they can even take stock of the situation. The experience may be waiting there ready to erupt almost in spite of the person's best efforts to contain it. This can be quite an alarming introduction to past life therapy if you are not expecting it. The best approach, if this happens, is to let it unfold. It does not serve to resist and try to stop the energies from expressing themselves. Again it is a matter of trusting that what is taking place is right and allowing the experience to flow. Afterwards you will remember everything and can have time to assimilate the experience.

Some years ago, I worked with a woman in Finland. Her entry into a past life experience was immediate. She accessed a life where she was gassed in a Jewish concentration camp during World War II. As you can imagine, it was quite intense. Her body went into the experience surrounding her death quite spontaneously without her feeling that she had any control over it. Her body was contorting and moving quite violently. At first, she was shocked and bewildered, and was very confused about her experience. I needed to steady her, interrupt the process and talk it through with her. Once I had done this, she relaxed and allowed her body to be the channel for these memories to be released. The further she went into the experience the more she actually began to gain enjoyment from the way that her body could serve her.

Each time she went through the experience of her past life death, it seemed to release a further layer of pent-up emotions, thoughts and energy conglomerates from inside of her. The material from the past life was not very pleasant, but because it was from the past, she could let it go. I remember that in between sessions, this woman would go for long swims in the beautiful lake nearby. It was necessary for me to talk with her a lot to help her understand the process of what was happening to her. After a handful of sessions, her body became quieter, and less emotion wanted to come forward, until she realised that the work around this lifetime was complete. By the end of the week, she felt a lot happier and more settled.

This woman had been living much of her life in fear and had been unable to make decisions that would help her to move forward in her life. In the regression, although quite terrifying in its contents, her body was able to release much of the fear that she was carrying, influencing her life now. With every movement and contortion of her body, as she went through the past life story, she felt instinctively that she was unburdening herself of energy blocks that she no longer needed.

When she started, she needed encouragement to trust her body, but she soon learnt to do so. Her normal rational critical mind did not know quite what to make of it all at first, but the feeling of inner freedom that the experience gave her helped her rational mind to accept it.

It is quite typical for our rational critical minds to be judgmental of past life experiences and not very sympathetic. This reaction comes out of fear, especially if we have been depending upon this faculty to cope with our everyday life. Past life experience shows that part of our minds that it does not have all the answers and cannot be supreme. Our rational critical minds may not want to accept this. If possible, we need to learn to let all the various facets of our minds, including our subconscious and our rational critical aspect, to co-operate together. It is not healthy for us when any particular faculty dominates the others.

By studying the content of what is given through a past life experience often a lot can be learned, even though this will not necessarily be at all obvious at first. Typically, the most telling elements of learning inherent in the past life, are only revealed slowly and often quite subtly. Again, we need to build up a trust in our inner senses so that we are open to perceive the learning that our inner consciousness wants to share with us.

Some people do not need to go through the whole story of a particular past life in a regression session. There may be a fragment from a life that contains some material that, when appropriately supported, precipitates an energetic release of some kind. This freeing of blocked energy may be the main thing that a particular person needs to make some personal discoveries and move on in life. Concentrating upon a particular episode from a past life can then be what is pertinent and sufficient for that client. Usually, when doing regressions, I like people to experience a particular past life thoroughly. When approaching the exploration of a given lifetime, there are a number of crucial elements of the past life that can benefit from investigation and be relevant.

Childhood

Events from a past life childhood are important, because often it is from childhood that the foundations for life are laid. Sometimes the initial image comes from a significant moment in childhood, and it is possible in the regression to just allow events to move forward. However, it is more frequently the case in my experience, that the initial image will be from some moment much later in the life, and there will be a need to retrace steps so that a fuller perspective of the life becomes apparent.

It is quite common to find that some disturbances in a past life have important roots in childhood events from that past life. By drawing out these experiences, the understanding of that life as it unfolds can be helped considerably.

How we react to particularly challenging situations related to our childhood can be very relevant to internal belief patterns that we adopt, which have quite a strong determining affect upon how our lives turn out. We are not necessarily products of, for example our parents' conditioning, and we have a choice as to how we react to any given circumstances. It may be quite an important step in our evolution as souls to learn how to withstand pressures from our parents and be true to ourselves even at a young age. But this can be very difficult and challenging test for our character, if we are abused or suffer bereavement and other deprivations. In these cases, we might have to reach out for help from others in order to overcome our problems.

In any given experience, we face lots of choices and temptations not to be true to ourselves. These can be like crossroads in our lives and present us with dilemmas as to how we act. Often the choice of yielding to temptation, knowing deep inside that it is not right for us, feels the easiest option. With regards to our parents, we can easily slip into a pattern where we do what they tell us, modelling our behaviour upon theirs rather than asserting our true individual self.

If a person does not solve a dilemma successfully or in a manner where he or she can feel peace, then this produces ripples that carry on into other events within that lifetime. There will be several incidents where essentially the same dilemma is being faced within that lifetime. Once a pattern is established of reacting to the dilemma in a particular way, this will tend to be repeated. As a person experiences these repetitions in regression, they become very much more aware of the consequences of any entrenched pattern of behaviour and how it affects the lifetime as it progresses.

If this pattern of behaviour has any particular resonance with a person in their present life, and the way in which they behave now, then revelations from that past life can be very instructive. Often, the past life childhood can have many similarities with the childhood that the person has experienced this time, and can consequently bring to the surface vulnerable present life memories. This process can aid people's understanding of their life now.

Traumas

Another aspect of regression that needs attention, is residual trauma left over from any given past lifetime. This is not usually very easy for people to face and can be emotionally quite painful. The best attitude to have when going through such experiences is to remember that they belong to the past and essentially can't hurt us now. Therefore, it is helpful in the process to have the attitude I have outlined, of being like a channel whereby these experiences can flow through us.

Earlier in this chapter, I gave the example of the Finnish lady who went through a past life regression relating to a traumatic experience from World War 2. From what she shared with me later, it appears that her present life became much less constricted as a result of accessing and releasing the fears associated with this trauma. I have found such an outcome to be quite typical with many clients. By expressing as much as possible of the emotions, thoughts and bodily sensations associated with regression experiences containing high levels of trauma, going through even the most awful experience can be quite liberating.

As with my Finnish client, people might go through murder, rape or torture, and although the whole experience can be unpleasant and very intense, with much bodily reaction, they will typically still feel much better for it afterwards. The releasing of energy from these experiences allows us to feel lighter and freer.

Some past life therapists do not like their clients to experience traumas from a past life and tend to either encourage their clients to watch them as an observer from a distance or to avoid them altogether. I do not feel that this approach is especially useful. Watching a trauma from a distance may give you insight and understanding on a surface level but there is no energy release or deeper appreciation of the dynamics involved in the experience.

To gain most from this therapy, it is better to choose a therapist who feels comfortable and familiar with the cathartic process of past life energy releases, and is willing for you to go through that wherever necessary. You may need to cry; your body might want to shake or squirm; you could feel the urge to cough and splutter or even to scream; your body may go very cold or hot; you could even feel the uncomfortable urge to laugh. It is good to trust your instincts and let your body do what it needs to do. All these are the body's releasing mechanisms and there is nothing to fear in bravely allowing this. Afterwards you may need to rest or sleep to let things settle. Given the chance, your body and inner consciousness will act to help you in your healing process.

With some people, emotionally cathartic release is all too readily accessible. For others, learning to allow the body to be a channel for traumatic past life experiences to flow through takes time and is only accomplished gradually. You need to trust that you are supported from within and will only be given those experiences to face that you are ready to integrate. The biggest barrier is fear. When you feel afraid, there is a tendency to try to push the fear away or ignore it in the hope that it will disappear. It is better if you can actually breathe with it and allow the fear to be there. This could feel very uncomfortable at first, especially if your body starts to shake uncontrollably. However, doing this will help your process to move on and you can learn what is within that fear; your perspective on what it was that you feared may then change. This in turn can give you feelings of strength and confidence. In my role as a therapist, especially when my clients feel anxious, I try to be as gentle and as encouraging as I can. To keep the flow of breathing can be a very important part of the process.

When you are going through a regression session and your therapist asks you questions that bring up uncomfortable body sensations or resistance in your thoughts and feelings, this is a sure sign that there is some trauma around the corner. Because of the pain involved in traumas, there is a naturally protective instinct within your sub-conscious, wanting to shield you and protect you from experiencing that pain. Therefore, a part of you will not want you to experience the things that, for your growth and inner liberation, you might need to experience most.

You may find that everything in the experience suddenly becomes all vague and unclear. You could feel that there are many reasons why you shouldn't continue with the regression. When your therapist questions you about your experience, your response could be to go blank. Your body will be your guide though. As you draw closer to the source of the truth contained in a particular trauma, your body could feel increasingly uncomfortable. Then, at some moment, the thoughts, feelings and imagery of the traumatic event might come tumbling into your mind. When you can acknowledge that openly, there will be an energetic release within your body and you will feel better.

Sometimes the process involved with releasing the energy blocks from a past life trauma can be quite complicated. When undergoing this for the first time, the way that your body chooses to release the trauma energetically can feel particularly disorientating. Some of the experiences you could have include breathing changes, sweating, strange body movements and energy sensations. You don't need to worry when any of these sorts of reactions occur. It is best if you can actually encourage it. Then at some point, it will settle. You need to trust that this is the mechanism of your body helping you to heal.

I have sometimes had to retrace my steps and go over earlier experiences from a client's past life to build up a more complete picture before that person can relive a trauma fully. The way that people experiencing a past life react to traumas is always linked to earlier experiences. For example, if a client experiences a past life event where as a man, he witnesses someone that he knows in that life being killed, many background details are needed for the person to relive that trauma fully. It is necessary to explore the relationship between the man and the murdered person, and any other pertinent experiences that he has had to do with killing. Other dynamics besides these could well need to be explored too.

Extreme experiences like rape, torture, humiliation or failure can be very difficult to endure. Often, these experiences have layers to them with hidden thoughts and feelings and various perspectives that will only emerge over time. Traumas are like wounds to the soul, needing sensitive careful handling, and also time for recuperation after any inner operation undergone in releasing the blocked energy.

If you have been through something similar in your present life, to the past life trauma, then these more extreme experiences are difficult. Some level of understanding can be gained from the past life experience to help you come to terms with the difficulties you have had in your present life. Any cathartic release related to the past life can also help cleanse you of parallel energetic blockages in your present life.

If, in a given past life, you are dealing with specific dilemmas, then the strongest traumas from that lifetime may bring those dilemmas into sharper focus, and the emotional and mental reactions may be more intense, with greater repercussions than at other times.

Going through this in regression, it is important to face the truth of how that past life character reacted to the dilemma, even if they made what would appear to be the wrong choice. The learning within our subconscious minds with reference to our present lives will be greater when we consider these past mistakes. We will be determined to do better this time.

It is not easy for any of us to face our mistakes and shortcomings. As I have already outlined, I believe that there is the yearning for our souls to go through just about every possible type of experience, good and bad. Therefore, to be in tune with our soul we need to be open to that possibility in ourselves. For those of us who have lived many lives, it is very likely, for instance, that we have been mass murderers at some stage in our evolution, and also that we could have manipulated and hurt people. There could also be many positive past lives where we have been kind and good, able to meet our challenges. To confront such truths about the range of our experiences from our past can be very humbling and an educational experience for our egos.

The most significant lives in our evolution are usually those where we have been able to turn an experience around - we may have started out by adopting some limiting behaviour but were able to change this into something more positive.

In one of my own past lives that I have accessed, I lived in Roman times within a wealthy Roman family. There was much corruption, opulence and cold ambition. In the early stages of this life, I just blended into this consciousness. One day, my son was drowned and I was devastated. This served as a wake up call for me. I blamed myself, feeling that the kind of life I had been living had contributed to his death. Consequently, I questioned my life at a fundamental level and chose a different path. After that, although most other people close to me did not change, I lived a productive life of integrity and compassion.

There were earlier lives, including one in Rome, where I had not risen above the circumstance surrounding me. So this lifetime was very strengthening to my soul. The death of my son was a trauma from which, had I not responded in the way that I did, I could easily have become bitter and more corrupt - and that life would have felt wasted.

I have not felt the need to go thoroughly through this past life, because it is one where I learnt my lesson. The ones where we didn't learn our lessons tend to hold the most value for us now.

In my own therapy, I have been much more interested in thoroughly investigating a quite recent past life in which I was a German judge, who was cruel and cold towards the people on trial in his court. This character felt very foreign to me, but it reminded me how much I intensely dislike being judged wrongly. Obviously, somewhere inside me, I had the capacity to make cold judgements towards people too. I felt compelled to study the patterns of how he came to be like that, so I would not repeat any of that behaviour.

In regression, it is easier to experience scenarios where we are victims of somebody else's wrongdoing than where we have been the perpetrators of some suffering to others. When we cause suffering to another, there is a part of us that is exactly aware of what that other person is feeling. Depending on our personality in the past life, we can close off from being aware of that information. But somewhere inside, we will not like what we have done. Typically, we will feel guilt, because our actions are in conflict with the loving relationship that we basically want with our fellow human beings.

The only remedy for guilt is forgiveness. In the regression process, finding forgiveness is usually something that can be best achieved after the death of the person that you were in that past life. But forgiveness is not necessarily a simple thing to accomplish. If you think of situations in our current time, some people find it almost impossible to admit that they may have made mistakes, to say 'sorry' and really mean it. In regression, this may be slightly easier because the past life experience is somewhat removed from our identities now. The realm of spirit, where people go when they die, tends to be a loving and peaceful place where almost anything seems possible. But offering and accepting forgiveness can be quite challenging. Inevitably, offering forgiveness to someone else means that we have to find a place within our hearts where we also forgive ourselves. To accept forgiveness from another, we have to own up to our own weaknesses and mistakes, the hurt that we may have brought to another. In short, this means that we need to open our hearts to places of inner darkness within us. Ultimately, this involves confronting our fear of what is acceptable to us and moving those boundaries so that we can consciously embrace more of ourselves.

Visiting memories in a past life regression where we have gone through a forgiveness process, can have a deep impact upon our being. It helps us appreciate other people's pain and hardship more fully, and also gives us the opportunity to practice forgiveness in our everyday life now.

The Death Experience

What happens when we die is a mystery that we can all anticipate. Ideally it is the moment when we need to let go of all our attachments from our earthly life and move on, whether we like it or not. From the perspective of regression, it can be very instructive to go through the experience of a past life death. There can be many emotions, thoughts and feelings caught up in this experience.

In regression the process of dying can occur suddenly or be a long drawn out process, in the moments leading up to the death, the thoughts and emotions that are in us may have etched very deeply upon our being. There are many kinds of deaths that can occur. Death can result from natural causes or from an accident, but quite often people experience lifetimes where death happens as a result of some violent act.

The most difficult deaths to go through tend to be those where there is a struggle, where people do not want to die. Struggling prolongs the process of death but people do not easily accept the experiences that want to unfold following death.

In the course of our lives, our belief systems tend to shape our experience to a large extent. We attract experiences to us on the basis of what we expect inwardly. Therefore, we can delude ourselves considerably about what is true and real, especially in our conceptions surrounding death. But when we die, we are confronted with some very fundamental truths about our existence. From the evidence of past life regression, our consciousness does survive death. Many of my clients who have been through several past life regression sessions have shared with me that they no longer fear death. It is a process where deep inside, people usually gain faith that the experience of death does not need to be feared and that there is an afterlife.

In regression, I have found it important to allow the death to be experienced as it is, even if it is not very nice. Sometimes the experiences around dying are also connected with traumas of various kinds. These can feel very messy and ugly. Alternatively, people can relive deaths that are filled with energy of great peace and acceptance. Assimilating experiences such as these can be deeply healing.

It is one of the beauties of reliving past lives that we are able to experience all kinds of personalities, human dilemmas, thoughts and feelings. Some of these can feel more familiar, and some less. Such experiences can only broaden our appreciation of life in general and our own soul in particular.

If we are stuck in our lives with thought patterns that operate quite rigidly within us, past life regression can help to liberate us from those patterns. When someone else is involved in causing us to die in a given lifetime, it is possible to react with strong negative thoughts and emotions towards that other person. This could be one of our soul tests from that lifetime. Our life can easily be considered as our most precious asset. We will naturally not want someone else to take that away from us. This kind of soul challenge in a lifetime can be a lesson about our attachments. Going through a difficult experience like this can prompt people to question at a deep level what they hold onto in their present experience.

When people experience a lifetime where they are killed or where fate seems to conspire against them to end their life prematurely, they can feel it is unfair and react bitterly about it. If they have felt hurt, they may want to hurt those that have hurt them. Sometimes, people may feel a grievance with God, and decide on some level that they do not want to go along with God's plan for them any more. People can feel cheated by death and want some form of justice that they can impose. These emotions and thoughts can gather around a death experience, creating residues that then have to find expression in the future.

At a deep level, we may have planned the manner of our death, but then, when we come to experience it, we might rebel and reject it as something we don't want. When we cannot accept what we have planned from deep inside, the implication is that we are in conflict with ourselves. This could have built up during the course of that lifetime where we repeatedly refused to act according to our inner prompting. When we die, this can then be a culmination for all that has gone before. Some part of us will be aware that we have been living a lie, and we could feel guilt or even hate towards ourselves for that.

Feeling hate towards oneself can be even more insidious than hating someone else, although the two are frequently interlinked. When we hate ourselves, we do not feel ourselves to be worthy of receiving love or anything good in our lives. We want to punish ourselves, and even sabotage worthwhile things that we could achieve. With these feelings, at death, we could feel deeply ashamed and isolated, not wanting help of any kind.

We might enter a past life where we are the victim of somebody else's hate. There may be a person who is very cruel, who kills us. We may decide as we are dying that we want that person to pay for what they did. This in turn might set off another lifetime where we are in a position to hurt this other soul. Because of the residual resentment from the previous life, we may do just that. Deep inside, we know that they should have shown us more compassion, and we feel bad with ourselves for not doing so in return. Our guilt over being unnecessarily cruel to this other soul may then set up a further life where we are victims to that soul again, and so it can go on. Typically, it is in the moments approaching death when we are tested as to whether we wish to perpetuate the energy of violence and hate, or not.

Issues of self-respect, and learning to love and accept others uncondit- ionally, are all part of the lesson for us in those experiences. Often these aspirations are not so easy to accomplish. We could have issues around those themes that we still need to address. This adds poignancy to the past life experiences.

In our past incarnations, we might not have always found death easy to accept - we may need to assimilate lessons from those experiences now. When going through a past life regression, I feel that it is best to just allow the experience of death to happen, moving any thoughts or feelings that we have about it to one side as much as possible. We can then experience how we handled the death experience in a past lifetime, and can learn from it.

The Spirit Realm

When people experience regression, in the moments leading from the last stages of dying to the first experience of having died, there will be a change. Often, people are rather bewildered by this at first. From grappling with various emotions and thoughts and physical sensations, it is likely to suddenly feel quieter. People may have an awareness of looking down on the body and feel a sense of detachment. This might not be so obvious for somebody who does not want to die. The turmoil of emotions and thoughts could continue even though the consciousness has left the body. But in most cases it will become clear that the connection with the physical body has been severed and this will be associated with a degree of peace.

In sessions where clients have accessed past lives of characters who do not believe in life after death, these people can experience death initially as something grey and bewildering, until they are ready to reach out for help.

In general, soon after leaving the body, people feel lighter and gain clarity about delusions that they have been living out in that lifetime, perceiving aspects of their lives that were not in balance and harmony. Typically people will experience themselves going upwards to somewhere brilliantly light and peaceful. This is what I would call the 'Spirit Realm'.

For people going through regression, coming into the spiritual realm can feel quite wonderful in comparison with the burden of the physical incarnation that preceded it.

Here people may meet with the energy form of spiritual helpers and guides, and others with whom they had interacted in that past lifetime. This feels very healing; the love and peace help to balance the difficult thoughts and emotions that the person had to endure during the course of physical incarnation.

I usually question my clients, when they enter the experience of the spiritual realm, about the nature of their purpose in that lifetime and the lessons that they needed to learn. Sometimes when I ask this question, the spiritual guide of my client steps forward, and they feel the love and the wisdom of that guide there to help them. This can be quite a humbling moment when mistakes and wrong turnings from that lifetime are fully realised. If the person has been through a traumatic experience, then the guide can be needed initially just to comfort the person and allow them to rest.

Revelations relating to that lifetime come to us in spirit to help the whole experience make sense. It is important to open up to this information as much as we can.

We can become aware of the imperfections in significant relationships from the lifetime where we have been, sometimes communication has been difficult and important things withheld. Then it may be necessary to meet these souls in spirit to redress wounds and unfinished interactions from the physical incarnation.

These souls can appear in some form to your inner awareness spontaneously so that you recognise them, whether you want them to be there or not. You may feel some anxiety and trepidation about this being there, and need the support of your therapist. It may also be that you feel the presence of your spiritual guide there to assist you. At this moment, the most important thing is to speak the truth of your feelings and receive what they want to convey to you. Once you have been able to do this, especially if you have had to overcome an inner barrier of fear, you may feel quite liberated.

A soul who has hurt you very badly during that past lifetime may appear. You might not want to have anything to do with that soul, even in spirit. However, by facing this soul and conveying your truth, you will become stronger and often more peaceful.

One process that can be very useful concerns difficult relationships, where the other person is still in the physical when you pass into spirit. It may be necessary to move forward to the time when this other person leaves the physical body so that you can complete the communication that is needed. Some of my clients have felt that they needed to come down with their guides to a special place where the transition from the physical to the spiritual takes place. Generally, the soul concerned will react to you in quite a different way to how the interactions occurred during the experiences of physical incarnation. The soul is likely to be more loving and understanding, and often very sorry for what happened during the lifetime. It will be like meeting that soul more truly, and for that soul to perceive you similarly. In the spiritual realm, the veil of delusions that we carry in relationship to each other while in physical incarnation is considerably lifted. We can learn much from these experiences.

Present Life Soul Links

Typically, the souls with whom you have a strong energy bond in a past life can be souls with whom you are connected in the present life. The energy from one lifetime can resonate with the next. So freeing the blocks in the relationship from the past can help release shackles that are still there in the present.

I once had a client who went through a past life experience where she was slowly poisoned and eventually smothered by her husband in that life. She experienced that she was helpless and had no energy to resist what this man wanted to do with her. My client recognised that the soul of this man was the same soul as her husband in her present life. In a group process, with a lot of help, we were able to encourage this client to reach out for help and move on from that state of consciousness where she was so stuck. She felt very afraid and despairing and needed a lot of help and reassurance. One other person from that life, whom she recognised from the past life experience as having contributed to her death, was there in the group with us. They were both aware of the connection from that past life.

This person felt a rush of energy inside her that she wanted to help my client, and try to remedy what she had done in the past life. She was able to lift and help support my client off the floor from where she had been stuck and thus help with the healing process. For my client to feel that others could help her and that she did not have to stay inert in that position of fear with this soul who was poisoning her and making her feel helpless, supported her tremendously. Within a week of doing this regression, that client finally left the abusive relationship she had been in for twenty years and started building a life of her own.

In regression, it is possible to identify souls from a past life with whom we are connected now. This is a delicate process and not everyone wants to do it. At a subconscious level there may also be resistance to doing that because of fear. However, I believe that making such identifications can be helpful. Becoming aware of how our existence over lifetimes is interweaving with that of other souls is a beautiful thing, and can only enable us to appreciate our lives more fully. We just need to have the confidence and inner belief that we are able to make such identifications in a regression process.

One client, with whom I have done a lot of past life regression, sees these soul identifications as images of people in their present day form superimposing themselves upon the images of personalities from the past life setting, thus getting her information. For myself, it is more an intuitive knowing. Thoughts of a person in my present life can come into my mind while I focus upon someone from the past life. I may also feel unusual body reactions that help with identification when my soul is present in a lifetime that another person is accessing.

Often it is not obvious. I need to empty my mind of preconceptions and expectations as much as I can when I am doing this, and then my intuitive capability for making a correct identification flows more easily. If my will becomes involved I can make mistakes.

In any given regression, it is not always clear to me who all the people involved with me from the past may be, and I am sure that not all of them are necessarily in my life now.

When we experience strong feelings in particular relationships from within our present lives then this can trigger memories of specific lives involving those souls from the past. On some levels of our being, we will know this, and instinctively be aware of the connection.

Besides relationships, there can usually be much learning when considering the links from a past life with the present. When your therapist asks you questions to this effect, there may be many thoughts and impressions coming to you where there are parallels from the past life with the present. Many of these concern beliefs or instances of behaviour that is similar.

It can be surprising to realise some belief pattern prevalent in a past life is still evident in your present existence. Once acknowledged, the behaviour arising from the pattern of this limiting belief begins to change.

In the case of my client who was poisoned and smothered to death by her husband, the limiting pattern in her case concerned a belief where she felt helpless and trapped by fear. She had felt unable to resist the will of this man to hurt her, and too weak to be able to move out of a situation where he would continue to do that. By energetically helping her to move beyond the position where she felt completely stuck and helpless in the past life, she was able to make the move in her present life that was to change it.

The learning from these links between lives can be very deep - your therapist may help you to clarify them but you need to do the integrating yourself. If you give yourself some time and space afterwards, realisations come that help you to feel more settled. It takes a while for all the various realisations and experiences of a past life regression session to filter through all the layers of your subconscious mind. In addition, your rational critical mind wants to judge and assess what has taken place. Therefore, you can be occupied with the experience you have had for some time.

At the end of a thorough past life session it takes a while to adjust to your present circumstances again. It is advisable to rest for a while, as usually there is a lot to digest.

Chapter 6

First Experiences

As part of my work I lead past life workshops. These can be held over the duration of a day, a weekend, or even as a residential week-long workshop. Over the years, I have led many such courses in various locations. Some people prefer the privacy of individual sessions for doing past life work. For others, group work has the advantage that people can witness each other's experiences as well as go into their own. Collectively, people can then encourage each other to open up.

With the one-day workshop, the format is such that I generally start with a group meditation. From there, those who want to explore the experience of their meditation further can volunteer to do so in a one-to-one situation in front of the group. Typically, people who participate in these workshops are new to regression, and there is the opportunity for them to engage in the past life processes as little or as much as they want.

From one of these workshops, I asked four of the members of that group if they would include an account of their experiences in this book. In the workshop, all four of them took the plunge and were willing to do in-depth work in front of the group after the meditation. I believe that they were all quite surprised by the intensity of what took place. Each of them had experiences and things to learn that were distinctive. What follows are their accounts.

Linny
I am the mother of two children. Bringing them up on my own has been quite stressful. However, I have been involved with reiki and holistic

therapies and these have been important for me to feel that I am on a spiritual path. I have noticed the compassion that I have felt towards the Native Americans, and a deep upset about the wars in which the white people killed so many of them. Coming into the workshop I wondered if, through past life regression, I could learn something more about this. I also reflected that in myself I have often felt that I belonged somewhere else, and I didn't know what that meant. The other thing that I shared concerned a dear friend who had died eighteen months earlier. The day of the workshop would have been her fortieth birthday. This felt significant for me.

As it happened, the past life that I entered had nothing to do with the Native Americans. What came to me in the meditation was that I was a builder living in the mountains, working hard, directing people who were moving stones and rocks in carts. I was aware of my mother in that life as someone who argued with me. She wanted me to be more involved in the affairs of the local community. But I preferred to be on my own, doing my work and not mixing with others very much. At my death, I was lying on a table with a fever. Two people were trying to help me and, after I died, I just hovered there above them.

The meditation was like a visualisation and seemed like a typical meditation. I was not shocked at all, and even wondered if it could be a figment of my imagination.

Something in me propelled me to volunteer to be the first one to develop the experience with one-to-one work. Paul asked me what part of the experience had the most energy. I felt drawn to the experience of my past life death. Closing my eyes, I now recognised that one of the people trying to help me then was my mother from that life. Suddenly, I was there. I could feel the emotions welling up inside of me. I loved my mother and I was so sad not to be able to fulfil her wishes. My body was twitching and my hands shaking. I couldn't stop it. I kept sobbing and sobbing. Then at the point of death, I physically felt that I couldn't breathe. My chest was getting tighter. All at once it eased off, and I knew that my body had died, and I was looking down on them.

I hadn't expected the emotions. It felt that it was me, feeling heartbroken, and I didn't want to move on. I wanted to stay with my mum because I felt that she needed me. As my sobbing eased, I became aware of my fear of the unknown. I didn't know what could be waiting for me now that I had died. That was another reason for me to stay close to my mum.

As I acknowledged this, I became aware of light. This rapidly became very intense. The involuntary flickering of the muscles in my face was out of control. I had never had an experience like that. It was so, so bright, extremely breathtaking. When I went through, into the light, I jolted up physically. For a moment, I thought that I had gone back into my life as that man. I had no identification with my consciousness as Linny.

In this spiritual realm, I felt that we didn't need to speak. I felt my perceptions to be open, and I just 'knew'. When Paul asked me what they were saying, I didn't know how to respond. I didn't have to speak. The energy of the spiritual realm felt very different to the physical. It was very loving and peaceful.

Later, I met with the soul of the woman that was my mother then, when she passed over. The interesting thing is that in my present life, I have a difficult and distant relationship with my mother. So to feel love of such intensity towards my mother from the past life felt very different and new to me.

Paul asked me if I had a connection with this soul in my present life as Linny. As I considered this, I could sense that she was not one of the people in my present circles. But then the knowledge flooded into my consciousness that I was going to meet her in the future. This awareness made me feel very happy. Having lost my friend eighteen months earlier the feeling that someone, with whom I felt very close as a soul, was going to come into my life comforted me. The fact that I felt so clear about this knowledge completely astounded me.

After the regression was over, I was surprised to feel very focussed in the here and now. When I got home to my children I had to keep stroking them, appreciating them and reassuring myself that they were there.

The past life experience from this workshop has made me more aware that things do not last forever, and I need to live as much as I can in every moment. I have always believed in life after death, but this experience has made me believe in it more strongly.

Joti

I knew had past lives – it was a gut feeling. There were some people with whom I felt so close, like I had known them for aeons. There were also things I could do in life that came naturally to me, even though I was not qualified in them. An example of that has been teaching. My children too, have been triggers for my curiosity in past lives. One of them said, when he was four years old, something like, 'It smells like war here'. How would he know what war smelt like?

I wanted to know about my past lives to gain some insight into myself and who I am – I knew that there was so much information out there to tap into, but I didn't know how to do it. I needed some guidance and felt that this workshop would be a way forward for me. Not knowing what to expect when I would do a past life meditation, I was worried that I would just make up something to suit my 'ego'. Consequently, I asked my guides to take me to a life that wasn't spiritual' but would give me guidance to understand my purpose in this life. Within me, I wanted to experience something I knew I couldn't have contrived; I wanted the proof.

When Paul talked me through the meditation, I struggled to see the meadow at first. I found this strange because I meditate regularly. Instead, I felt that I was a mass of colour and energy. When I was asked to walk through the door I could see a door but, rather than walking through it, I felt a sensation of being pulled through a tunnel of pulsating purple colour. Meanwhile, my eyes were flickering with rapid eye movement.

When asked to look at my feet, I was surprised at how easy it was to see my surroundings and myself. It didn't feel like watching myself - I was that person; I could sense the emotions and see through their eyes. I was astonished at the detail I could see – as if it was yesterday, and fresh in my memory. Going through the various stages of that life was tough and emotionally difficult – I knew that I couldn't have made anything like it up. Each new experience felt strange. When asked to think about the lessons of that lifetime and about its links to our present life, it was so clear, so obvious – I knew.

In the meditation, my first impressions were of being a boy living in Bombay. I felt myself to be 9-10 years old; I was not wearing shoes and my clothes were old and torn. Considering myself, I got the feeling that I was quite content, mischievous, but not a bad boy. I had a free spirit. At this time, I was playing 'tig' with some other children. I was a Hindu.

Moving forward to a scene a few years later, the scene was not so happy. A group of militant Muslims had attacked our village and there was a lot of fighting. I was with my younger sister and we were trying to get away. My sister was behind me when I heard her scream. When I turned back to her, I saw that her leg was caught in a metal contraption, one used to trap animals. This one had been laid out purposefully to trap humans – it was like a metal jaw with rusted jagged edges. Trying to prise open the jaws, I found that I couldn't, it was too tight for me. I tried to shout for help, but nobody came. People were too scared and concerned to get away from the Muslim fighters. The emotions were so intense; I felt despair and anger watching my sister scream out in pain. All I could do was hold her.

When the meditation ended, this particular memory of my sister being trapped stayed in my mind, and the emotions were strong in my chest. I knew that I had to revisit that time; I couldn't just leave it like that. I had to work through it. Otherwise, that feeling would have stayed with me – it was such an urgent feeling. I was pleased but anxious when Paul said he would carry out one-to-one work, knowing that it was going to be an emotional ride.

Closing my eyes, I was there again at the moment where my sister was trapped. The emotions flooded through me. I couldn't stop myself from expressing them. Going forward to the moment of her death, I felt deep anger towards the Muslims. We hadn't done anything wrong, they didn't know us, and I didn't care about their religion.

Later I became a militant myself, responsible directly and indirectly for the deaths of many Muslims. Going to the moment where I was about to shoot one of them, the power of the emotions almost overwhelmed me. I could feel the urge to kill and have my revenge, but as Joti, I hate to hurt anybody. It was such a struggle to allow those feelings that were so foreign to me. Yet I also felt that struggle in the character that I was then. A part of him did not want to fight, but wished for peace.

This struggle found a resolution when later on I was confronted with one of my friends who had been shot. As I held him, again I felt intense sadness. I had had enough. A realisation hit me that this fighting was not working. Holding my head in my hands, I had feelings of remorse and sadness.

Later I found myself talking to some militant leaders; I tried to propose a truce, but they just laughed at me and told me that I had gone soft in the head.

My death occurred when a man came up to me while I was at a market. He looked at me in the eyes and pulled out a gun, shooting me in the stomach. 'That's for killing my brother', he said. The pain in my stomach was intoxicating and I felt as though I couldn't breathe. I was hot all over and trembling.

Eventually, I could feel myself hovering above my dead body, looking at my blood-drenched hands covering the wound in my stomach. I felt light and was surrounded by white light. It felt such a relief to be over that life. I felt like I deserved to die for all the suffering I had caused. I saw my sister and felt overjoyed. I didn't want to let her go; I felt such love for her. When Paul asked me to see the spirits of those that I killed, I felt such shame I didn't want to look at them in their faces. When I finally did, they were sending me love and forgiveness. I felt peace.

The connection that I feel from this past life to my present one is through my current work as a community worker. My work is on many levels. One key role is with the ethnic minority communities, bringing people and communities together. I have gained respect in the community for the work that I carry out. I work on a strategic level, on a voluntary basis, as a trustee in a charity that works to create cultural understanding and

71

respect. Where I live now is in the heart of the Muslim community. I believe that I have been given an opportunity to help those that I hurt in my previous life, to propose peaceful solutions to possible situations of conflict.

With Paul's prompting, I recognised various soul connections from that life to this. Two significant ones were my current partner who was someone I shot, and my youngest son who was my younger sister in the previous life. Other souls that I recognise are people with whom I currently work.

When I came back into being Joti, I felt weak and overwhelmed by emotions. It was a hard life to live through. I was glad that I had done it, and felt relieved to have coped with it, although a residue of guilt was still there. I was shocked at how real the experience felt – the emotions and the vivid scenes. I never expected something so intense. I felt vulnerable and 'naked'. It was so difficult for me to feel the impulses from the past life where I wanted to kill others. This is something that I could not condone now.

In the closing meditation, I went within to an ancient temple where there were colour-healing chambers. This was an inner place that I had visited previously and I felt safe. Stepping into a chamber studded with emeralds and green light I felt peace, and the words 'I am forgiven' came to me. Coming out of the meditation, I knew that I was forgiven. It was another thing to forgive myself.

Afterwards, it was essential for me to tap into my support network. As soon as I went home, my first step was to write up the experience as fully as I could, to let it leave my mind and to sleep that night. I was too exhausted to speak to anybody in detail but the next day, I met up with a trusted friend to share my experience – he helped me put it into perspective. With the Reiki that I do I sent healing back to that past life, to help me move forward from the strong emotions.

From my experience, I understand the vehemence that I have felt against wars going on in the world. Wars do not help. By opening to this part of myself, I am eager to learn more. I look forward with expectancy to the next time I can enter into a past life meditation.

Eleana

I have always believed in reincarnation. It is a fascinating subject and I have a huge interest in it. In my family background, there are a number of psychics and healers, so I suppose it is natural that I would be interested in these things too. Prior to the workshop with Paul, I had been to one other workshop where we did a past life meditation. This had felt a bit like putting my toe in the water. It was as though I was an observer standing on the outskirts looking in at the past life story that came up for me.

With the initial group meditation in Paul's workshop, I could feel myself stepping in more fully because I felt a greater connection to some of the feelings that were involved in the experience that was there. But the logical part of my mind was still present, observing the snippets of my past life story, trying to link things and work it all out.

When I later offered myself to do some one-to-one work, the actuality of the experience then was completely different to what I had supposed with the logical part of my mind after the meditation. This astonished me, and has strengthened my belief in the reality of past lives.

In the meditation, I saw three different doors. One of these doors had red around it though and seemed hot. This particular door appeared to me to be the most challenging option, but I still felt that this was the one that I needed to go through.

As I did so, I found myself as a woman in a burning bedroom. I was in a big old house. Physically I noticed my breathing change, shortening because of the fire. Inside I felt some panic that I wouldn't be able to get out. I was a woman in a night-gown. At the door to the bedroom, a gentleman appeared. He was concerned for us to get the children out. I sensed that they were not my children and I was not particularly concerned. However, we did all manage to get out of the house.

When I was led to an earlier phase of the life, I was aware of resentment that I felt towards my father and sister. There was an argument due to me wishing to take food to the poorer people that lived in the woods. We were quite wealthy and I wanted to help those people. My father did not want me to do it.

Later on, I lived in a wooden house in the woods, where I died as an old woman. The death felt very peaceful. There was a white energy and other spirits were saying 'Where have you been?'

From the glimpses I had of the later stages of this life, I recognised it as the same one that I had explored in the previous workshop. The fire in the bedroom was from an earlier stage in this life.

With the logical part of my mind, I decided that this must have been a straightforward life where as a result of the fire; I went to live at the edge of the forest. I had no notion of the difficulties and darkness within this experience.

Watching others go through the one-to-one work, I felt tremendous emotion in support of their experiences. However, I also felt the urge to do my own work and I did not know what to expect.

But then, when I closed my eyes, all at once I was there in the bedroom with the bed on fire. It was as if I was here and there at the same time. At one point I tried to open my eyes, but they wouldn't open. Paul asked me questions about the surroundings, and I had to force myself for a few moments to pull myself out of the experience somewhat to answer him, but then I was there again. My breathing was getting quicker and I felt the panic that I needed to get out of here. However, there were other feelings too.

Suddenly I knew that I had started the fire myself. That knowledge had been completely hidden from me before then. I spoke this awareness aloud in a very matter of fact manner. My logical mind was being overruled by a deeper part of me that 'knew'.

Soon I was sobbing my eyes out. I did not want to be there anymore. I didn't like the snobbery, the nastiness, and the segregation of the rich people from those who were poor. Then I remembered that my father had been angry with me. My sister had told him that I had taken linen stores to people of the village. I felt betrayed by my sister. My father always made me do what he said.

Paul prompted me about my mother. Suddenly I felt huge distress. My mother had not been well, not right in her mind. The Doctor had had her chained to the bed. And then she had been taken away. I felt such a lot of sadness, not knowing where she had gone.

The bed that I had lit was the same bed where my mother had laid. I wasn't even sure that I wanted to get out. My driving force was that things in this house had to end. The children in the house were those of my sister and I felt no closeness to them.

After seeing that the house had been burnt to the ground, I was taken to my death when I was very old. After my body died, it felt very light and breezy. I was part of a circle with other Spirits. I felt that I knew them all very well.

It is clear to me that there is still much for me to discover about this life. I feel that I will need to do some further work on it later.

The one-to-one experience felt very different from visualisation meditations where I would imagine things. I was connected to a part of me that knew the answers to what was being asked, as if I was totally recalling something. The emotions that accompanied the experience made it vivid and real. In the course of my present life, I have never felt a release of emotions like that.

Lynne

I have always believed in reincarnation from childhood, and I have had a strong wish to gain knowledge and insight about myself. Spiritual growth is the most important thing to me. Yet everyday things, like raising my two children, have taken up much of my time, making me feel frustrated and confused at times.

Before the workshop with Paul, I had touched upon one or two of my past lives in other groups and also had a soul reading about some of my past lives and how they are affecting my present. In the workshop the past life that emerged was quite different from any of those.

The initial meditation was quite foggy for me. I had vague images of being a priestess with robes on, working at a temple. There was one other character of which I was very much aware. This was a male priest. On one hand, this priest was charismatic and I felt very much drawn to him. However, I also felt used by him, and there was much resentment from the other priestesses for the fact that I was favoured by him. In the end I had my clothes ripped off and my throat cut by the priest, resulting in my death. I was left with the feeling of being overwhelmed by the power of this priest.

In the way that I perceive things in meditations, I do not tend to see images very clearly, but I can feel emotions keenly. Although in the initial meditation, I did have feelings, especially towards that priest, in the one-to-one work that followed; these were felt so much more strongly and in depth.

As Paul suggested that I focus upon the priest, I perceived him as tall with a powerful, dark and consuming energy. He appeared to live on power, absorbing that from the women. Yet he professed to be something else, a spiritual teacher and guide, someone of the light.

I noticed that I felt different from the other women and isolated. I put my trust in him and he sought me out when I was alone, for sexual contact. This was against the laws, but it felt right and I gave him everything.

We engaged in sexual practices. On one occasion I was lying on the altar. There was chanting and singing from the other priestesses. Then the priest touched my heart with a ceremonial knife. It was a wonderful, floating sensation. I had a special role, and had been chosen.

Later, I was aware of the deep resentment of the other priestesses. They were challenging his position in the way that he was relating to me. I felt fearful but kept hoping that he would protect me. Then he accused me of seducing him, and cast me aside. Even as they cut my hair and prepared me for a ritual, I believed that he would save me. But then he did not, and my trust was betrayed.

On the altar, I was pushed to my knees. He looked at me in anger. I felt that I couldn't trust male love. Holding my head back, he cut my throat. As this happened I could feel, as Lynne, a physical sensation in my throat. It was not painful but felt like a cutting and tearing on an energetic level. With this I saw an image of bleeding and felt my consciousness slip away. My heart beat very quickly before the death and then afterwards slowed right down. It felt a relief to be over that life.

Then I became aware of light and warmth, with a gathering of souls. There was a female spirit holding me by the hands. I sensed the words coming from her that I needed to trust my self and my inner wisdom at times of isolation, and not seek wholeness from somebody else.

Paul encouraged me to go to the moment when I would confront the priest in Spirit when he passed over. With his energy in front of me, I had a feeling of a black empty hole in my lower abdomen. Breathing into this, I felt that I despised him. There were tremendous emotions of aggression that I had to express. As I did this, I felt this dark energy lifting from me, shifting the energy and bringing light into it. This made me feel much lighter and better, bringing more fluidity of energy into that region. Then I felt considerably more at peace, helping me to complete the experience.

I am aware that I still have issues in my relationship with men in my current experience. The feeling of my throat being cut lingered with me for some days, only gradually fading. This past life experience has left a big imprint upon me, but there are still questions from it that are unanswered. In the days that followed, more details came to me. For instance, when I asked inwardly about how the priestesses came to be at the Temple, the information was given to me that girls were taken away from their families when young, and placed there. In some ways, it was an honour, but it was also quite brutal.

I hope that this experience of a past life will make some difference to my life. Usually transformation works slowly inside me. It is certainly not an experience that I will easily forget.

General Comments

Each of these experiences brings out distinct themes illustrating some of the potential that is inherent in past life regression.

In the case of Linny, her experience undoubtedly had a profound effect upon her faith. The spiritual experience she had was real beyond doubt for her. It gave her the belief that at a deep level she had the capacity to perceive truth, and that she was not alone.

With Joti, although her experience was quite shocking for her, it helped to give reasons for the ideals and work that was so important for her today. It helped her to gain perspective, insight and understanding about her work situation and the strength of her feelings against war.

Eleana became aware of how visiting a particular past life memory a number of times can reveal further layers of truth that may not be evident at first. Like Linny, she experienced her inner capacity to 'know' things, but also saw how the mind has hidden depths that she had not realised were there.

In the past life that Lynne went through, she was helped to release the suppressed emotion of anger that was still associated with the abuse she suffered then. She felt this energetically, and thus she was able to become aware of the psychotherapeutic healing potential of regression work.

All four participants found their experience to be accompanied by a massive outpouring of emotion, particularly in the one-to-one work. As a therapist, one of my aims in the one-to-one work is to find places where my clients feel vulnerable within the episodes of the past lives. Usually these moments of vulnerability hold the key to unresolved problems that need healing. By encouraging my subjects to give attention to their inherent feelings and thoughts, they can go inside themselves and become aware at a deeper level of what is taking place. Often, these moments contain elements that have been suppressed and full of emotion. Each of these participants was very trusting, willing in consciousness to explore these feelings, and thus they all felt positive afterwards that they had gained from their experiences.

Chapter 7

Tanya's Story

I would like to introduce a case study of Tanya, a woman who attended two of my past life workshops. In the account she gives here, she describes the past life experiences she had in the first workshop. Over a two-day workshop, I can usually explore issues more thoroughly with participants than I can in a single day with a group. She writes about focussing on the experience, going back to formative events, going through the main challenges and critical moments of the life, her death experience, meeting with other spiritual beings after death, and linking the past life with her present circumstances now. Her story is clothed in emotional intensity, passion and drama. As an outcome of her experience she has gained an insight that she now applies to her everyday life.

Meeting Tanya

Tanya is a dynamic person with a big heart. In my workshop group, it was clear from the outset that she would apply herself to the process one hundred percent. In her sharing at the beginning she told us that she was going through a lot of change and personal growth in her life. As a recovering alcoholic, she had had much to focus on in order to create a more positive life for her self. Other avenues of support in addition to the past life work had contributed strongly to help her make forward steps.

However, having worked with a number of recovering alcoholics with regression, I believe that the transformational process of regression work can have a galvanising effect upon people in this situation. It serves to remind us at a deep level about our responsibility to create a constructive life that is true to our inner purpose, and the suffering that can result when we don't do that.

Here follows Tanya's account.

Tanya's Past Life Regression

My first experience with past life regression therapy took place during a weekend workshop, which I attended with several friends. I was curious to see if this would provide further proof of the existence of the soul, that there really was a part of me that was not dependant on this life, this body and this personality.

My own spiritual search had been put on hold for many years as I struggled with alcoholism and other problems relating to an inability to accept life on life's terms. A year before this weekend, I had come into recovery and begun working the twelve-step program of Alcoholics Anonymous. This included making a decision to turn my will and my life over to the care of the god of my understanding. I took this step after what I believe was Divine intervention in my life and since this time, my spiritual journey has become of primary importance to me.

I did not go on this weekend for healing. If I had thought about it, I would have said that I was already doing enough work on myself, that I had dealt with all major issues in my life, and that I had the tools to deal with anything new that came up for me. Certainly, I did not expect anything profound or deeply emotional.

The life which I describe began to come to my awareness through my feelings, as someone else was relating a past life experience of their own. In the life that she described, she had been mother to a child who was taken from her and sacrificed. She also talked about how much she despises people in her life now that hurt children.

As this woman was talking, I found myself becoming increasingly uncomfortable. I felt many powerful and unexplained emotions surging through my body - feelings of grief, guilt and remorse, and an over-whelming desire to say 'sorry'.

My friend's recall of that life was clearly very painful for her, and the events she was depicting were quite tragic. As I began to cry, I knew that this was partly empathic, in response to the strong emotional atmosphere in the room, but I was also aware of a vast well of pain in me, which I did not understand. The only thing that was clear was that I desperately wanted to say 'sorry'. It was vitally important to me that everyone there should understand just how sorry I was feeling. The thought that I was going to have the opportunity to apologise was exciting as well as frightening. At last I was ready, I had enough faith in the inherent goodness of myself and the universe, I had people with me who I trusted would not judge me, so that I would be able to admit what I had done.

As Paul began to direct me into the past life, he asked me to go into the experience that had the most energy. I could see many images in my mind, the strongest of which was an impression of water, fast flowing water, and a wooden box, just under the surface. The box was below me so that I was looking down on it. Although it was closed, I knew that there was a body inside. My feeling was that I was responsible for the death of that person and I assumed then that I was trying to drown them.

Paul guided me back to the time when I was putting the body in the box and I became confused. As I was putting this person into the box, I could see that he was already dead, and my rational mind could not accept this. Why was I doing this to a person that was already dead? What was the point?

Then I was directed back to a time when this person was alive and well. I saw him sitting at a large wooden table in a kitchen. There were stone walls and a fireplace, herbs hanging on the walls. This was our home and this young man was supposed to be my son; I was his father. He was happy, laughing, looking at me with bright eyes. At that moment, he was holding a piece of fruit in one hand and a knife in the other, using the knife to cut and eat the fruit. I looked at him and knew that I was going to kill him with a knife, because I had to do so.

I had to kill him because he was not my son. He was nearly sixteen years old, and for all of his life, I had believed him to be mine until his real father had told me the truth. Once I knew the truth, it became obvious to me that it was real. Things I had not understood before suddenly made sense and so I believed this man and what he told me. I felt incredibly stupid. My whole life and everything in it was based upon lies. I felt as if everyone was laughing at me and had been for years. Every time I looked at the creature that I had thought to be my son, I was reminded of what I total failure I felt myself to be. I had to kill him. He was an abomination, and couldn't be allowed to live.

Paul suggested for me to consider my wife. She was very beautiful, I thought, with long, curling, strawberry blonde hair, pale skin and rosy cheeks. I loved her very much, but she was very unkind to me. She laughed at me, made fun of me, ordered me around and criticised me constantly. Despite this, I had always believed that she loved me, really, deep down. I had clung onto memories from our early time together, but even these were now crumbling away, tainted.

Going forward to the time when I killed the boy, I was aware that we were in the kitchen by the fireplace. I had the knife in my hand and he was standing there in front of me. He was talking to me, but I had to block out the words from my mind. I couldn't engage with him, I just had to kill him.

Suddenly I thrust the knife forwards into his stomach as hard as I could. I don't know what I had been expecting, but I felt uncertain about what to do next. He didn't die immediately. Instead he looked at me and I looked back into his eyes. There was great fear there, a look of total incredulity. I wanted to take it back, just for a minute, feeling that I wished to explain what I was doing to him and why it was necessary. I wanted him to know that I loved him, and that it wasn't his fault or mine, but just the way that it had to be. If only I could explain it, then he would understand. But there was no time. I had to stab him again quickly so that it would be complete; there was no going back now.

When I was sure that he was dead, I fetched a large wooden box from the outhouse. Once I had emptied this, I put the body inside. I had to get the lid shut so that I could nail it down. My idea was that I would put it in the river and let it float away from there. However, I had trouble getting the body inside, finding room to tuck in the arms and legs. It was necessary for me to take off his shoe, but then I got the lid closed and secured.

Paul suggested that I went forward to events relating to the consequences of this murder, but I was unable to see or understand any future situation clearly. I felt that I had become insane, retreating into a world of confusion and pain, full of guilt and remorse, but unable to face the reality of what I had done.

Going to the time just before my death, I was thin and ill, covered with sores, scratching a stone floor with my fingers until they bled. I wanted to die, knowing that it was coming, and I couldn't wait for it to happen. The moment of death was experienced as tremendous release. I felt that I was free at last, felt myself rising from my body and being carried so gently away from all the pain and trouble of life. Soaring through the sky, the colours were rose, gold and midnight blue. I was bathed in a light that went right through me and made me pure again.

I was directed forward to the time when I met with the soul of the boy that I had killed. When I saw him, he was beautiful beyond description. With no hesitation, he came to me and embraced me with total and complete acceptance and love. It was not so much that I was forgiven by him but that he had never condemned me. He conveyed that for him, there had never been anything to forgive.

During the whole of this experience, I had been crying and shaking. Paul had been telling me continually to breathe through my mouth, and I could feel this helping me to release deep emotions. As the regression came to an end, I found myself utterly drained, yet also invigorated. I felt a calm clarity inside me and knew that I had done something very important.

There were still lots of questions about the life that I had experienced, things that I didn't understand. At the completion of the day, I went away and spent the evening on my own, allowing my mind to drift so that more details of the life came to me. Most importantly, I realised that I knew the soul of the real father of the boy as someone from my current life. This person was someone to whom I had always felt drawn and yet also strangely guilty and uncomfortable around. For weeks, I had been meaning to contact this person, but for some reason, had decided to put it off until this weekend was over. Although the past life has not helped me to know how to heal our relationship, it has allowed me to understand my feelings better and I now believe that a time of healing will come when it is right for us both.

During the following day, while having a private session with Paul, I asked the character from my past life, what message he had for me, and I received the following:

"Do not be deceived by appearances, it is all love - even if it does not look like it, it is love."

This message made a lot of sense to me. For as long as I could remember, I had felt that it was not right for one human being to judge another. It had always seemed unfair to me to make judgements about other people without having total understanding of them and the context in which they acted. As we can never have this total understanding, we can never judge fairly.

I realised that whilst the crime committed by my past life self was terrible, within the context of his life and experiences, what he did made perfect sense and he did not feel that he had any choice.

This is all part of an important lesson for me at the moment - that I can love everyone, regardless of what they do or appear to do, that I can trust that everyone is doing the best that they possibly can, and that despite appearances, all is love.

Chapter 8

Choosing the Right Therapist

To engage in individual past life therapy, the relationship with your therapist is a very important one. You want to feel safe with your therapist and able to trust that person to support you. To go into regression means surrendering many of the psychological control mechanisms with which you normally direct your being. Therefore, you will be very vulnerable and you will need to feel that your therapist is sensitive to your needs, and acting according to those needs as much as possible.

In addition, you will want to feel that your therapist has sufficient knowledge, skills and inner wisdom to be familiar with the various states of soul that may emerge with your regression.

Your therapist will be your companion on your very own sacred inner journey of potential discovery and illumination. Because of this you may feel close to your therapist and feel that this person is special to you. Equally you might want to feel quite dispassionate, comfortable with keeping a professional distance in your relationship. Whatever you feel in this regard, it is well to remember that the regression experience is your story, your soul memory and your learning. Your therapist, and of course other people close to you, will have stories, memories and learning that belong to them, and these will be very different from yours. The task of your therapist will be to listen to you, support you and perhaps, to be your friend, but you have your own path to tread and no one can share that with you completely.

Methods of Guiding a Regression Session

Past life regression can be guided in a variety of ways. Some therapists prefer a passive approach, letting the experiences unfold for their clients with very little intervention. Other therapists tend to operate with a formula of standard questions and objectives to direct the client, whatever their client is experiencing.

Another approach that the therapist can adopt is to be dynamic, intuitive and flexible in their way of operating as a guide with clients. Here, therapists attune to their clients, oscillating between being passive and allowing the process to unfold on one hand and, when it feels required, intervening on the other. If the client is stuck or avoiding the surfacing of an experience, then these therapists prompt or actively encourage the client along some particular avenue of exploration. Such an approach can be a more co-operative one, with both client and therapist working actively together to take a process forward.

I favour this form of therapy, although it is more demanding in terms of skills and responsibility for the therapist. It is important for clients to feel that they are responsible for their own healing process. Therapists adopting this approach successfully need to be good listeners. They need to be careful, so that they are attuned with their hearts to serving their clients and not merely indulging their own agenda. In my own practice I also try to listen to guidance from within myself, asking inwardly how I can best help a person at a given moment. Some of the thoughts and urges that I have received when I do this have surprised me greatly, but they generally work.

Qualifications

When choosing a therapist, you might feel the need to check out his/her qualifications. There are many impressive sounding titles that therapists can put next to their names. An increasing number of organisations purport to offer training in past life regression. Also, as aforementioned, there are many different approaches to this work, some of which are surely deeper and more meaningful than other ones. How do you make the right decision?

When seeking the right therapist for you, it is helpful to talk to any that you contact about the experience and training that he or she has had in this field. It is helpful if your therapist has been extensively through his or her own personal past life regression experiences and learnt from them, and had had some degree of supervision. When people have experienced past life regression for themselves, they tend to have a greater understanding of what other people go through.

I urge you to choose someone whom you feel can listen to you, not someone who may want to dominate you. Trust your instincts to make the right decision.

Past life experiences can be very intense. If your therapist is really with you when you go through the regression, it is likely that they will be affected by what you experience as well. So it is important to feel that your therapist has the necessary support and maturity to be able to process his/her own reaction to what you experience.

Once, I received healing from a very sensitive psychic who noticed that, at the very edge of my aura corresponding to the region of my solar plexus, I had formed a hardness that seemed like a protective layer or shield. This healer perceived the layer to be something that I had constructed energetically to help me to cope and be detached enough when working with my clients. Obviously I had done this without consciously realising it, to enable me to stay centred when my clients were dealing with strong emotions and releasing distress. Admittedly it has been necessary for me to learn as much as possible to be able to keep my own balance when working with clients, so that I can truly serve them. However, over the years, I have noticed that I have developed the capacity to withstand even the most extreme outbursts of feelings from my clients during regression, knowing that this is an essential part of their process. I am sure that other therapists, as they develop experience, will have constructed similar forms of energetic protection.

To summarise, whilst undergoing extensive training and supervision is important for this work, I do not feel that this will ultimately determine a therapist's true worth. Of greater value will be your therapist's soul awareness and psychic sensitivity. They also need clarity of mind, and an open heart that wants to care for you and help you.

Whilst it is useful and important to learn about a therapist's qualifications, you need to trust your own instincts to help guide you to the right person.

Overcoming Difficulties

When engaging in a series of past life therapy sessions, there can be times when you question whether or not you want to go on. You might be uncertain about where the therapy is going; it may be difficult for you to cope with the inner disturbance it triggers; it can be hard to share your experiences with anyone else, making you feel lonely. Especially in the time immediately prior to going into your session, you might think of all sorts of things that you could be doing rather than going into that therapy situation again.

A lot of this can come down to fear. Our everyday self does not welcome change, and likes everything to be familiar and in its place. Very often, past life therapy can initiate revolutionary change within our inner being, and this can be, especially in the initial stages, very disorientating. It is very important, if you are struggling with the therapy, to feel able to talk this over honestly with your therapist. If you are troubled by an aspect of the work you are doing, your therapist will not necessarily be able to read your mind to know what that is about. You may need quite a lot of support to process the experiences that come up through regression, and it is not always wise to try to do this alone. The emotional and mental aspects of past life experiences can affect people's mood for quite a long time after a session is over. Therefore, it is helpful to feel able to approach your therapist with any matter that concerns you connected with your inner work.

Your therapist might also make mistakes and may need you to point something out about your process, so that he or she can be more sensitive to what you are experiencing. Some of my clients, who have gone on to become friends, have since confessed that they were in awe of me when we were working together, thinking that I knew everything about them. Such perceptions are inaccurate, of course; I am glad when my clients can both value me and also regard me as human, and therefore not perfect!

We need to feel empowered in the process of past life regression, and not give away all decision-making about the direction of our inner work to our therapist. A balance must be struck here for, if we do not trust our therapist to support us, we will make little progress in terms of letting go into experiences where we could learn something valuable.

A worthwhile therapist encourages us to build confidence in our abilities to sense inwardly what we need at various stages of our therapeutic process. We will only have short concentrated bursts of input from our therapist while working together. In the time outside our sessions, we will be trying to cope with thoughts, feelings and sensations arising from our past life work, on our own. Therefore the more skills we can develop to manage our process independently the better.

Journal writing is one approach that can help us to sort out problems in our minds. Another technique is to practice the art of inner listening. Sometimes I have found with my own inner work that I can be troubled by a problem or something that I don't understand relating to a past life experience. If I ask my inner consciousness a question about that problem frequently, at some point later, I will receive an answer. This is a skill that can be developed. You may find at first that some of your own prejudices and expectations infiltrate the guidance that you receive. But if you keep practising staying open to listening inwardly, then the guidance may improve. You find after a while that you can distinguish between your own thoughts and genuine guidance. Using this technique you can learn to contact your Higher Self or perhaps your Spiritual guide. It is also something that you can do yourself and could be a useful backup to the therapy that you are undergoing.

When you are processing a past life experience, your emotional and mental reactions to situations are not necessarily going to be very stable. You are likely to be more emotionally volatile than usual. You may be inclined to project aspects of the inner dilemmas that you are trying to resolve onto others. This can include your therapist or anyone else with whom you share your life. Tapping into inner guidance to help you may ease any difficulties of this nature, so that they can be settled.

With past life therapy there can be all the usual projections that can occur in a client-therapist situation. For instance, the way that your therapist interacts with you may remind you of other people or relationships that you have had in your life. If these other relationships have not been positive, this may colour the way that you feel towards your therapist. For instance, if you have had an abusive father and then work with a male therapist who has some characteristics like your father, it is possible to project behaviour onto your therapist and not see him for who he is. Also, the way that you present yourself can trigger emotional reactions in your therapist. It would be the responsibility of your therapist to work out any problems in this manner so that he or she can still serve you appropriately.

In general it is important to keep the relationship with your therapist as simple and open as possible. There will be enough inner material coming up from the regressions, needing to be processed, without having more to deal with in the relationship that you share with your therapist as well.

There has often been a phase in my relationship with my long-term clients where there has been a need to address personal issues to work out some things. I am sure that this is quite common. When I have been able to discuss and work out these difficulties with my clients, it has been very healing. I cannot pretend that I have always succeeded.

Some of the problems I have had include my client becoming infatuated with me, feeling that I am trying to control them, or not listening to their problems adequately. The best way to counter these problems has been to be honest and frank, but also kind. Generally my clients in these situations are not meaning to create harm, but need help in some aspect of their selves.

We all have the capacity to hurt as well as heal. The relationship between therapist and client is a delicate one on both sides and needs careful handling. In my own work as a therapist, I feel that it has been quite a helpful thing for me to admit to my clients that I have things to learn as well as them.

Past Life Issues

One skill that I try to develop in my clients is the ability to sense the present day identity of souls that appeared as characters in the past lives they have accessed. Some are more willing to speculate and trust their conclusions; others prefer to leave this aspect of inner exploration alone. However I do feel that, when these identifications have been accurate, it has given my clients the capacity to gain insights that they would not have otherwise gleaned.

Occasionally I have had a client who has identified me as a soul featuring as one of the characters in the regression he or she has had. Sometimes this has felt embarrassing, but I have tried to honour it. My senses have told me that on a few occasions these perceptions may have been a projection stemming from my client's subconscious and not necessarily real. However in most cases, I do feel that my client's perception has been quite genuine.

This is an area where I as a therapist have had to be very careful. Generally, when my clients have made an identification like that, I have been able to tell when it is true because my body has reacted, and I have felt tightness or tingling somewhere in my energy system. Often the thoughts of the identification have come to me before my client spoke it. But then, the challenge for me has been as to how I would respond to this knowledge with my client?

Sometimes the character identified by my client as myself has been quite a negative one and therefore shown me in a poor light. I have had to deal with my own discomfort surrounding this. However, I have found that the best approach for me to adopt in these situations has been to be open and honest, and to validate the perceptions of my client. To talk openly about the experience on both sides has usually been very healing and enabled my client's trust in me to be deepened. As a therapist, my aim has always been to help my clients to open themselves up as much as possible to learn about their own inner truth. I can only do that when I am prepared to lead by example.

A little time ago I had a young woman come to me for therapy. Upon meeting her I felt a great longing to help her. My feelings in this regard were much stronger than I usually felt. From her side I felt that there was a slight holding back, as if she wasn't prepared to completely trust me. I could tell from her profile that this was something that she carried with people in general. But I wondered if there was something specific towards me, about not trusting me too.

Some months after my initial meeting with her, she came with her partner to one of my past life evenings. From her meditation she managed to access a life from ancient Egypt. In this lifetime she had had a very cruel father, who eventually literally drove her mad. As she shared about her experience I noticed my own body reacting and, although I did not want to believe it, my inner senses indicated to me that I was the soul who was her father in that experience. During our tea break I talked with this woman and, although it is not my usual practice, I felt a compelling urge to share with her my perception - so I did. She listened attentively and was quite silent about it. Inside I felt very sorry; I wanted to make it up to her and help her but I did not say any more. For many months after this evening, we did not meet.

Eventually she contacted me to inform me that she was about to leave the area and wanted to say goodbye. Earlier that day I had been doing some regression work where I had encountered for the first time memories of a recent life. In this past life I had been a young boy who was cruelly murdered. As I talked to my client on the phone, it occurred to me that she was the soul who as this man in my past life had killed me.

The coincidence of my past life experience with the phone call of my client seemed remarkable. There had to be a reason for this. As we talked about our previous meetings, it became clear that she did not feel finished with the Egyptian past life that she had accessed. She decided that she wished to have another session. I felt that this was quite brave of her, considering what I had disclosed to her. Somehow I felt that she trusted me and had appreciated my honesty with her.

In our session she went through much more thoroughly the details of her relationship with her father in the Egyptian past life. There was a great release of the negative feelings that she had been holding onto, both towards him and herself as the young man from this experience. Letting her do this in my presence and with my support seemed very powerful. As a therapy for her, releasing such a lot of pent up aggression from within felt very important. When she returned to normal consciousness, there was a very open, loving and healing atmosphere in the room.

Then I felt that I wanted to tell her about the past life that I had just learnt about where I had been a boy who was murdered. I asked her if she would mind if I got some assistance to regress more thoroughly through this past life as a balance to the experience we had shared already. She agreed. It was traumatic for us both to go through that and to realise that my killer in that past life was her soul, then in the guise of a cold, rough man.

After we had discussed this, something felt completed on a very deep level. My client shared with me that previously she had always felt an edge to her relationship with me, but now that edge was gone. What I felt was a deep respect for this other soul and I felt very grateful for the experience.

Generally it helps us, when choosing a therapist, to feel that he/she is also able to share the more vulnerable sides of his/her nature with us. We need to feel that our therapist can be open and honest about his or her feelings, especially when honesty and trust are expected from us.

As a seeker it is probably as well, if you have difficulties with your therapist, not to opt out at the first sight of trouble but to persist and try to communicate. There could be much for you both to learn. Walking away from a therapist with whom you feel you have difficulties, without trying to work out the relationship, will probably result in you being less likely to open yourself to help from the next therapist who comes your way.

The Beliefs of Your Therapist

The belief systems of your therapist can have a significant influence on what you are able to achieve with past life regression. Some therapists who do this work do not even believe in reincarnation. Others say that they believe in a form of genetic memory but not more. Depending upon the belief system of your therapist, there could be certain areas where your therapist feels comfortable and others where he or she does not.

The expectations of your therapist can shape or mould to some extent what you will experience. There will be a tendency on the part of your inner consciousness to want to conform to your therapist's outlook. Your inner consciousness will not want to open to places within it where it does not feel accepted. For your inner consciousness to open, it needs to feel safe and you need to be aware of what is there. If, from inside, you sense that your therapist does not feel comfortable with what you need to access, then such experience will remain hidden. I believe that our inner consciousness is very protective towards us.

Your therapist's questions will also influence what experiences come forward. It is important, as much as possible, for your therapist to ask open questions where your inner consciousness has space and freedom to present its own response. Where questions are loaded and an answer assumed, this may bring out false and created experiences rather than genuine memory. It is the responsibility of your therapist not to place any pressure upon you where you may feel that you have to answer questions in a particular way. But you need to assert your rights with this as well.

At a sub-conscious level, you are likely to be aware of how your therapist will tend to interpret your experiences. To gain the most from past life regression you, as a seeker, need to check within, that you do not feel limited in this way by your therapist. It is worth ensuring that you feel

comfortable with a therapist's outlook, before you commit yourself to therapy with him/her.

Although you as a seeker may wish to please your therapist or produce experiences to match your own inner expectations, this does not imply that what you experience will only be created from your imagination. What helps to build people's faith in this work is how past life experiences so often bring forward surprises and experiences that were not anticipated.

Therefore, as a practise, past life therapy is about learning from within and opening to let these experiences reveal themselves without condition, rather than imposing our own beliefs to manipulate what we may be inclined to experience inwardly.

On a final note, I feel that it is important for your therapist to be on his/her own path of exploration and inner growth. Only then will s/he appreciate the potential growth and inner understanding to which you are aspiring.

Chapter 9

Reactions and Outcomes

Reactions

When we undergo a session of past life regression and channel through us the memories of that lifetime, the energy of those experiences enters the subconscious mind of our present day self. This is bound to affect and disturb the equilibrium of how thoughts, feelings and beliefs are arranged within us. As the energy of the past life experience continues to infiltrate our subconscious minds, new thoughts, feelings and beliefs may form. Energy patterns are generated within our minds by the thoughts, feelings and beliefs that we hold. We can alter those patterns by our will, and by choices and decisions that we make.

Normally we are not in contact with the patterns of our deeper subconscious mind, but the patterns of being that operate here influence how we are. Through past life regression, we can make changes in these deeper layers of our being by confronting similar patterns that might have existed in the past. By reliving events from the past where certain patterns were established, we make new decisions relative to those patterns and thereby alter their form within us now. If we are true to ourselves, this process releases us from limiting structures within our minds.

A process of adjustment follows, while our inner mind tries to come to terms with the knowledge revealed in the past life experience. Eventually this process of adjustment completes itself, but it can take considerable time – in my experience it takes hours, days, months or even longer. Generally the assimilation process is complete when thoughts and feelings associated with the past life no longer hold our attention, and we become occupied with other things. After my own past life sessions, it has usually taken a day or two for the experience to settle. The more difficult ones have taken a little longer.

While the integration process is taking place, we may experience various signs and symptoms. Although the process of lying down and living through a meditation-like experience seems innocent enough, it can leave people feeling quite exhausted afterwards. Alternatively, when someone has had a very positive experience, where much has been resolved and new levels of self-acceptance have been reached, then that person may leave the session elated and even intoxicated. In such circumstances, he or she has an abundance of energy and feels happy for a considerable time.

Some people dismiss a regression experience or are sceptical as to its reality, but it is likely that the experience still has a substantial impact on their sub-conscious selves. When people embody the impressions of another personality from another time - all the drama, mistakes and trauma that this involves - much of it feels quite foreign to our present day sub-conscious minds. If we feel afraid or resist accepting those impressions in some way, the result may be a shock reaction within our sub-conscious minds. Where there is a strong resonance from the past life, that links with present dilemmas and challenges, the realisation of past mistakes and painful suffering can have a shattering effect upon our inner belief systems. This is where we will have to decide at quite deep levels within our being, what to do about it.

During the integration process, people can feel in a strange mood. They may be more tired than usual. Often, people will notice that they have a heightened awareness and sensitivity while they integrate a past life experience. Those people who are elated could feel a zealousness to want to change the world, and a belief that anything is possible. Our bodies may even react by showing symptoms of illness, which is how we cleanse ourselves of impurities and allow change.

In an example of this, one of my clients accessed a past life where she had lived in ancient Egypt as a male political leader. In this position of authority, the past life character misused his power through greed, killing many people. He felt very cold to my client.

The contrast between the personality of this past life character and my client's present personality was quite stark. In her present life, my client has lived a very simple and harmless life. Yet, when she went through the regression, she could accept the past life as it emerged, to be her soul. On the surface at least, she found it to be very interesting, but after the session was over her body reacted to the experience very strongly.

My client was not able to return to her work for over a month. Initially she needed to sleep a lot, but then she suffered from stomach pain and diarrhoea. Doctors diagnosed food poisoning but it was very difficult to trace from where that had come, because no one else had fallen ill and other people had been eating the same food.

When she came for her next session, after her recovery, I tested her inner consciousness; these tests indicated that the illness had stemmed from the past life experience.

My client did not regret the regression work we had done. She felt the session had made a positive difference in her life. Now she felt able to cope with more and felt stronger in herself. She noticed little things that used to irritate her, did not bother her any more. Her concentration had become much sharper, and in general she felt a sense of inner peace that she hadn't previously. Interestingly I noticed that the past life character had died of food poisoning, suffering symptoms similar to those she had endured after her session with me. Indeed I believe some of his victims were poisoned too.

In this case, I feel that the illness my client suffered was purifying; she could obviously accept it and allow it to be. Thus it served its purpose. During the actual session, she had not released any of the emotions connected with the experience at the time. Obviously it needed to find an outlet afterwards. This particular reaction was quite extreme - usually any post session reactions are less debilitating than this. My client however, was very clear that she wanted to go through this past life experience, and expressed no regrets about the reaction that she had.

I must appreciate my client in this case because I feel that she was very courageous, and it says a lot for her character that she was able to accept the experience and its aftermath without resistance. It has not always been my observation that my clients will do that.

Regression experiences relate to our past and thereby connect to experiences that we have already been through. On an inner level we may have mastered lessons that are associated with a given past lifetime or else we may be still struggling to do so. The effect of experiencing regression is to bring knowledge from our soul held at a deep inner level to our normal conscious awareness. Thus, through this process, we make a link from our deep inner being to our surface consciousness. This helps us to become more fully aware of our wholeness as a being and results in personal inner growth.

If we do not accept what a past life experience is trying to communicate, the power of the experience may lead us to feel fractured rather than whole. Rejecting the learning from a past life, when it is presented to us, can make us feel very uncomfortable because we are then in conflict with essential knowledge from our soul. This conflict may result in us suffering more severe reactions than otherwise. I believe that difficult reaction to past life therapy usually results from inner conflicts connected to the experience. On an inner level, our consciousness will naturally try to resolve those conflicts, but may not be able to do so if there is too much fear. We need further help if these things are not resolved.

When we sleep, we dream to process experiences in our subconscious minds. If fear needs to come out of our system, our bodies may tremble. Then the fear is released from within us. When we feel irritable or sad after a past life session, tears can be the method that our inner consciousness chooses to cleanse ourselves of those emotions and associated thoughts that have been held inside us.

When a past life session does not settle, the reason may be that there are still elements from that experience needing to be brought to the surface and processed. Because we do not like to be afraid, our subconscious instinctively tries to shield us from unpleasant experiences. This can result in important details of the past lifetime being omitted without the person even realising it. However, without these details, the overall insight and release needed from the experience may not be possible, so the experience remains incomplete. Internally a part of the person knows what is missing and naturally wants the story of the past lifetime, and the healing from the experience, to be completed. Thus, the uncomfortable memories that have been suppressed are likely to be stirred anyway.

When suppressed experiences want to come to the surface, uncomfortable bodily sensations, disturbing dreams or even flashes of memory connected to the past life experience that will not go away, can occur. The person undergoing the regression has to judge what to do about it. Very often it may be beneficial to have a further session of therapy. This can help those remaining details to be expressed, so that the experience can be laid to rest.

Occasionally a particular past life requires a number of sessions to fully cleanse us of limiting beliefs and residues associated with it. As we become more experienced at going through regressions, we learn to recognise when an experience feels complete and when it needs further work. Therefore, I recommend seekers not to be too fixed and rigid in their expectations when approaching past life regression. The nature of the experiences that lie within us can be very unpredictable.

If you have a past life experience that feels incomplete, you may decide that you do not want to deal with it all now. If your life is complicated and you are trying to manage many demands, it might feel too much to put additional energy into the past life experience as well. With some clients, I have been able to ask their inner consciousness to file away experiences that still need processing, so that when the time is right these can be dealt with later. Often, when this suggestion is put to people's consciousness they will feel an energy shift indicating that this filing away has been accomplished. However, this does not always work. Seekers need to have respect for their inner consciousness, and if an experience will not be put aside, it is in their interests to give it the attention it needs.

With inner work, it is important for seekers to develop a healthy relationship with their inner consciousness. On one hand, there needs to be openness to what the inner consciousness can offer. Life will be much poorer while we do not have a conscious connection with our internal being. If we try to suppress experiences that are there, we may suffer from psychological problems or even illness. But on the other hand, if we let the streams of consciousness in our inner worlds dominate us, we may become very confused and disorientated. Our ego self needs its own clear boundaries so that we can adequately deal with the physical side of coping with our responsibilities in the present time. For people who are psychically sensitive, it is very important to have daily tasks and activities that are grounding so that they do not get lost in their inner worlds.

Our inner consciousness needs our outer personality self as an outlet for experiences that are disturbing us inside, and also to purify inner limiting belief patterns that are not in harmony with our soul needs. From the other side, our outer personality self needs to be open to our inner consciousness to learn self-understanding and to gain access to the soul wisdom that exists within us.

When our body reacts to past life regression, our inner consciousness gives us signals that help us learn. Our body also shows symptoms through illness or discomfort, alerting us to some inner cleansing still needed or in process. The healthiest attitude towards our body reactions and our inner consciousness is to regard these as our special friends. Some people have described the sub-conscious as being like a child. As such, it needs much love and encouragement as well as acceptance. It will not work for us if we are critical of what we feel inside or if we try to ignore it. Unless we listen to our inner consciousness when it calls to us, it will just try other means to get the attention that it needs.

It could be, for example, that we need to come to terms with some violent or abusive tendencies within ourselves. We might, for the most part, feel quite calm in the course of our everyday life, but particular situations act like triggers for those violent feelings to surface. Clearly, we will probably not like those feelings, and may feel quite disturbed by them. Our natural response is to want to get rid of them. However, if we are unprepared to take responsibility for those feelings, we will blame the person or situation that has acted as a trigger, citing this as the cause of the problem. The origin of the violent feelings may lie as a residue from a past life. Accessing the memory and expressing the emotions inherent in this could be an effective means of dealing with it.While we continue to avoid searching within, investigating what that part of us needs, the uncomfortable feelings could worsen. We might feel stressed, tense, or even become depressed without fully realising why.

Depression is a state of mind that often manifests when people are afraid, and when they try to hold in their feelings and reactions. Doing past life work helps provide the necessary stimulus to release those feelings, and can also give us the understanding to enable us to shift the patterns of thought wrapped up in the depression.

Sometimes in therapy work, we need to learn new coping strategies to work through our problems. If we avoid opening ourselves to search inwardly for the means to resolve inner tensions, life precipitates a crisis forcing us to adjust our outlook.

We can ask ourselves inwardly as to what the lesson is that we have to learn when we face any type of problem, especially if we don't know how to deal with it. By asking for inner help, we open ourselves to insights and understandings that come into our mind in response. The answers that we need may lie in our past lives if we are prepared to look in that direction.

For instance, if we find ourselves feeling consistently disturbed by the behaviour of someone else in our life, we may have met that soul before in other lives. If we are interested, it might be beneficial to seek out the source of these disturbances by regression. Doing so could both help us understand the deeper dynamics in the relationship, and also release the inner difficulties we feel in relation to that person.

Once there was a colleague with whom I was in conflict. I found it hard to be calm in this person's presence, so I sought help through regression. When I approached a past life in connection with this, I felt this soul to be my main protagonist in the lifetime that I entered. In this case, I was the victim of this soul's urge for power over others. There have probably been other lives where the dynamic has been reversed. Anyway, after this regression, my reaction was initially to feel even more negative towards this person, than I had before. However, after a day or two, this reaction subsided and I felt more detached from this colleague, more neutral, and this helped me a great deal. I believe that my response to the process was quite typical.

Outcomes

When a past life experience has been fully processed, there can be a number of possible outcomes that take place. In the example I gave from one of my own regressions, I described how I felt more detached in relation to the woman with whom I had been having difficulties. In the case of a client, who accessed a life as a murderer in ancient Egypt, on finally digesting her session, she felt calm, strong and more at peace with herself.

From my observation, the outcomes of past life work can be quite subtle. I believe that they do make a difference. The re-patterning that can take place in our minds when we do regression can initiate considerable change in our lives: we feel inclined to embark on activities in a way that we did not do before; our thoughts and feelings about specific matters in our lives alter; our approach to relationships and work shifts; things that previously occupied us do not do so anymore.

The changes in our character and outlook on life may be more noticeable to others than to us – some might even feel threatened because we do not abide by the same old habits that we used to.

Past life regression enables our soul to have more space to express itself in our lives. The main benefit, in my experience, is that I now feel more fully myself. Many of those who have ventured to try this remarkable therapy feel the same, I am sure.

Chapter 10

Tracing Fears and Phobias

Irrational fears and phobias can result in a wide range of unwanted behaviour, including extremely violent nervous responses. Even when people try in vain to stop themselves from reacting, certain situations and associations act as triggers that can result in very unpleasant bodily sensations. Examples of these include fear of heights, enclosed spaces, water, spiders, and specific types of people, to name a few. Fears and phobias are unique to every individual. Generally no logic can be applied to control these fears; they manifest in spite of any efforts that we make to stop them and this can make them very frightening. Their roots exist in our sub-conscious minds - to alleviate these problems psychologically, we need to connect with this part of our selves.

It has become clear after investigation that some of these fears and phobias stem from people's early life, experiences that have left a strong emotional imprint. For many people, the origin of their fears and phobias is much more mysterious. I believe that it is quite often the case that these difficulties are the residues of traumatic past life episodes.

Two case studies, of clients who sought help from me through past life therapy for specific phobias and fears, follow. The first of these is Marc, who saw me privately for help with a problem he had around people whistling. Angie, who attended one of my weekend workshops, relates a conglomerate of fears and phobias from which she has suffered, and how her past life regression session impacted upon those.

Marc's Story

I have always considered myself to be a rational man. In terms of my attainments, I am well educated and work in a large teaching hospital. To an observer, I have always tried to appear well adjusted. But for as long as I can remember, I have had one major problem that has proved not only embarrassing, but incredibly disruptive. My problem has been such that I could not tolerate people whistling. As I write about it, I struggle to understand how this could be so debilitating, but the reaction that I have experienced every single time this has occurred has been so extreme that I have spent thirty years dreading such incidents.

Although I have been unaffected by people blowing whistles, or by noises like kettles, if a person whistled any tune within hearing distance, I would immediately fill with rage from the very core of my being. My whole body would become tense, my fists would clench and I would be unable to concentrate upon anything other than stopping the noise. The anger would be so great that I would feel the urge to physically beat the person who was attacking my senses. I hated the effect this had on me. At other times I was adamantly a peace-loving man, but whistling turned me into someone quite different. It made me feel foolish, as if I couldn't be true to my own principles.

The rational part of me knew that it was inappropriate to attack people and that it was a problem in me. Generally people didn't mean any harm when they whistled, but I reacted all the same. Whatever understandings I tried to impose upon myself about this made no difference to the problem. The only option I felt I had, when people whistled, was to remove myself as completely from the sound as soon as possible. For every moment longer that I had to stay in their company, I seemed to tip more and more towards a state I can only describe as temporary insanity. As a result, over the years I have forced myself off trains if someone whistled in my compartment, I have abandoned trolleys of shopping in supermarkets, and I have even walked out of restaurants before finishing my meal. Thankfully friends and family have generally been considerate enough not to whistle around me, although I have been at the mercy of anyone who wished to take advantage of my problem. This alone has made me feel very vulnerable.

There have been times when I have felt enormous despair about how I could resolve this problem. So when I participated in a workshop led by Paul, I felt drawn to ask him if he could help me. When he cautiously suggested that some individual therapy with him could help, part of me remained sceptical that something so entrenched in me could ever be shifted. However, I knew from working with Paul that quite remarkable things could happen to people when they opened up their inner consciousness to that possibility.

Within the workshop, I had my first experience of one of my past lives. Afterwards it took me a number of months to come to terms with this and accept it as real. I knew that I needed this to feel settled in me before I could approach Paul with my problem. Finally, the time felt right and I contacted Paul to make arrangements for our first session.

Initially we spoke about various details concerning my life, and Paul was able to obtain the information that he needed. From as long as I could remember I had hated whistling, even when I was a small child. My father used to whistle when I was little, and it was hard to tell him then what I felt. I am confident that he is not the source of the problem, for I know that he never meant me any harm when he whistled.

Paul suggested that it may stem from a past life, but he wanted to try a more open approach with me to go inside the dynamics of what I was feeling. He suggested that I lie down, close my eyes, and that he would whistle to me, and for me to try to allow any images, thoughts and memories to come into my mind in response to this. With some apprehension, I agreed.

To further facilitate the process Paul induced a light hypnotic trance and, even though I still was aware of my surroundings, I remember feeling very comfortable and relaxed. Then Paul started to whistle.

It is difficult to describe the fear invoked by such a simple tune but, as soon as he began, I was filled with panic. Physically my whole body was shaking, my breathing became shallow and rapid, my fists clenched, and I was overwhelmed by a need to escape. I could see quite clearly that I was seated on the edge of an armchair, alone in a room. It was possible for me to sense that I was a little boy, perhaps eight years of age. The source of the whistling was immediately apparent.

I knew that it was really Paul who was whistling and that he would not hurt me. But in my mind's eye I could see a man that I feared greatly. He was in his late sixties, with straight hair, a pitted complexion and a large nose covered in broken blood vessels. He was wearing overalls, a tweed jacket and cap, and he was working on the window frame of the room in which I was seated. As he whistled I became increasingly anxious.

Paul tried to coax me to move forward into how the scene unfolded next, but I found this very difficult. Part of me wanted to save the little boy from pain, aware of the fact that I was trying to script the story to allow his escape. Paul gently confronted me about this and reminded me that this memory was far in the distant past and didn't need to hurt me any more. What I needed to do to help myself was to re-experience the memory of what really happened all those years ago.

Gradually I allowed the scene to unfold and, with my body quaking in fear, I described to Paul the events of that day. From the perspective of my adult consciousness I felt that I was expressing myself quite inarticulately, but it was the thoughts and feelings of that eight-year old boy that were foremost in my mind. I told Paul that I was afraid because, when the man finished working outside, he would stop whistling and come for me. It was clear to me that he had abused me before, and he was about to do it again. With difficulty, I was able to describe the scene as the man did indeed come into the room. A struggle occurred as I tried to run past him, but he held on to me tightly whilst I tried to kick and punch. I told Paul how he pushed me backwards against the wall and held me there effortlessly with the superior strength of a grown man. As my body convulsed, I saw the man's face coming towards mine and felt revulsion as he forced his tongue into my mouth. I was also aware of him groping me.

This was as far as we went in this first session. Paul suggested that going back through all the main elements of the interactions with this man would help me to detach myself from the traumatic associations that I had with whistling. I needed to come for a second session. Already I felt as though something had lifted inside of me.

108

The second time, I went straight back to the life in which I was abused, and Paul guided me through events that had occurred over a period of four years. Firstly, we established my situation.

I was in the care of my grandparents in a small village where there were few other children. I lived a solitary existence apart from the company of my dog, a gangly, black and white mongrel that I adored. As is so often typical, it was the dog that enabled the man to get close to me initially, as he held him by his collar and forced me to collect him. At first, the touching was quite occasional and subtle. Instinctively I felt that it was wrong, but was afraid to speak out against an adult as he wasn't really hurting me. I just felt uncomfortable and confused.

Gradually the touching increased. Sometimes Paul whistled to help trigger the more traumatic memories and I would feel terror at this man's approach. He seemed to be a handyman and, as I heard him working around the village, I would just try and run away. I simply could not bear the sound of him. The experiences progressed from touching to sexual abuse, and the longer it went on, the less I felt able to resist. There was no-one to tell. I told Paul of the sense of helplessness I felt and how I spent my time alone, dreaming of moving away to a safer place. As that child, I could only bide my time, and try to stay out of harm's way.

Paul asked me to describe the worst instance of abuse. I knew that this happened at age twelve but, when Paul asked me to describe my feelings, I discovered that I no longer cared what the man did to me. Somehow I had resigned myself to him using me for his self-gratification. I no longer valued myself or made any attempt to express my discomfort. Paul questioned me further about this, asking me to go back to the first occasion when I made this decision to give up. This event occurred when I was ten - alone in the house - and the man used this opportunity to assault me yet again. I remember letting him get on with it thinking that, if I didn't struggle he would get it over with sooner. A sense of numbness came over me as I detached myself from what was happening. Lying there afterwards, I felt dead inside.

Next I moved to a later time and recalled that when I was thirteen, while he was doing a job in another part of the village, the man had a heart attack and died. So that was how the abuse ended. But the damage was still there inside me.

Paul now focussed upon the feelings and thoughts I had had during the time of the abuse, and tried to encourage me to express them. As I repeated certain words and phrases, they felt almost like mantras penetrating deep within me. A lot of it was about honouring my individuality and respecting myself and my own needs, daring to communicate how I felt. I had directed anger and hatred inwards that no longer needed to be there. With each expression of repressed thought and feeling, the numbness in this boy dissolved a little more, until I finally felt free and could much more be myself.

There were strong resonances with my present life. Without realising it, I had spent much of my present life trying to suppress my feelings. To avoid upsets I had been trying to satisfy everyone else, with little regard for my own value as an individual. In short, it became clear that I had suffered in silence through more than one incarnation.

When I came out of the trance, Paul whistled and I hardly cringed. Even though I had not approached Paul with a desire for any therapy concerning my self-worth, having not even acknowledged in myself that this was a problem for me, we had in fact discovered something fundamental to my happiness in this life.

Now I am consciously asserting myself in my relationships with my partner, friends, family and colleagues. In this regard I have made some significant breakthroughs that have quite astonished me. It is a learning curve, but I am excited about the future. In addition to this I can now tolerate whistling. I still don't like hearing it, but I am not filled with rage or fear any more. In fact, my usual reaction now is to laugh.

Angie's Story

I'm Angie. I'm 35 years old, have never married, and have a 10 year old daughter, Georgia. I was with Georgia's father, Geoff, for 7 years, and now only maintain contact with him to arrange my daughter's visits. After Georgia was born, I soon came to realise that there was no future for us as a couple. He was spending longer at the pub, making no effort to find a job, and would often take himself away on holiday to Greece, leaving myself and Georgia at home with no money. After several unhappy years with Geoff, I decided one day that I had had enough, and needed to make a clean break from him. Georgia and I left and moved to a town ten miles away, so that I would be well out of his way. He didn't drive, so would be unable to come knocking on our door at all hours. It was a bad period in our lives, which thankfully time has healed. At the time of my regression work, I had established a very happy relationship with Keith. As far as my health is concerned I had been diagnosed with Menieres syndrome, which affects my balance, and over the past few years I had suffered from panic attacks, although I could never understand why these happened.

I had talked with my sister Jane on several occasions about past life regression, as it is a subject by which we are both very intrigued. We believe in life after death, and had always been very curious to try regression. By chance, my good friend Peter happened to mention that Paul was doing a weekend workshop in our area, and asked if we would be interested in attending. Immediately I phoned Jane, who was very keen - with each other's support, we put our names down on the course. (It was very much a case of "I'll go if you will"). I knew that Paul had been working with my friend Peter for some time and Peter rated him very highly. I suppose that the only reason I chose to go on the course was through pure curiosity, as I had a happy life and did not believe that there were any problems needing to be addressed through regression therapy.

Peter had told me that there would be ten people attending the workshop. The first day would be a group session, and the following day would be a one-to one session with Paul. That is all the information that I had, so I was totally unaware of what to expect.

After Paul had introduced himself, and everyone else in the group had given their names and reasons for attending, we were taken into our first group regression. Slipping subconsciously into the meditation very easily, I was soon ready to go through the door that Paul had suggested would lead us into our past life. Upon closing the door behind us, we were asked to become aware of our clothing and surroundings.

111

My vision came to me very quickly and clearly. I was outside a small cottage, which I had the impression was my home. I was feeding chickens with a basket on my arm, feeling very happy and contented with my life. It was the kind of simple lifestyle that I would quite like now. I was aware of the sound of running water, which was coming from a water wheel on the side of the cottage. Then I heard a small child and looked up to see a young woman, which I sensed immediately to be the same soul as my sister, Jane. She looked much as she looks now, except that she had very long hair in a plait. I sensed that she was still my sister back then, and I acknowledged her by her name at that time, Elizabeth. Then the little girl, of about three years old, came running towards us calling 'mama'. This girl, I sensed, was the same soul as my daughter in the present day, Georgia. Putting my arms out to her, I was upset that she ran to my sister and not me. In that life, she was the daughter of my sister, Elizabeth and her name was Maisie.

I found this all very odd, as I was seeing my sister Jane in a previous life, still as my sister, and my own daughter Georgia who was then my niece. Another strange fact to arise later was that when Jane and I were chatting in the car, she told me that if she had ever had a daughter of her own, she would have called her Maisie. She had never told this to anyone before.

Further on in the regression, I was asked to move forward to just before the time of my death, to become aware of my situation and how I was coping with it.

At this point, I had a totally different feeling about my life. I was very depressed, lonely and frightened. Standing at the side of the water wheel, I was looking down into the water. The water was almost pulling me down. It was at that point that I knew that I was experiencing the moments immediately prior to my death. I knew that I would be jumping into that water within the next few instants. Starting to panic, I made myself come back to my present surroundings quickly. I couldn't breathe very easily and felt very light headed and scared.

When Paul brought the rest of the group back to our normal conscious state, I was quite distressed by what I had experienced, feeling shaky and very hot. I felt as though I had lived through a most terrifying nightmare, one which I certainly did not want to revisit. Everyone in the group was asked to recall their experiences. When it came to my turn, I could recall vividly what I had seen and the terror that I had felt.

Paul asked for a volunteer to be regressed in front of the group as a demonstration. After what I had experienced, there was no way that I was going to volunteer to go through that again, especially with everyone else watching me. A couple of volunteers did put themselves forward, to go into more depth and detail of what their past life contained. My sister Jane was one of the volunteers. These one-to-one demonstrations tended to be very strong emotional experiences that affected me very much. After watching those regressions, I had more of an idea of what my private one-to-one session would involve, and I wasn't much looking forward to it.

At the end of the day, Jane and I were comparing notes in the car on our way home. Jane was able to share what it felt like for her to be actively working with Paul while reliving the past life, allowing the expression of what came to her inner consciousness. It reassured me that she felt that she was still in full control of what she had said. However I still knew that, as soon as I went into regression, this horrible experience would come back to haunt me, and I didn't know why. That night, I didn't sleep well because I was very frightened about my regression the following day. Somehow, though, I knew that I had to go through with it.

On Sunday morning I picked Jane up and we made our way to the country house where the sessions were taking place. Jane was quite excited and was really looking forward to her session. I, on the other hand, was most definitely not.

After waiting for what felt like a lifetime, it was finally my turn to sit with Paul. He could sense that I was feeling very anxious and calmly tried to put me at ease. Paul explained that I needed to revisit this earlier lifetime again in order to put it to rest. As I closed my eyes, within seconds I was back reliving my previous life. There was still much detail of that lifetime of which I was unaware, so Paul asked me to go to the event that could have caused my depression.

I was standing in a crowded church, wearing an ivory coloured wedding gown, feeling very happy. After a few moments in the church, I suddenly had the sense of being alone, and I knew that my intended was not going to arrive. Trying to pretend that it was no big deal and putting a brave face on it to everyone in the church, deep down I was devastated. Only I knew that I was pregnant at the time. I knew that it was not an option for me to have a baby out of wedlock. Waiting until everyone had gone, I decided that I only had one choice available to me.

After returning home, I walked straight to the water mill. I didn't want to jump, but I felt that there was nothing else that I could do. I counted to four and then jumped. The water felt very cold, and I suddenly started to lose my breath. At that point, I remember looking up from the water to see my sister, Elizabeth, and her daughter, Maisie, looking down at me, and calling my name, which was Tilly. At that particular moment, I knew that I had made a mistake and wanted to get out of the water. My dress was caught around the wheel and I was loosing all strength. As I was slowly being dragged under, I felt myself panicking more and more.

Paul kept suggesting to me to move forward, and at one point I started to feel more peaceful. I knew that it was all over and that my body had died. The whole experience had been so emotional for me that I now felt quite drained and tired. I was aware of some 'being' waiting for me. I could not make out the gender of this being, as it did not appear human. It had a stick and was pointing to the ground with it, as if showing me a map. I knew that it was showing me where I would be going next.

Paul brought me back to the room again to my normal consciousness. He explained to me that although I had released a lot of emotion and I had been shaking throughout, it was important for me to cleanse myself of all the fear, difficult thoughts and feelings surrounding this experience. It was his suggestion that I needed to go through the death experience of this life again. At first, I wasn't happy about this and started to cry, but then I agreed to his plan.

I went once more to the point where I was about to jump in the water. It was still a bad experience, but somehow not as bad as the previous time. The emotional outpouring was much less this time. I was aware of Paul urging me to try to keep breathing steadily through it all, and I felt relieved as I passed into spirit following my death.

Paul suggested that I went forward to the moment when I could meet with the spirit of the man who jilted me. Initially I felt apprehensive about this. But I was surprised to see that this person who had ruined my life then was Geoff, the man who had made my present life so miserable. In the spirit world I felt able to forgive him, and he apologised for leaving me and prompting me to kill myself. I felt released by this, and then went on to meet with the spirit of my unborn baby. This was very emotional for me, as I had felt guilty. But she was very happy in spirit and said that it just wasn't her time. She also forgave me after I apologised to her.

Coming back to my present state, I felt quite shaky and traumatised. Paul gave me some healing to calm me down. However, I knew that something very significant had unlocked itself within me.

At the time of writing, it is now two months since my session with Paul. I have noticed that the relationship with my ex-partner, Geoff, is now a lot less strained. I feel more forgiving towards him and he in turn has been has been less aggravated by me. The panic attacks have been manageable, and the balance problem is currently under control. The biggest breakthrough for me is that, at 35 years old, I now feel able to commit to marriage - something that I had always previously feared.

Chapter 11

Past Lives and Our Hidden Nature

Human beings are complex personalities. We express a wide variety of qualities according to different social settings. In the company of certain people we relax and feel able to assert our needs easily. With others, we feel tense and inhibited. We could well have a range of sub-personalities that come to the fore under particular circumstances. Sometimes we are consciously able to choose one or other of our personality characteristics to be more prominent. However, probably not all of our sub-personalities are compatible. Depending on the situation, we may feel a compulsion to express ourselves in a particular manner, believing other forms of self-expression to be inappropriate.

Possibly, some of our inner sub-personalities are in conflict with each other: a controlling part competes for attention with a very passive, child-like and needy aspect of our nature. One part might win out, while the other aspect tends to be suppressed. But if we suppress a part of ourselves, we will not be happy - and if that part wants to express itself, it will probably still seek avenues to do so.

The sub-personalities within us may have built up as reactions to pressure, and our responses to conditioning imparted to us by others. We can model ourselves upon others, as we tend to do when we are children. When we encounter circumstances where we feel afraid, we may choose to adjust our behaviour so that we conform to what feels safe. Again, this can result in suppression of some important aspects of our nature.

At times our sub-personalities have links with our past lives. If we have within us a former life where expressing particular qualities led to a traumatic outcome, we might be reluctant to allow those qualities expression this time round. Yet it could be the path we have chosen as a soul to overcome our fears, so that this side of our nature can be lived out.

Our inner path might very well be about reconciling aspects of our nature that are in apparent conflict, so that we can be more at peace and at ease with ourselves. To do this we need to be able to acknowledge, understand and accept various strands of our character, so we can sense how they might be able to come together.

In the following account, I want to share about Marilyn, a former client. She had within her, a hidden aspect of her nature that she did not allow others to see. Yet the drive for this side of her to be expressed was immensely strong. By suppressing it, she was causing herself much distress. Marilyn tells her story of how this side of her was unlocked by accessing one of her past lives where her hidden self was much more in evidence. The outcome of her accepting this part of herself resulted in some dramatic changes in her life, including the break up of a very unhappy marriage to which she had been clinging. Afterwards she felt free to be herself in a much wider, deeper and stronger sense.

Meeting Marilyn

I met Marilyn, a community nurse, in her late forties. My impression was that she had a generous heart and had enjoyed the opportunity she had been given, through her professional life, to care for people in need. She appeared to have worked hard to maintain a respectable image both within her family and to her associates and friends. But this pressure within her to conform to other people's expectations of her had had its cost. For many years she had been entrenched within an unhappy marriage, unable to shift herself from it. There had been this hidden aspect to her nature that she had kept secret. She had felt that it would not be safe to express the longings of this hidden self to the world.

It was while I was using hypnosis with Marilyn, to trace the root of this hidden side to her personality and the fears preventing it from being expressed, that she first encountered an experience of one of her past lives. Here is her story.

Marilyn's Past Life Experience

I first encountered Paul when contemplating trying to kick my habit of smoking. I literally picked him out of the telephone directory. On speaking to Paul, I instinctively felt that he was genuine and trustworthy. This was to be my first experience of hypnotherapy and I was intrigued to find out whether it would be a 'painless' way of giving up the dreaded weed.

At our first session, Paul and I spoke for a long time about my beliefs, faith and general philosophy of life. I acknowledged my belief in God, agreeing that I had always wondered about past life experiences, and whether they had any bearing on or relevance to our present lives. So far, my life has been a mixture of sadness and happiness, as I'm sure most people feel about their lives. Paul suggested that I might benefit from hypnosis as a way of bringing to the fore deeply held feelings and their causes. Doing this amazed me, and at first I was highly embarrassed by my reactions. Being a person who valued her privacy, I was quite astounded by what I disclosed. I was aware of everything Paul said, and of my responses - tears flowed down my face as I felt the pain of love, hurt and rejection. I spoke of my need to love and be loved in a way that I would never have allowed myself to do, in any other situation. Most alarmingly too, I was aware of my body reacting to the pain as if a physical pain was being inflicted upon it. The whole experience felt like a tremendous release. It was a relief to confront the issues that I had felt so acutely in my life, issues of loneliness and not feeling accepted to be myself. The outpouring had a cleansing effect, and I began to see things more clearly afterwards. It also became apparent that the smoking issue was itself a symptom of my life situation and would be dealt with when the time was right.

At a subsequent session, I explained to Paul how I had always felt that there were two quite distinctive personalities within me and that the

118

conflict that these personalities caused was of some concern. On the one hand, there was the personality that I and those who know me were used to experiencing. This person conformed to the role that family, friends, employer and society in general expected. She worked hard, often too hard, in a continuous effort to 'give' to other people and in an attempt to fill her life in a meaningful way. The other persona was much more complex. I feel that I have spent a lot of my life trying to repress this 'other self'. Conversely, however, this 'other self' was the one which I felt to be the more real me. It was a much more wilful, impulsive, natural personality but also one which I feared would appear to others to be immoral and out of context with present day society.

Under hypnosis I re-lived the horror of certain childhood experiences. One of these included attempting to cross a swing bridge over a deep ravine. This had been at the insistence of my father, with whom I had always had an uneasy relationship. As I crossed the wooden slatted bridge, holding on fiercely to the rope handrails, I looked down at the swirling water below. The bridge swayed in the wind and I was overwhelmed with sheer terror. Although I couldn't hear what my father was shouting, I could see him making gestures, displaying his obvious annoyance at what he saw as my cowardice. I lay down on my stomach for what seemed an eternity before inching slowly back to the safety of the bank. The experience of re-living this under hypnosis left me feeling quite sick and shaky at the time. I was aware of my body going completely rigid and perspiration breaking out on my body and hands. After the therapy, I found that I could think about this experience without fear. It also helped me to rationalise my father's treatment of me as a child and to think of him in a more charitable way. He recently presented himself, unannounced, at my house to stay for a few days. To my surprise, I found that I could tolerate his presence in my home much more easily and that he did not have the same unsettling effect upon me that he had done in the past. I suppose it would be true to say that I was letting go of those past childhood experiences and even beginning to forgive him. I was also starting to feel braver about being more assertive in relationship to my husband, and less regarding of the pressures that he put me under.

In a further session, with the help of hypnosis, I felt myself begin to sink deep within to what I can only describe as my soul. At this point, I actually began to feel that I was another person. This person, younger than I am now, was naïve, but had a much greater affinity with the natural world. I'm not sure of the era that she lived in, because she herself, does not seem to be aware of dates or times, only seasons and the difference between day and night. She wears drab, loose fitting, coarsely woven clothes and lives in isolation from others in what appears to be a single roomed dwelling made of stone. Her thoughts and feelings come into my head, although they don't always make much sense. Sometimes it is like watching someone through the wrong end of a telescope as they go about their daily life. At other times, I am that young woman. I know what she looks like. She has long, thick, straw coloured hair, which has waves in it. She is much stronger than a woman of today would be and she has certain mannerisms that I can actually recognise myself doing.

Since starting these regression sessions, I have had flashes of this previous life whilst going about my daily life. It feels like these 'flashbacks' are not new insights, but rather re-visiting of experiences. They are sometimes invoked by other instances. Whilst alone at the bottom of my garden recently, as it was beginning to go dark, I became aware of the birds singing as they prepared to roost for the night. For a split second, I was no longer in my garden, but in a glade in a wood and I heard myself say quietly "sleep well". Twice I have felt a hand on my shoulder and turned, expecting to see an older woman there. I know that it is my mother - not the mother I have now, who is twelve thousand miles away, but the mother of the girl. I know what she looks like too, but I only 'feel' this knowledge, as I can't see her directly. Whilst I was eager to know more about this past life, part of me was fearful of what it will uncover.

At some sessions with Paul, I chose not to be hypnotised for fear of what it would reveal. I suppose it would be true to say that sometimes I did not feel spiritually strong enough to peel back any more layers. Some of the encounters are physically and emotionally shocking, and at the time do not make sense. At one session, quite early on, I felt as if I was being choked. I became aware of a huge, thick plank of wood being pressed down onto my chest. It was an effort to draw breath into my body. I felt fear and helplessness, but also a sense of injustice. During this and at other times when I felt frightened, threatened or insecure, I became aware that I am unable to speak out in my defence. Curiously this is something that affects me in my present life too, so I believe that we carry idiosyncrasies with us from one life to another. Paul tried to help me with this, because, although I was frightened, I knew that I needed to express the truth of my feelings more fully in my life today. I recognised that there were to be more traumatic experiences by the sick feeling of dread I felt, as I allowed myself to sink into trance. But I also knew that it was important to experience these events to enable me to further understand the person I am, and the person that I had been.

I was very afraid in my life with members of my family, and friends, that if I allowed myself to express what I truly felt, I would be rejected. My past life self continued to bravely be authentic and open in the life she had lived, but she then suffered the most appalling traumas from people who did not accept her.

One of the most horrible sensations was the feeling of being raped. The physical pain that coursed through my body was nothing compared to the feeling of degradation and humiliation. At one point, I was aware that I was willing myself to die. But then I became aware of a woman's voice in my head saying "leave this place, go to the woods". I then felt an experience of floating and letting go, returning to my body when the experience was over. For quite a few days afterwards, I remember feeling a vague ache in my lower abdomen and a sense of shock. Strangely though, I now feel that this past experience didn't somehow matter. I felt free from it and that it wouldn't bother me again.

Regressing to a past life is a bit like piecing together a jigsaw. Until you have most of the pieces in place, it is impossible to know the inner person. That is what it felt like when I regressed to my past life, I was uncovering an inner person hidden deep within me, rather like an archaeologist scraping away layers of earth to uncover buried material.

I also became aware, at one point, of being incarcerated in a damp, cold, dark room, which seemed to be some sort of prison. It smelt foul and I became acutely aware that I, too, smelt of dirt and decay and that there were fleas crawling on my legs. I remember feeling shame for the filthy state that I was in – so much so that when I had surfaced from trance, all I wanted to do was to go home and have a bath. I had to stop myself from telling Paul not to look at me, so strongly did I feel that I was a dirty mess and that other people could see it. I also felt a strong need to be able to see the countryside. Again, this is something that is part of my present life. I have never felt happy in a town or city, often seeking out the solace of the natural world.

At further sessions, happy experiences began to surface. I felt love and joy. I saw a little girl, just beginning to walk, on fat, wobbly legs. Then I felt the despair of having that child threatened and finally being taken away by the man who was its father. Whilst not everything is clear about this girl's life, it was obvious that she lived on the fringe of her society and was in some way paying the price for it. I noticed how much I had placed myself in a respectable job in my present life so I would not be on the fringes as she was. Even though I so much wanted to express myself as she had done, I had been afraid of repeating her suffering.

As I continued my sessions with Paul, I became aware of changes within myself. I felt happier with the person I am. Generally I was much more confident around people, although I still feel shy with people who exude a certain power or charisma. Others have commented upon the changes in me, saying that I appear more self-assured, more outgoing and less submissive. One day, I will give up smoking and it won't seem quite the challenge that it did a few months ago.

After Thoughts

A short time after Marilyn wrote this account her marriage ended. Doing this greatly challenged the side of her nature that wanted to be respectable - to appear to be doing the right thing socially. She had to endure judgements from others who did not agree with her decision and so it was not an easy time for her. Staying true to her self through a difficult process and surviving – even thriving - has perhaps been the ultimate lesson for her to learn and live out.

Chapter 13

Helen's Story

I could produce many examples illustrating the effectiveness of short term past life therapy – I have chosen Helen's, a woman who attended one of my workshops.

From the outset, Helen was very open to doing past life regression with me. She could have followed up the workshop sessions with further past life work on a one-to-one basis, had it felt right for her. As it was, she expressed enthusiasm about her experiences, and continues to view them in a positive light.

She explored two past lives during her weekend with me. In the following case study, she describes one of them. Both have proved to be highly significant, providing a firm impetus for her to initiate important changes in her life, and her approach to it. The second past life, not mentioned here, concerns her links with members of her family and is more personal. It is clear, from her story and the past life that she shares in her account, that the insights she has gained have challenged her in a far-reaching way. I imagine that assimilating this will need considerable time - therefore the amount of regression work that she has done so far is quite sufficient for now.

Meeting Helen

Helen was both nervous and excited when she applied to attend my weekend past life workshop. Something in her was pulling her very strongly to do it. Yet I felt her approach to be quite innocent as well. She did not have any pre-conceptions about what she would discover, but instead a burning curiosity to be aware of her inner self.

It did not need much preparation for her to become aware that there was certainly a past life waiting for her to access. To her surprise and delight, she was successfully able to go through all the various stages of exploration. Interestingly her way of relating to the character that she saw as her past life self, was to see him as someone separate from herself - yet she recognised and felt that she was this character. This occurrence is quite common, especially when people are accessing past lives for the first time. Some people need to feel safe within the regression, and to be slightly removed from the experience.

The outer appearance of the past life character she writes about is so very different from the person she is today. The scenario of being an old man living hermit-like in a mountain could not be more dissimilar from the busy life that she maintains today. However, the inner dynamics of that character reminded her so much of how she feels herself to be, in the present time, that this is where she could learn.

Here follows Helen's account of her experiences of this past life in her own words.

Helen's Past Life Regression

My interest in past lives began when I read a book about a lady who had experienced her past lives, and had researched her most recently recalled life in such depth that she went on to meet the children that she had had then. It fascinated me to think that this could be true and I began to wonder if I might have had past lives myself. The thought excited and overwhelmed me.

I didn't think that I would ever find out about the past lives that I might have had, as my life did not cross the paths of past life therapists - or so I thought. Within my circle of family and friends, I didn't really have anyone with whom I could discuss the notion of past lives, so it became more of a personal research project. I read a range of books about past life experiences, still never ever imagining that I would have any kind of opportunity to find out about my past lives.

It seemed by chance that I met Paul on a stall at a show in Manchester. When I saw that he did tasters of past life therapy, I knew straight away that I wanted to make an appointment with him. During the session, the impressions that came to me were quite rich, and I decided that I wanted to find out more. Picking up one of Paul's leaflets, I booked several weeks later for a weekend workshop of past life regression. I felt nervous because a whole weekend seemed like a big commitment.

Coming to the workshop, I had mixed feelings. Even though I had read many articles about past life regression, a part of me was sceptical as to whether I was really capable of experiencing my own past lives. Going into the meditation and listening to Paul's instructions, I remember feeling very calm. When nothing came to me immediately, there was already a train of thought entering my mind that it hadn't worked. But before that thought could entrench itself, I was picturing myself as an old man. I experienced the old man as separate from me, in that I was looking at him, and yet I knew that it was me. It was a bit like watching me on video.

As the old man, I was crouching down with my arms wrapped around my folded legs. My head was bent over and I was rocking on my feet. My feelings seemed to be the feelings of the old man; I felt isolated and alone. I felt that I had given up everything - deep down, I knew I was waiting to die. The old man was extremely thin and bony. He was wearing rags and had long, thin white hair with a beard to match. As he sat rocking by the embers of a fire, outside a cave, he wasn't bothering to eat or drink. When Paul suggested that I become aware of the old man's daily activities, he just couldn't seem to move. It seemed like that was it for him.

Paul suggested that I go to an earlier time when my character was happy and well. Immediately, without feeling that I had any time to calculate where I would be, I saw a young man, well dressed in a bustling market. He was alone, and I got the strong feeling that he was looking for someone, anyone with whom he could talk. It seemed like I, as the young man, was looking for someone to share about life. I wanted to find out the reasons for being. Everyone around me was caught up in buying and selling things. No-one appeared to be at all interested in discussing anything that to me was meaningful.

As I digested this, Paul moved me forward asking that I go to the next important event. With Paul's prompting, it unfolded that, in this past life, I had spent my days wandering from place to place, searching for people with whom I could talk to about life and its meaning. I felt that I had something to share with people, and yet I only wanted to do that with someone interested enough, with whom I could communicate. In the end, as the young man had aged, he had got fed up and eventually turned to the life of a hermit, living in a cave. He had given up on life.

Paul then led me to the end of the man's life. I remember that, in my physical body as Helen, I was shivering with cold and my whole body felt stiff and achy. As Paul instructed me to take my last breath as the old man, I felt my body totally relax. It was as if I was suddenly filled with peace. The change from the old man's body was such a contrast to the warm peaceful feeling that I experienced now. There was a warm, golden light, and I felt as though I was bathing in it.

Before the end of the regression, Paul asked me about my feelings for the old man. I felt much more detached from the old man now, but I felt angry with him. Ultimately, I perceived that he had wasted his life. He hadn't really tried to make himself heard or known to others, all the time expecting other people to come to him. I felt that he should have spoken out, but he hadn't. There were things that he had wanted to do and share, but none of this was accomplished. In the end he had given up, and it made me feel angry and frustrated towards him. I also felt sad because I could see myself as the old man and knew that somehow this was me too.

Who can really prove that past life experiences are real and what they say they are? No one can actually prove that what I experienced was a past life or a figment of my imagination. However, having been through the experience, it is almost impossible to explain on paper the emotions I went through as I viewed the old man. It is hard to convey how it could be that I was watching myself as an old man. But that is the overwhelming feeling I had.

The experience has affected me in many ways. Afterwards I admittedly questioned its authenticity. My mind kept saying, 'Could it have been made up? Did I invent the experience?' Yet, despite the doubts, I always come to the same conclusion. Yes, it was a real experience. This is confirmed by the meaning the experience has for me and the effect that it has had on my life.

Before my regression, there were things in my life that I wanted to do. I had thought about doing these things but never really got around to them, never quite having the courage. I wanted to join a Buddhist group, meditate, and share my thoughts about the meaning of life.... I had been living with these feelings, yet not doing anything about them. I hadn't shared any of these ideas because, in my opinion, none of my friends or family was interested in such matters. So instead, I had kept them to myself, reading books alone, thinking things through alone, without even telling anyone that this was my interest. The past life experience was like a huge wake up call to me

I had been angry that the old man had wasted his life. Furthermore, I was frustrated at his lack of effort in communicating his true thoughts. The more I thought about the old man, the more I saw myself reflected in him. I knew that this past life had an important purpose in my present life and it touched me deeply.

Since I have had this regression, I have been trying to live by being more true to my feelings. I have joined a Buddhist group. Every day I meditate. Much more than before, I now share my thoughts and experiences with my husband and family. I have even dared to share my past life experience with some friends and work colleagues. It was a weight off my shoulders when I told my family about it.

Whenever I feel that I have something that I want to do or share or talk about, I am reminded of the old man looking back at me, and I try to take action instead of pretending that it is OK for me just to carry on and ignore my true self.

Chapter 14

Loraine's Story

To illustrate the benefits of past life therapy of medium duration, I am including the case study of my client, Loraine.

Loraine came to me for individual sessions through the recommendation of one of her friends, a colleague who had undergone both general psychotherapy and past life therapy with me over several months. Her presenting problem was about a need that she expressed to reduce weight. She did not appear to be excessively overweight by any means. However, she was very sensitive about her appearance especially in relationship to her partner, and it upset her tremendously whenever he made any remarks that were critical of how she looked. She was also concerned about turning to unhealthy food as a comfort whenever she felt under stress.

Loraine had a compassionate, bubbly and sensitive personality, and it was clear that in her life, both professionally and privately, she spent a lot of her energy trying to help and care for others. I sensed an underlying strength in her character, but also vulnerability. Although she had suffered a lot of trauma in her life, she tried to be brave to convince herself that she had come to terms with these things and was ready to move on. Already, when she first told me of her troubled past, I sensed that her weight problems might have quite complex and deep roots, far deeper than she consciously realised. I suspected that part of her knew this and wanted in depth help to understand her self more fully.

Once we began to engage in the therapy, it became apparent how much, on a sub-conscious level, the events of her past still troubled her. There was a huge turmoil of emotion welling up inside her awaiting expression and release. All this was weighing her down without her being consciously aware of it.

Only after the first few sessions did we consider past life therapy. By then, I felt that there could be dimensions to her problems that went beyond the confines of her present life. This hunch turned out to be correct.

Each session proved very intense for Loraine. She learnt a lot about herself that had not been previously apparent. As a client, she was very open and trusting and this was a great support in my work with her.

Ultimately, Loraine went diving into the darkest areas of her being. It took a lot of her energy to integrate these experiences and accept them. Exploring three past lives proved enough for her. She reached saturation point, needing time and space to fully come to terms with what she had done.

The most significant learning for her was about how much, as a soul, she is responsible for the reality that she experiences. Bringing in the dimension of past lives, she perceived that she had set up the horrible events that she had gone through in her present incarnation in her past lives. Therefore, there was no point in wallowing in self-pity about being a victim of other people's abuse. She needed to accept her life as it was and do what she could to make the best of it.

To understand this on every level of her being was a considerable task for her, and it has been of no surprise that after her third regression she needed time out to assimilate it all, and recuperate!

Because of the intense nature of past life work, it is often the case that people will not be able to sustain further regressions without having a long break for integration.

Thankfully, during the course of the work that we did do, Loraine was also able to attain her goal of reducing some weight.

Here follows her story.

Preliminary Sessions

In recent years, I thought that I had dealt with my painful childhood memories. I had tried very hard to sort out my relationship difficulties, and establish myself in a worthwhile job helping others, that gave me respect and security. But now I realise that I had only put the lid on what was within me. While outwardly I had been attempting to convince myself that I was OK, I had closed myself off from the turbulent mass of unresolved thoughts and feelings that were swirling about inside.

A friend of mine had been to see Paul to conquer feelings of inadequacy and low self-esteem stemming from her own life traumas. Somehow, she had blossomed beyond belief. Paul's work had had a truly amazing effect upon her that was outwardly evident. My friend had emerged, more youthful, more assertive, and more at peace. I felt strongly that Paul could help me too.

There was one problem that I felt I had, and this was with food. I felt food to be an obsession in my life that was driving me totally crazy. It pre-occupied my thoughts and feelings to a degree where I did not like myself for it. Desperately, I wanted to escape the clutches of this obsession and finally break free from the feelings of misery that it was creating inside me. I was somewhat overweight and did not feel comfortable. My partner would make remarks and inwardly I felt ugly and unworthy because of this. Food seemed to have control over me and I felt that I had no power to resist it.

I had never tried hypnotherapy before, but I felt willing to do whatever was necessary if it would make any positive difference to me.

In my initial session, Paul asked me questions to gain a profile of my life. We looked at my patterns of eating and all the things that drove me to food. I noticed that whenever I felt the least bit emotional in any way, I would turn to food as a crutch to lean on and distract me from the feelings that were there.

I did not like talking about myself very much and when we touched upon areas like my earlier relationships, my parents and childhood, I could tell that there was an awful lot of unhappiness inside me.

One topic that came to light concerned an abortion that I had undergone, seven years previously. As Paul questioned me, I realised that I had never properly grieved over this trauma I'd endured. Gently, Paul suggested that sometimes experiences that we have not digested completely, can weigh us down energetically and physically. At the time, when we first talked about it, I was not aware that it was causing me difficulties, but at the same time, it felt like unfinished business.

Over the following week before my next session, thoughts of this abortion kept popping into my head. Increasingly, I knew that I needed to unravel this issue and suddenly, as I drove to see Paul, these thoughts became a very strong, potent force that I felt I had to resolve.

When I went under hypnosis, I could hardly believe the power of my reactions. Sheer anger and immense pain erupted and tumbled out of me. So intense were my emotions that I felt afterwards strong waves of embarrassment, with an impulse directing me that I could not possibly face Paul again.

I struggled to overcome these fears. My sensible self reminded the other parts of me that other people must surely go though similar processes. If I was to be truly healed then I had to let it all out and, if that meant shouting and screaming, then so be it.

This session unlocked a flood of thoughts and memories from inside me: all my life, I had had an obsession with wanting a family. If people asked me about this, I invariably told them that I wanted to be everything to my children that my parents were not to me. It seemed so vitally important to make this statement and repeat it as often as I could. I felt as though I had a mission to make up for my own suffering by having a child of my own.

As a young child of five years old, I was sent away to boarding school. Because of this, and perhaps some other reasons too, I had spent my life feeling unloved, rejected and abandoned. I blamed my parents and spent so much of my young life feeling thoroughly miserable. As an adult, I feel that I have played out that issue of abandonment many times, constantly forcing my partners to abandon me, or sometimes abandoning them, as it would be less painful that way.

Having this overwhelming need for a child was a major factor in the break up of many of my relationships. Many of my ex-partners probably thought that the only reason I wanted them was so that I could have a child with them. I felt like a total failure when it came to relationships. As well as having a child, I desperately wanted to sustain a long term relationship. But as time went on, it seemed less and less possible. As I got into my thirties, the length of my relationships got shorter and shorter, because the biological clock was ticking, and I wanted at all costs to have a child.

Then along came the pregnancy, when I was 34 years old, right out of the blue - a genuine one night stand with a friend that I had known for a long time. The pregnancy was not intended; the use of contraception and the morning after pill both failed. I was alone, and unable to tell my friend for fear that he would want to go ahead with the pregnancy. My instinct told me very strongly that it was not right to have a child with this friend. So I chose to abort my own child that I had so desperately wanted. I abandoned it as I felt that my parents had abandoned me, and I still don't know why I made this decision to this day.

At the time, the only tears I cried were as I was going under the anaesthetic. Afterwards, I pushed it into the back of my sub-conscious mind, rarely giving it a passing thought until my hypnosis session.

The grieving that I experienced in that session was immense. Something in me seemed to open as I released all the distress that I had locked away. Suddenly, I could sense the presence of the spirit of the boy child that I had aborted. He had such a loving energy; he even seemed to be pleased to see me, and able to forgive me. The tears of relief heaved out of me.

Since that time, I have had frequent visions of my boy smiling down at me from some beautiful, serene place, flanked by the spirits of my dead grandparents. I now feel able to put my past pain behind me, and finally come to terms with my actions.

My present partner has a grown up family. When we met, he was adamant that he did not want to have any more children. Initially this broke my heart, and I felt that I had to reject him as I had done with others in the past. Subsequently, we had three months apart before I somehow realised that I needed him in my life, even if we didn't have a child together. I had not given up hope though.

Through the hypnosis session with Paul, it finally came to light that the family that I had always yearned for was no longer necessary. I felt at last that this intensive desire was fading and could be laid to rest.

My next two sessions with Paul were at least as harrowing as the one concerning the abortion. They focussed around themes of sexual abuse.

The first one concerned an incident that happened when I first went to boarding school. I was sexually abused by a number of older girls. It was really a most humiliating, awful and frightening experience. There was nobody to help me or protect me, and I was only so little that I could barely understand what was happening. I cannot write the details of what took place.

In the hypnosis session, my body reacted to this memory with a tremendous release of deeply held pain. For much of the time, my body shook with fear. There was so much anger that I had never dared express as a little girl. Part of my anger was to do with God. If there was a God in this world, how could He allow an innocent child to be treated like this? Not only did I feel abandoned by my parents but also by God. Who was there to love me, nurture me and protect me? I was alone and had no choice but to develop an independent coping mechanism. Externally I was a survivor, but internally I was crumbling.

After this session I did not feel good, but I knew that releasing all those suppressed feelings from this time was worthwhile.

The next session concerned my relationship with my father. I loved my father very much. I admired and adored him; he was everything to me, and then one day the bubble burst and he failed me. One day, when I was a young teenager, he kissed me on the mouth sexually. It was something that I found absolutely shocking, and my trust in him disappeared at once. I did not react outwardly at the time and haven't done so since. All the feelings I held about this stayed inside me.

It was a very difficult thing for me to approach with Paul, but I am glad that I did. Hypnotherapy, in the way that Paul practises it, seems to work like no other therapy that I have ever tried. In these sessions, I released intense emotions - first of anger, followed by tears of sheer pain - and then finally I felt a profound calm and overwhelming peace, difficult to put into words. With Paul's gift of healing following these sessions, I really felt unburdened and able to be at peace with those haunting life experiences.

Following these sessions, I felt that there was still more to do. I felt much better in myself, and freer to be me. But I was still struggling with my eating. With vague feelings of unease, that sometimes troubled me, I wondered what would come next.

First Past Life Session

Prior to my work with Paul, I had a total disbelief in the existence of past lives. In my mind, I felt myself to be one of the world's sceptics with regards to this phenomenon. Although my aforementioned friend had recounted her own past life experience to me in great detail, it was not something to which I could relate. Yes, I was fascinated by the tale, but that was all.

Never for one moment did I imagine that I could be headed for a past life experience of my own, but that is exactly what came to light in my next session.

One thing that I noticed was that my own inner consciousness would tend to prepare me for my sessions in advance. So, in the hours before, and especially while I was driving to meet Paul, I would tend to anticipate the emotions and issues that I would have to address. Therefore, it had become clear to me that the agenda of my therapy was being driven mainly by the needs of my own inner consciousness. Occasionally, I would have fears about what I would say to Paul in our sessions, but

134

these always faded as the time of our meeting approached. Thoughts of what I would need to confront in myself would preoccupy me so much that it would be a struggle for me to think of anything else. By the time I actually entered the room with him, these thoughts and emotions would want to tumble out, and it would be a great relief to let that happen.

Before this session, I remember vividly telling myself that I was not going to cry, because at every other session I had let go of buckets of tears, and I just wanted to be calm enough not to do that. But even as I expressed this thought to myself, the tears began to flow, and they kept flooding out all the way to the session. I was hardly able to even see to drive. The tears I let out were not of sadness, but of an intense anger, anger so vehement that it frightened me.

During the course of my life, I had carried a lot of anger. Particularly, I was angry about how often things went wrong for me, frequently stating over the years that 'it is just my luck!' Even my friends adopted this statement and used it to reinforce the conception that I had of my unlucky life.

The issue that troubled me was one that had already come up earlier in my work with Paul but this time, the feelings surrounding it felt much stronger. It concerned my faith and my relationship with God. I was angry with God. The tears were to do with my desperation, because I so much wanted to connect with my faith and believe in a higher force or power, but the more I tried, the more it seemed to elude me. All during the preceding week, I had been trying to bargain with God, asking Him to manifest things for me in certain ways as a proof of His existence. I needed something concrete, so I could trust and find my belief again.

As I lay down for my session with Paul, my anger at God exploded like a missile being launched. All the pain of my life where I felt that God hadn't been there for me was seething, and I felt an acute sense of rejection and abandonment.

Gently, Paul asked my consciousness to take me to the source of this pain and anger, and that was how I began to experience the memory of the past life. As I started to sense what was happening, I wasn't frightened, and I decided that I would surrender myself to the memory that was emerging as fully as possible.

The feeling of this lifetime was one of poverty and sheer misery. My mother abandoned me. Off she went with another man and left me with my father. His hurt and bitterness was then dumped upon me, and I was made to follow in my mother's footsteps. This meant that I had to lead a life where I was fulfilling all my father's wants and demands, from being a slave in his home to sleeping in his bed. I had to perform all wifely duties to him, and had practically no contact with anyone else. As a result, I was deeply unhappy and felt immense loneliness. It was an empty existence that was made only vaguely comfortable by my intense obsession with food.

During the day I would sit and eat bread, as if this was some way of taking the pain away. Every time my father came in, he would call me a 'fat wench'. He would laugh and ridicule my eating habits and appearance constantly. This just drove me to eat more. And the more that I ate, the fatter I became. The well of unhappiness inside of me grew bigger by the day.

I could sense the parallels of this with my present life - the fact that eating was then my only comfort. It made me cry.

The further I went into this life, the more I had this sense of a deep, black depression surrounding it. When I was directed to the time of my father's death, very little changed for me. I still felt destitute. There was no relief from the sorrow that I felt. I was still living an existence of dark despair and unhappiness. Going on to the end of my own life, I felt fat and alone, and still had an aura around me of dark depression.

Experiencing the emotions of my own death in that life was harrowing. All I could see was intense darkness. There seemed to be no escape, and it felt impossible to penetrate. My whole being was immersed in it. Finally, I realised that the reason for this darkness was my lack of faith. This felt terrifying. The darkness was trying to absorb me.

I tried to fight because I didn't want this. Desperately, I tried to let the light in. At first, some of the black shifted to grey, and then an amazing thing happened. I felt this beautiful light from above me, and I wanted to reach it. However, as the light was drawing me from above, I felt that the darkness was trying to pull me from below. At that moment, an incredible itch started on my right foot. I felt compelled to push my foot along the floor in an attempt to relieve this intense itching. Concurrently, I was shouting aloud at the darkness, 'Go away and leave me alone'. This struggle went on, and all I felt was that the darkness was trying to consume me. Physically I found myself kicking out with my feet very aggressively, violently shouting over and over again, 'Leave me alone'.

Then, almost without warning, the light became overwhelming in its intensity, so that it seemed to take me over completely. The power of it was incredible and almost instantly, the darkness and the itching stopped.

Tears of joy and peace, like none I have ever felt before, were flooding my body, cleansing me of my pains. There I was, standing in a place that was serene, and I felt enveloped in pure love. I was being held and hugged affectionately by the spirit of my dead father, who was now smiling at me. Becoming aware of my appearance, I was lovely and slim - no longer that fat miserable wench that I had been in that lifetime.

In this realm of light, I was radiating the energy of love and happiness, which I had never experienced before. Here I felt really protected and loved. Through my efforts and the wish of my higher self, I had been reunited with this part of me and rescued from that life of pain and despair.

When I came out of this past life experience, I was crying tears of joy, and I wanted the feeling to last forever. What I knew now was that God was with me again and I no longer needed a sign. Feeling this presence, my anger had been abated.

Afterwards, as I reflected upon it I marvelled at what I had been through. There were still some cravings for food that I did not like but inside, I felt as if some enormous progress had been made in my development.

Second Past Life Session

Following my first past life session, I knew that there were still many stones unturned. For a week or so I felt on a real 'high', and then my mood started to spiral out of control. A depression was looming. Days of blackness overwhelmed me. This was associated with episodes of anger that flared up here and there. I knew that the mood preoccupying me anticipated the next therapy session that I was approaching. Several issues were involved, and they were quite specific.

For as long as I could remember, the need to be financially secure was fundamental to me. Behind it, I recognised that I had a great fear of being without money and because of this, I had stayed in the same job for many years even though at times, I felt trapped in it. The feelings of being a prisoner of my job were particularly strong now.

One of the main facets of my work was to help mothers and young families. What I noticed was that I was feeling an extreme adverse reaction to having anything to do with these people. Needing to answer questions about parenting and motherhood was driving me crazy, and I just didn't feel that I could cope with it anymore. Previously, I had found this aspect of my work to be very worthwhile, but now I was despising it.

Concurrently, I was directing a huge amount of anger at my manager. I saw her as a control freak. Any authoritarian position that she took was like waving a rag to a bull. Even though I tried, I couldn't hold back my emotion. Often my reactions were exaggerated and directed towards her at quite inappropriate moments. This made me feel out of control and frightened. I felt compelled to get to the root of these disturbing responses that were suddenly coming up so much in my everyday life. My next past life revelation certainly provided that.

As I went deep into hypnosis, I began to feel intense stabbing pains in the middle of my back. It was really uncomfortable and very frightening. As I focussed on it, I knew that it was a memory of a knife going into my back. I was about to die.

Paul encouraged me to back track to a time before this stabbing, and details of this bleak life began to unfold.

I was sixteen and my mother was an alcoholic. My father was a weak, pathetic man, who could not stand up to my mother. He did nothing to help and support me. One day, my mother demanded for me to go out and work. I heard the words in my head, 'We need money, money, money... We must have money.' It was down to me to earn the money she needed to support her alcoholism. Without knowing anything else to do, I went begging in the streets, but this was not what she had envisaged. Consequently, she sent me off to sell my body as a prostitute.

While I was doing this job, a big black man befriended me, telling me that if I worked for him, he would help me earn the money that I needed for my mother. I trusted him, believing this to be the way for me to escape from the life of hell into which I had become entangled. But, however bad my life had been until then, it was about to get worse with him.

This man took intense control of me and locked me up. I never received any of the money that he had promised. He frequently tortured me, whether I had done anything wrong or not. The pain of these beatings got worse and worse. Sending me out to sell my body, he gloated, living off the money I made. My life with him felt terrifying.

One day, he raped me and I became pregnant as a result. Going through this trauma in hypnosis felt completely real. It was as though I was pinned to the floor. The more I tried to resist him, the more I felt that there was no means of escape. I screamed. Tears of terror overcame me. I tried so hard to force this man off me, but all my strength was gone and I felt helpless to do anything. Arching my back in an attempt to repel him had no effect at all. Afterwards, I was overcome with grief.

However, I then had an interlude of solace. The man left me alone while I was pregnant. There were no more beatings, and no more work. I even began to feel a glimmer of hope.

Once the baby arrived, the love that I felt for this little being was all consuming. For me, my love for this baby made up for all the previous pain that I had endured. Now I had a beautiful daughter to whom I could give all my attention. She was going to be my life. I could experience myself sitting there endlessly, holding her close to me and treasuring every moment.

During one of these moments of closeness, he came into the room in a rage. He was insisting that I had to go back to work. We began to argue, and soon, his rage escalated into violence. I tried to plead with him that I couldn't work because I needed to look after the baby. He would not accept this.

Coming over to me, he forced the baby out of my arms. In spite of my desperation, he strangled my baby, right in front of my eyes. She became limp and lifeless.

Intense pain, so overwhelming that words could not describe it, were surging through me. There were tears and sobbing out of control. I felt destroyed, utterly and completely.

I tried to run, to make my escape, and that is when he came after me, and drove his full force at me, and plunged a knife deep into my back, again and again. As I was lying on the floor, whatever was happening to my body, I chose there and then to give up and die. I had lost my glimmer of hope. My beautiful daughter had been taken from me and there was nothing more to keep me alive.

Recalling these events, I can honestly say that during the hypnosis session, it felt like I was going through that reign of terror for real. I was sobbing gut-wrenching tears that were uncontrollable in their expression. My body was physically exhausted from all the emotional turmoil, and I felt grief like I never had before.

After my death, I came to a place of serenity. Peace and light were absorbing me, lifting my emotions through a crescendo of pure happiness. All the pain and terror that had been thrown at me during that lifetime seemed to be released. More importantly, I was reunited with my beautiful daughter. I experienced myself holding her in my arms once again. While doing that, we were both bathed in what felt like light and everlasting love.

Paul directed me to go forward to the moment when my soul in spirit would meet with the soul of the man who had killed me in that life. I could sense that some 'time' had passed because my daughter accompanied me, and she now appeared to be six or seven years of age. Despite my trepidation, we approached him with the energies of love and forgiveness. He was obviously sorry for what he had done, and I found the experience of this meeting to be very healing.

As I was finishing with this, I became aware of another spiritual being that was with me. I saw this being as a beautiful woman. I sensed that she was there for me, that she knew me and was supporting me with love. I could see her standing there, and she had long white hair and a warm smile. It came to me that her name was Martha. She was my spiritual guide, and there to accompany me and help me on my journey through life. All I needed to do was to reach out for her, and I sensed that she would be there to help me find peace in the midst of all my struggles.

When I finished my session, I felt that I had been to the root of so many of my fears. I felt that I understood now about my various reactions to the situations that had been bothering me, and felt much more peaceful as a result.

In the following days, people remarked on a feeling of 'calmness' about me, and a sparkle. My interaction with young mothers that I encountered in my job felt easier and I didn't experience the same upset with my manager anymore. I felt like my energy was flowing. With regards to the past life, I felt as though it was no longer walking hand in hand besides me, but laid to rest in some serene place.

I felt a strong motivation to learn to meditate and adopt a deeper, more spiritual outlook on my life.

At last, in the days after this session and before the next one, I began to reduce my weight, managing to lose nine pounds in this interval. It was hard work, but I appeared to have the strength to do this now, that had previously been lacking.

Third Past Life Session

Somehow, I knew with my instinct that there was something further that I needed to explore with Paul. As I approached my next session with him, I suffered a recurrence of feelings of black depression, of being judgmental and controlling towards some of those nearest and dearest to me. I was not looking forward to this session. Something within told me that it would be very difficult.

Now that I come to write about it, I realise that it has taken me a long time to pluck up the courage to put pen to paper. This is because the experience was so full of negativity and pain, but not stemming so much from other people's actions as my own. Facing the darkness in my own character to the extent that I did in this session was something that I never expected to happen.

As I went into hypnosis, I felt a very uncomfortable feeling and a difficulty in swallowing. Around my neck, there was a tight sensation, as if I was choking. This felt very real and frightening. I was being hung.

Prior to this, I sensed myself to be forlorn and all alone, shackled in a dungeon, with metal clamps on my wrists and ankles. It was very dark and drops of water ran down the walls from the roof above me. The atmosphere of the place was unpleasant, and it felt as though I had been there a long time. Yet I was only a youth, a teenage boy. What had I done to get into such a place?

With Paul's help, I began to trace the main earlier events of this lifetime.

At the outset, I had been a sad, isolated little boy. Much of the time, I was physically abused and ridiculed by my mother. My father had abandoned us and my mother took this out on me, beating me constantly and despising me. I think that for some reason, I reminded my mother of my father. She regarded him as having been mad. In my present day mind, I reflected that my father then, could have suffered from a mental illness and genetically, I suffered with the same tendency. My mother judged me that I was evil, that I had the devil in me, and that I was no good. I felt useless and helpless in her presence.

Sooner or later, I began to believe the messages that my mother instilled in me. She was my model and I wanted others to feel what I was feeling. Consequently, I started to torture other children. I wanted them to suffer like I had done. Compulsively, I liked to witness these children becoming frightened and vulnerable, and what I could do to them. It gave me a strange feeling of pleasure to have control over them. The way that I treated my victims grew ever more violent.

These children were younger than me and so I was stronger than them. When I beat them, I actually laughed as my mother had done as she dealt blow after blow upon me. In my mind I justified my actions because they were no different from how my mother had treated me.

The feeling of control over these children made me feel very powerful. I felt compelled to find more victims. I became very excited while engaged in acts of torture, and as an activity, it became more and more frenzied.

Paul directed me to the worst incident of cruelty, and I recalled the experience of killing two children, a boy and a girl. They were only killed after extended sessions of torture where they were tied up, the details of which I am not going to write. Needless to say, they were both terrified, and I found it funny. Somewhere deep inside, I knew that what I had done was wrong, but the thirst in me to kill and hurt others was too strong. To get rid of their bodies, I threw them into a nearby canal.

It is not clear to me whether they were the only children that I killed. I would prey for them in the darkened streets. Somehow, I suspect that there were others that I killed too.

My downfall occurred when I was asked to baby sit for my little brother while my mother was out. He was crying incessantly and I couldn't stand it any more. There was an overwhelming force in me telling me to gain control and put an end to his crying. This I did, by violently shaking him until he was dead. Even though I protested to my mother that it was an accident, she took me to the authorities mercilessly and accused me of being infested with evil spirits. Thus, I was locked up in that cold and lonely dungeon. Much later, I was hung for my crimes.

Going through death was a tremendous relief for me, but I needed to climb a ladder to reach the place of peace where my soul wanted to be. It was so hard to accept myself for what I had done, but there were other spirits there reaching out to me to help me and support me.

I was directed to go to the moment when I was confronted with the souls of my victims. They were there in front of me and it was so hard to look at them. From each of them, there came the energy of forgiveness towards me, something that I hardly dared to allow myself.

This place of peace was overwhelmingly supportive. Even members of my family were there. It was just what I needed after the dreadful existence that I had lived prior to my death.

Once I came out of the hypnosis, I could sense clear links between that lifetime and my present one. Immediately I recognised the souls of the boy and girl that I had killed as two people that were very influential figures in my life today. In my heart, I wanted to make amends for the terrible hurt for which I had been responsible in that former time. It made me question how they could tolerate to be close to me when I had done that. My esteem was very low and I had to somehow forgive and love myself. I never wanted to let anything like that happen again.

In my present life I had not been given an appropriate opportunity to have children. Now this occurrence seemed to be a very important lesson for me. For that reason alone, I needed to accept and embrace my life as it is. The impact of this session was sobering and humbling. I felt that I had gained a much deeper understanding of myself but it was not easy.

Afterwards - Author's Notes

Loraine had further sessions with me following this work. It took her some time to digest what she had experienced, especially in that last regression. Before her next meeting with me, she had lost another five pounds. Her weight was no longer a problem. Now she questioned whether she was a good person, and whether she was worthy to be loved. She had a great need to consult with her guide Martha, and found this contact to be very comforting. The main guidance from Martha was about Loraine's need to consolidate on the cleansing process that she had already been through. Loraine could accept this. She still needed support.

I believe that the sessions with Loraine helped solve her presenting problem, relating to her need for weight reduction, whilst also facilitating a deep transformation in her life. Her outlook has become much more spiritually minded, and she is aware of so many more things from within herself that have given her a depth of self-understanding. Confronting her inner darkness was a very brave thing for to do. Until then she had avoided facing this, instead becoming angry and blaming others or God for her troubles. Now it was much clearer to her how much she was responsible for the well being of her own life. The challenge she now faced was about how she could usefully apply those understandings she had gained to the routines and patterns of her everyday life.

Chapter 15

Jane's Story

As an example of long term past life therapy, I am including a piece from my client, Jane. Jane is a woman with whom I have done past life regression for many years. At times, I have questioned whether or not going into further past lives has been an indulgence for her. But, having perceived a genuine and continued interest from her in her own soul journey, as well as what she has gained from these explorations, it felt right for her. Tracing over the work that we have done together over the years, it appears that she is a soul who has made many mistakes within her physical incarnations. The tendency towards perpetuating these mistakes has become entrenched as a pattern within her. She has needed to go through, and endure, the memory of her past actions as a cleansing to enable her to create a more constructive way forward for herself. She has shown a great deal of courage to persevere, especially when she has felt that everything in her past is dark - for this is not the case. In her heart, she is a very sensitive and loving soul who has a desperate need and drive to make up for times from her past when she could have given something positive to others but did not.

In the following account, Jane shares about one of the darkest lives she has encountered within herself - all the more terrifying because of it being so recent. It is just one small chapter within the overall work that she has done with me, but it has made a significant difference to her, as she relates here.

Jane's Dark Past Life

I had always felt that I was one of life's victims. I hated everything around me, I hated my life, and I hated my marriage and job. But most of all, I hated myself.

I was a failure. Everything seemed to conspire against me, and 'they' or 'it' was the cause. Stuck in an inner darkness, I developed a deep self-loathing and depression. Several times, I was on the verge of suicide. In my mid-forties, my life was going nowhere, and all I could see ahead were years and years of ever increasing misery and sadness.

Somehow, I realised that I needed to seek help. Knowing that the conventional approach would be to throw tablets at myself, I looked for a viable alternative and eventually saw Paul for therapy.

When my work with him started, I became aware that there were huge gaps in my memory. Paul helped me to begin to access a very difficult past that I had shut away. As I worked with my inner child, I discovered a pattern of sexual abuse and violence. I gradually worked through this, taking very small steps at a time, but making progress. My life began to change. I left my marriage, gave up my job, and moved on. I was beginning to find myself.

However, even with the deep and traumatic work that I was doing, still in the background was this sense of always being the victim. I became full of self pity. It seemed that the more I uncovered, the more unjust it all seemed. I neatly 'boxed up' all my experiences prior to therapy in a dark and shadowy past. It was a place of utter darkness and I shut the door on it all, feeling bitter and angry in myself that I had had to undergo such awful things. 'Why me?' I wailed. 'What did I do that was so wrong?'

In the course of my work with Paul, I did some past life work that helped me to gain inner awareness and understanding of myself. From lives in recent times that I accessed, there was nothing in any of them that appeared to hold the key to the magnitude of suffering that I had endured in my life now. In fact, the three most recent incarnations I recalled all appeared to be horrible 'victim' lives as well.

To cope with myself, I continued to try and shut away my past so I would not be reminded of it, even though there was an inner part of me that knew this was wrong. Every time I confronted some fragment of the darkness in my past, I felt a little lighter. Because of the pain of these memories, though, I tried to keep a lid on it all. But I couldn't completely shut it away. Events kept coming into my life that triggered past memories. There came a point when I decided that I would have to deal with this more fully.

In my mind, I began to see a 'freeze frame' image of myself aged about nine or ten. This wouldn't go away. It hovered in my inner vision persistently and I felt scared whenever I focussed on it. Although I was afraid, I knew that I needed to address this with Paul.

I saw myself standing in my school dress at the bottom of our cellar steps in our family house, looking through a doorway. This was where I was frozen. I could feel the fear.

With Paul's patient guidance, I entered into the memory of the experience on the other side of the doorway. There I found something so terrible, so awful, I struggled to accept the events that I witnessed. In this cellar, a group of people were practising satanic rites, and I was being used in a ritualistic way, sexually and violently. The terror and fear that I felt took me to my absolute limits. I struggled to cope. The worst realisation was that my mother, as well as my father, was involved. Up until now, I had only identified my father with the abuse that I had suffered as a child, my mother appearing to take a disinterested standpoint. But the shock of seeing her participating in naked rituals was devastating. Somehow, I couldn't doubt the reality of what I was experiencing. The feelings were just too overwhelming for me to consider that they might have been contrived by my fantasy. Once more, I began to feel bitter and angry. Why had I had to suffer so much? Why? Why?

Following this, other images began to appear in my subconscious, images which at first I denied. From my experience, I knew that it was a past life. I spoke to Paul about it and we agreed to go into it. It was a life of violence, murder, sadism and satanic ritual.

148

I discovered myself to be a young man in England, around the early nineteenth century. My father was a wealthy landowner who bred fine horses. There was not much love in my life, and my father was very cold to me. The one woman who did care about me was cruelly banished from my life by my father because I had dared to visit her in her home. This woman had acted like a nanny to me, much more understanding of me than my own mother. The effect of losing her was to close down my heart.

As a teenager I became bored and indolent, drifting into looking for excitement with a group of like-minded young people. Although I regarded these as my friends, by this stage I did not trust anyone. When my father introduced me to the local Masonic Lodge, this enabled me to become familiar with ceremony and ritual. But I could not be bothered with the small part given to me in these meetings; it was all too tame.

Another young man that I identified as being called 'Monty', was there too. Together we found an old deserted barn, and with some other young men, we began to meet there regularly to practice satanic rituals and black magic. As the experience unfolded over several sessions, what I saw was utterly horrific. I found myself, as that young man, raiding graves for human bones and skulls. The power of the rituals, aided by sexual activity, raised a force that was very real and terrifying. We began to kill animals to obtain blood for the 'Master'. This progressed to human sacrifice. We simply kidnapped vagrants and prostitutes, people we felt were OK.

It is very hard for me to acknowledge the feelings that were going through me during these sessions. As that young man, the lust I had for power was overwhelmingly intoxicating. Seeking that power was a substitute for me of the unfulfilled need I had for love. I had an ambitious nature and, like my father, I felt that I had to be in control. As I approached each of the murders for which I was responsible, my body shook violently with fear. I cannot write all the details of these experiences. How could I have allowed myself to become like this? I was so bad and yet I couldn't deny the sense that this person was myself.

As my thirst for power grew, I killed Monty in a jealous rage. The strength in me was demonic and his death was gruesome. Afterwards, I set the barn alight and burned everything.

Meanwhile I had established a 'private' practice of my own, under our stable block, where I used and killed my own victims. Not being satisfied with this, in time I decided that I needed to be in the nearby big town, in order to improve my position. My father's estate was too remote. To be able to afford this, I needed my father's money, lands and property. Over a period of time, I callously killed all the members of my family, my mother, father, brother and sister, so that I could have what I wanted. Once they were gone, I was able to inherit everything. I sold the estates and moved on.

In my present life, I have often suffered because of feeling a lack of family in my life. Now I understand the connection.

Further on in that life, I established myself in a large mansion in the town. The money I inherited secured my position as a proud and respected member of the local council, and a regular member of the local lodge. Secretly, though, I continued my satanic practice, using my money to pay others to acquire me victims as tribute to the 'Master'.

Much later, I met another man through the Lodge and we became good friends. We fell in love and established a relationship. He moved in with me and we practised rituals together, always involving sex and sacrifice. One day, my friend went out and did not return. His mutilated body was found floating in the nearby river. This event prompted me to feel acutely afraid and lonely. Increasingly I feared for my own safety. My procurers were demanding more and more money, and blackmailing me. Eventually a mob came to my house, screaming for my blood. I tried to escape but was caught. They took me outside the town and killed me.

The experience of this life was so dreadful, so awful. But, like a light switching on, a sudden realisation came to me. I was no longer a victim; all that had happened to me in my present life was brought into sharp focus. Understanding flooded in and I felt a 'lightening' of my soul, a clarity that I had never experienced before. I felt different. The darkness that I had built up around my past was gone, and a huge healing had taken place.

I imagine that there are still residual energies left in my soul from that awful life, things that I will have to work through. Maybe I will plan them into my future lives, who knows? Now I am more determined than ever, to live the rest of this life following the path of healing, love and spiritual service.

Several observations have subsequently come to me about that life, and its relevance to my current experience. I have sensed that many of the people I know today were my victims in that life, and once again the balance is being made. Then I had no respect for anybody or life form of any kind: the only thing that mattered was my selfish need for power and domination. The only love that I felt was for my partner, and when he was killed I was left with nothing.

This horror and darkness is now in the past. My memories of this life are receding, and I am finding my way forward. I am learning to honour the past for what it has taught me as a soul, and I am looking towards the future.

Chapter 16

Developing Psychic Sensitivity

When we access a past life, we open our inner consciousness to dimensions, beyond the usual boundaries of our present life subconscious mind. We become aware of inner knowledge concerning our history and journey as a soul. We only achieve this by loosening the belief systems within us that confine us to the experience of three-dimensional reality, and opening to something more. Our relationship to our higher self and to the spiritual realm can become more accessible; we feel that our existence is not just what we experience in our physical bodies. We might even become aware that our consciousness exists independently of our physical bodies. Once this starts to happen, we can conclude that our mind is more like an energy field than grey matter inside our heads. Experiencing our own life as energetic patterns unfolding, we begin to perceive that all other life forms have their own energy patterns too. The capacity to discern the energetic forms of life beyond three-dimensional reality I call 'psychic sensitivity'.

To experience the memory of a past life, our inner channels of perception have to open more than previously. Once these channels are open they usually stay open, unless we make a very determined effort to close them. If we do further past life work, the channels may open even more. The next dimension of consciousness has a much finer vibration than our normal state of being. Making this connection is bound to affect us, possibly in a quite dramatic way.

There are people who are born with the gift of psychic sensitivity. People can suppress this during childhood, perhaps when encountering others who ridicule or criticise them for what they perceive. People with this gift inherent in them have described it as being like living in two worlds. Many people develop their capacity for psychic sensitivity once they begin to do inner work.

When this sensitivity starts to awaken, we no longer feel enclosed in the limited energy field of our present day personality, separate from others. Instead we become open to impressions within and around us, connecting us with others and our inner worlds. On the level of human interaction, we are more aware of the various layers of thought and feeling within us as well as the thoughts and feelings of others. We have to learn how to cope with this.

Past life regression is not the only tool that will enable people to unlock their potential to gain inner awareness. However, when people are able to immerse themselves in it, the experience of past life regression opens inner doors that had previously been closed.

When people decide to undergo past life regression, they have chosen it at a deeper level to open their spiritual awareness, because it is their path. But becoming more psychically sensitive, while making life feel richer and fuller, can also make life more challenging.

There may be various signs that we are developing psychic sensitivity. We might notice that we feel things more intensely than we did previously. When confronted with difficult situations in our life, we react more strongly. One likely consequence is that we will feel both joy and pain more fully. When people attack us personally or criticise us, we feel vulnerable to a greater degree. By opening our inner channels, we have a stronger sense of the need for right action and it disturbs us when we know that we have veered away from our own path. Another aspect of this sensitivity is to do with our own sense of energetic boundaries with others. We will feel more keenly when our boundaries have been intruded upon and not like it. When we tune in to other people, we will be more aware of their pain and hurt. Out of this growing sensitivity, we might feel the need to do something to help. Thus, with psychic sensitivity can evolve compassion and feeling for the plight of others.

Some people may not want to feel more sensitive as a result of past life regression. It could be chosen as more of a leisure time curiosity or something to do for social reasons. But I do not believe it is easy to engage in past life work superficially.

People can do very clever things with their minds. I have witnessed clients place past life experiences in separate compartments inside their minds, remote and separated from their everyday experiences. I feel that such an attitude defeats the purpose of past life work. The aim of past life regression must surely be to help us feel more connected with fundamental aspects of our being. If we deliberately segment these experiences so that they have nothing to do with any other aspect of our lives then we will not be doing this.

A lot of people in our modern age seem to compartmentalise their lives, so they may have a place for work, a place for family, a place for their social life etc. Such an approach to living makes it easier to cope and to concentrate upon very different strands of life experience. However, it will also psychologically split us inside. People with this orientation may find a place in their lives for spiritual work, but unless this is connected energetically to the other strands of their lives, tension and stress coming from these other spheres of activity will continue to play havoc. Such people could find that the only time they can find peace is when they attend their meditation class!

If we compartmentalise our past life memories then, when these experiences start getting tough, we will want to close them down so we don't feel affected by them. However, only so many experiences can be compartmentalised before beginning to impact upon other areas of our lives. Any type of suppressed experience only creates problems from within.

We need to realise that, even if we are unprepared to acknowledge the learning associated with a past life experience at a conscious level, it is still likely to affect us because it will influence our subconscious mind. Therefore, even if we do not feel inclined to take up challenges indicated by a regression experience, our subconscious will take these on board. Our lives feel increasingly uncomfortable, especially if we do not want to acknowledge the learning involved.

Undergoing past life regression is a serious spiritual path. It needs respect, requiring people to let the experiences permeate into all areas of their lives. People need to trust that this is safe for them to do.

In general, the best approach to have is to be prepared to take responsibility for the experiences that come to us. Even if it is a difficult experience, we must regard it as something that we have created. Everything in our life is here for a purpose. It is nobody else's fault. So if we struggle, we may need to ask for help both within and without. The best way to progress is to have faith that we can learn what we need to learn. Otherwise we will be fighting against ourselves and will not find peace.

Usually, past life experiences are very humbling because they teach us about our weaknesses, the areas of our being where we still need to learn. If we approach past life regression with a fixed agenda, where we feel that we want to find out something specific, our inner consciousness can reflect back to us awareness of memories that conform to our goals. The understandings that come to us could then be quite selective. Such past life experiences may confirm our prejudices rather than help us to grow.

When we approach past life regression with the desire to confirm our belief systems, we may not be concerned with the needs of others. Experiences from the regression might potentially challenge our view. However, if we have a particular view on an issue, nothing that is given to us by our inner consciousness is likely to change it. If we remain fixed in our attitudes, regression work can still stir our psychic sensitivity, but it might not create balance. We may feel things more intensely but not necessarily tolerate other views besides our own. We might also appreciate the 'truth' more as we want it to be, rather than as it is. Generally the process of past life regression does teach us to be more fluid in our views, sometimes even in spite of our attempts to be otherwise.

Let us consider some of the components of past life work and how they can help open our psychic faculties.

Beyond Death

When we go through the death experience in a past life, we will experience something of the next realm of consciousness - where we go when we die. We cannot experience this without connecting with it to some degree. Therefore our consciousness has to open to achieve this.

In regression the experience of passing through death is typically a very liberating experience. The consciousness opens so that life can be seen in a fuller perspective. There may come an experience of light or peace, and an overwhelming sense of love. When people experience these things, no matter to what degree, it affects their consciousness. An internal recognition occurs concerning the truth of what happens when we die. Consequently the boundaries of our self-consciousness stretch beyond what they were previously. Naturally, this results in us being more sensitive to subtle energies.

For us to open our consciousness is quite profound. It may be best for us if we can do it gradually. If too much comes too soon, we back off and get scared. However, with something as beautiful as the experience of spiritual life after death, we are likely to feel profoundly moved. We probably want to experience more. This could give us a considerable stimulus to seek further inner learning; we want to gain self-knowledge. But then we need to ask ourselves whether we are ready to take these steps.

Making Contact with Guides

When grappling with problems associated with our inner life, it is very important for us to learn to ask for guidance. As we ask for help inwardly, by listening we will receive intelligent responses. Connecting with our inner consciousness is another pathway towards the development of psychic sensitivity. Through training ourselves to listen to our inner being, we become more aware of the subtle energies within our system. This enables us to tune into others at a deeper level too.

Many people in our present age believe that we have with us a spiritual guide or guardian angel looking after us, giving us love and support when we need it. For many years, I have been helping people to make contact

156

with their guide. This has been a very rewarding process and I have come to believe that such beings do exist. I feel that we each have a spiritual being assigned to us that loves us and knows our soul. This being is there to protect our spiritual self and provide help for us when we ask for it so that we can be true to our path.

It can be very rewarding for people to make contact with their guide. This can bring with it strong feelings of being supported and loved. However, the only way that people can connect with their guides is by opening the channels of their awareness to that next dimension, so that their guides can be reached. Our spiritual guides do exist on a higher frequency of awareness. Therefore, sharing a living relationship with our guide prompts us to raise our vibrations higher than our previous state of awareness. This, of course, has the impact of opening us to become more psychically sensitive. By developing and maintaining our relationship with our guide, we learn about that dimension of consciousness and our awareness opens further.

One of the main catalysts for establishing contact with guides is past life regression. When people pass through a past life death, they rise up into the spiritual dimension of consciousness. They find that they are met by a very wise and loving being that turns out to be their guide. Possibly they become aware of their guide when they review that lifetime and its lessons. Undergoing a traumatic release from a past life also can trigger the appearance of a guide into the awareness of the seeker. I often ask my clients to be given something healing after confronting trauma. A meeting with their guides can then arise to satisfy an inner need for comfort. Typically people first sense the presence of a loving, peaceful light. From this presence may then emerge the recognition of that spiritual being as their guide.

For people to access the memory of a past life, they need to become aware of more subtle vibrations of consciousness. This, of course, is necessary to establish inner guide contact as well. The two processes are often very connected.

People can become aware of the presence of their guides via routes other than past life regression, including spiritual healing and meditation.

Generally, when people have made initial contact with their guides, experiencing past life regression can often be deeper and more profound. Guides can be very useful in monitoring people's experiences, and prompting aspects of regression that may need more precise attention. People find thoughts, feelings and imagery coming into their minds, suggesting what they need to investigate inwardly. It could be that this prompting is from the guide rather than their own instinct. Thus, guides also help shed light and insights upon necessary learning. People feel greater confidence to tackle more difficult and challenging past life experiences when they know that their guide is there. The feeling of protection and support that the guide offers give encouragement to people to go ahead with past life exploration if that is what they choose.

Guides can change from one life to the next. They have characteristics to distinguish them, one from another. When I have been through past life regressions to the legendary ancient civilisation of Atlantis, I have been aware of having a guide who appeared in the guise of a woman. She was a very strong presence. On her head she wore a head dress with esoteric symbols on it that were very mysterious to me. She had flaming red hair. There was something mighty about her appearance but also kind. Her energy contrasts sharply with my present guide Sebastian who, although very forthright in his communication with me and very honest with deep searching eyes, has the energy of a simple, humble person. I often feel him as someone quite close to my level, whereas my Atlantean guide felt much more remote. These different guides have also reflected my soul evolution and the inner needs that I have had during various stages of my learning.

Opening to the presence of my guides has helped me to be more inwardly sensitive, but it has also brought more peace into my life.

The mechanisms for making contact with our guides are not the theme of this book. However, in as much as this inner pursuit is relevant to past life regression, I feel that the most helpful thing we can do is to affirm that we do have inner assistance. We can try to build our faith in the existence inner guides and our higher self to help and support us in our regression process. Experiences occur that feel right. We can encourage our inner journey of discovery to unfold in harmony with our needs, by expecting it to do so. If we have doubts and fears, perhaps that something awful may happen or that evil spirits may take over, the best thing is to talk these issues through with our therapist. Keeping such feelings to ourselves makes us feel more afraid and the process that much more difficult.

Dark Lives

Past life regression can be very educational. I have realised through this work that nearly any kind of experience others go through in their lives, is something I know about in my soul through my past lives. I have been female in my past lives as well as male; I have hurt people and been hurt. It is all there. When I open my heart to the experiences that live in me, it makes me want to care for people and help them. Basically I feel that we all need help, and everything that we do is connected with what others experience; underneath we all want to love and be loved.

Going through dark lives serves to further awaken our inner sensitivities. When we relive a life where we have made mistakes, and perhaps hurt people or hurt ourselves, it is likely to feel very uncomfortable inside. We will feel how we 'should' have acted, and there will be an impulse in us to make amends so that we do not repeat the same mistakes. Exploring any such life more fully we discover that, underlying whatever difficulties were encountered in that life, there have been qualities or expressions that have been suppressed. Because these qualities were not brought out in the life itself, this led to frustration resulting in pain and suffering.

Reliving the experience in regression, it is possible to recognise the qualities yearning for expression. We feel the pain and suffering from whatever trauma was in play. Allowing this trauma energetically to come to the surface can release the blockages in the subconscious mind. If, as is likely, the suppression of those qualities is an issue in our present too, this release might free energy up enabling us to feel more whole and inwardly connected. Qualities suppressed in this way usually have an element of love within them. Therefore, when these elements are reintegrated and allowed to mingle with other qualities from our being, we become more sensitive.

Coping With Sensitivity

Some souls choose to develop psychic sensitivity as part of their life plan. This may be something that they have done before in other lives. They might choose this, intending to use this gift to help and serve others, or perhaps to experience the ways of the world more intensely.

When we live a lifetime where we are more sensitive than those around us, other people may not necessarily like us for it. They can easily be envious or jealous of our gift, and thereby be unkind or even cruel towards us as a result. Sensitive people can often be the object of ridicule, bullying or condemnation because of lack of tolerance shown by others. Someone with a sensitive nature will feel this very acutely. The challenge will be about how we deal with it.

To cope with the pain of other people rejecting us, we are inclined either to hide our sensitivity, pretending that it does not exist, or else we might want to fight against those who are trying to put us down. A middle way is to assert ourselves, our rights, and not cause harm to others. To learn as a soul to live a life where we can appropriately express a sensitive natures, we have to attune inwardly and conscientiously so we can follow guidance that will help us to act rightly. It may be necessary for us to go through many lives with a sensitivity theme before we can learn to do this gracefully.

From my experience with regression, it is common for lifetimes where the soul is psychically sensitive to hold a lot of suffering. Typically, souls can turn to violence or retreat from human contact, as the only means of withstanding the pain of other people's reactions.

With these possible traumas in the background, people may not want to embrace a lifetime where they are once again psychically sensitive. At a subconscious level, it will not feel safe.

Therefore, if it is the path of a soul to be psychically sensitive in their present lifetime, it is helpful to revisit some of the lives where that soul has been psychically sensitive before. This is pertinent especially where the lives concerned were traumatic. These lives could be very dark, and difficult to endure. But approaching such experiences helps to release the fear surrounding them. The channels for that soul to feel safer being psychically sensitive in the present, will be opened.

If we go through an experience where we feel very hurt by others, we might then have to hurt them back. For someone who is psychically sensitive, when we realise that we have hurt another human being, even if it is in a past life, we feel that pain very strongly. This can happen when visiting our dark lives in regression. As a consequence we are bound to feel that we do not want to cause hurt again. Our compassion is aroused.

People with psychic sensitivity have the potential to serve and help others tremendously. Such people are often very fine healers and teachers.

Do We Want to Be Sensitive?

It is a challenge for us to decide if we want to develop our psychically sensitivity or not. Once this inner perception has begun to open, there is a pressure from within for us to continue to develop it further. I believe that our souls want us to express as much of our essence during our physical lives as possible. A lifetime where we can become psychically sensitive, gives us a great opportunity. If we resist this for some reason, we might become very unhappy. The conditions of our life may feel increasingly uncomfortable; our life will want to flow one way and we will be pulling desperately in the other direction.

If we inwardly agree to continue our inner development, it can prompt lots of anticipated changes in our lives. When we open to our sensitivity, we sense more fully the scope of whatever soul path we have chosen. While we have in place inner barriers that suppress our sensitivity, we can easily be ignorant of the actions that our soul wishes us to perform. Once those barriers are removed, we can feel compelled to be true to whatever it is that we have to do.

When we have allowed the experience from a past life to come to the surface (whether that be a lifetime where we were psychically sensitive or not) other experiences may crowd around wanting to find expression too. This may feel like a can of worms or perhaps a box of treasures, depending on our outlook. But there could be lots of things stirring inside. All past life experiences have the potential to help us with our inner development, because they enable us to become aware of further aspects of ourselves.

To summarise, deciding to open up to past life regression can be an important step to take on our spiritual path. Doing this work is likely to affect our perception of our lives, and makes us more sensitive. It is not a process to be engaged in superficially. Once we have started it is likely - unless we are very determined - that there is no turning back because our awareness will have irrevocably opened.

Chapter 17

Johanna's Story

Johanna is a young woman who has an innate capacity to be psychically sensitive. She appears to have a strong yearning to develop this sensitivity. I was delighted when she joined a workshop I was leading, because I could sense that she had a high level of openness to exploring her inner worlds.

When we reached the regression phase of the course that I was leading, Johanna accessed a past lifetime where she had been psychically sensitive. This did not surprise me. In her present life, it seemed that she had issues about the difficulties she had in fully expressing herself, and her more sensitive nature. There were blocks and fears within her about asserting herself in some aspects.

The past life that she worked upon was tragic and traumatic, probably leaving a residue of difficult emotions and beliefs about what it means to be psychically sensitive. Going through this past life, she could feel the pleasure and sense of fulfilment that this personality felt,being open to energies and healing. She also became aware of the depth of suffering that this woman had to endure. Acting as a channel for the energies of this past life, Johanna released a huge amount of emotion – an extremely liberating experience for her.

For many weeks after these sessions, I believe that Johanna continued to need to adjust herself to changes that had occurred, in the ways that her perceptions had altered, and to accept this. With these changes, she also gained much insight and self-understanding. The story of her past life work and its outcome follows next.

Johanna's Approach to Exploring Her Past Lives

My first experience of past life regression occurred during a workshop called 'The Healing Circle' that I attended, led by Paul Williamson. Prior to this workshop, I had been interested in reincarnation for some time. I had acquired the belief that a soul is on earth to learn unconditionally to love, and to recognise being part of the Divine force. And because one life is just too short to learn that, one has to go through several lives to learn and integrate this in all kinds of different situations.

There was a yearning in me to develop knowledge about my past lives. I sought the help of two psychics, who channelled information for me about some past lives that I had had. Although I did not obtain any images of my own while they were communicating with me, I felt that there was a deep truth in what they said.

I read two books about past life regression, including Paul's book, 'Healing Journeys'. From this base I felt that I was well prepared for my own regression experiences. I have to admit though, that I doubted a little bit if I would be able to access images and whether it could work for me.

During the workshop I participated in two past life group meditations and an individual session with Paul within the group. During these sessions I explored one particular lifetime. The experiences were progressive in their intensity, and I would like to describe these and some of my subsequent reactions and reflections.

Johanna's Regression Experiences

To my surprise, images came to me immediately, as soon as I entered the first meditation. I saw myself as a woman in her early twenties, with brown, ruffled up long, hair. When I looked down I noticed that I was barefoot, wearing a ripped dress. I was going on a road, leading to a town. Further down the road, I could already see the town. Around it was a large city wall. The town was on a little hill. Instinctively I had the feeling that this scene was from the Middle Ages in Germany. For some reason I knew that I had to go to the town, and at the same time I felt very uneasy. I was afraid and had an aversion: I didn't want to go to the town.

Paul directed us to be aware of our home and I saw a hut, built out of wood, near a forest, outside of the town. In the hut were one big and one small room. All in all it looked quite poor, and everything was simple. There were some dried herbs hanging down from the ceiling. I saw a little boy, about four years old, sitting at the table in the middle of the big room. He was my son. I felt a lot of love towards him. It was clear to me that I lived by myself with my son in this hut.

I was asked to focus upon my childhood next. I became aware of growing up in a poor family with many children. There were older and younger brothers and sisters, so I was in the middle of them. My mother died early, during the birth of her last child. So I was left to live with my father, my brothers and sisters, in a house in the town. It was always quite dark in there. My father had to work all the time so that we would have something to eat. Otherwise, he didn't care very much about us, and he drank a lot of alcohol. One of our older sisters was responsible for us. But I didn't feel very close to my brothers and sisters. I felt quite lonely and unhappy.

When it was suggested for us to go to an important event, I felt that I was a teenager. There was an old woman who lived in our neighbourhood and I felt drawn to her. Meeting her, she taught me a lot of things and how to make herbal medicines. I liked this woman and I was always happy when I visited her. Seeing her, I was able to escape for a while from my grey family life. This woman became very important to me, and I missed her very much when she died.

When I was directed to the time approaching my death, I saw myself again on the road that led to the town. I had to go there to get some food for my son and for myself. Again I felt the aversion to going to this town that I had felt earlier in the meditation. When I entered the town, I noticed men there who were very loud and somewhat drunk. A few of them I recognised as people of position and influence within the town. As I tried to pass them, they shouted at me and verbally abused me. I felt danger and wanted to escape from them. Suddenly somebody pointed at

165

me, screaming that I was making herbal medicines and that I was a witch. At once there were men swarming over me and forcing me to go with them. It seemed to me that the men had been just waiting for a signal so that they could do this. My main thought was fear and concern for my son.

Then I got a picture of being outside the town on a hill, tied up on a wooden stick (or it could have been a wooden cross). This was supported on a heap of wood. Two other women were next to me also tied up like me. A crowd of people was standing around us, looking at us. Some were shouting at us, but there were also some people who had a lot of fear. Even though I was afraid of what would come next, my biggest fear and worry was still about my beloved son, that I would leave him behind. My heart was full of pain.

When I died through the fire, I left my body, floating upwards. There were some light and bright beings around me. They received me and I felt very peaceful in their presence, although the worry about my son was still there. The light calmed me down and explained to me that my son would be taken care of. 'Trust us', was the last thing I heard before the meditation concluded.

On reflection, even though I was quite affected by the scenes that came to me, they were still just pictures for me. Certainly I played a role in these images, but nevertheless I stayed somehow unconcerned. And yet I felt that behind the pictures there was a depth that made me feel nervous inside.

Later on we were given the opportunity for a second past life meditation. In this, it was simply suggested that we could go into whatever events and moments from the past life were most appropriate and relevant for us to explore.

Immediately as I entered the experience, I found myself in the hut that was my home. Inside my heart I had the strong feeling of being excluded from the people of the town; they treated me like dirt. As a consequence, I felt sad and lonely. But I was not completely alone.

166

There was a friend who sometimes looked after my son and me. He was a few years older than me and a bit stocky.

Once while he was looking after my son, I went to a meeting in the forest. It was a circle of women and we were carrying out some ritual. However, I did not feel very involved with them. Using the power and strength in that circle, I wanted to call out to the mother goddess to help but there were some women in that circle who I did not trust. There was talk amongst the women that we had to be careful because we were living in a dangerous time.

From the outset, I became aware that I had been making the herbal medicine mainly as a means to survive. People would come to me and I would sell them from my home. After a while though, besides my own sorrow, I started to feel the suffering of others as well. Because I was living with my son, alone, I had a lot of time to think about life and what human beings endured.

One day I was told a story about Jesus, in which He had placed His hands on people to heal them. Inspired by this, I tried placing my hands on a man who visited me for help, and discovered that I could channel healing too. Suddenly I developed a lot of sympathy and compassion for people, and felt that I could give something to them.

Again I went through the events that took place in the town before my death in more detail. Someone was screaming accusations that I was a woman selling herbal medicines. They were calling me 'Lisa'. After they had captured me, I was taken into a stone house and interrogated. I was hit several times and it hurt me very much. Trying to proclaim my innocence, they took no notice of me. Why did I have to come near these men? – I blamed myself. And all the time I was thinking of my son.

From the experience of my death, the main impression I had was of the guilt I felt in leaving my son. This impressed itself upon me.

The thoughts I had on finishing this meditation concerned the importance of that life in developing my compassion towards other human beings, in spite of suffering exclusion and rejection.

As I returned from this second meditation, I noticed how much more involved I had felt emotionally in the story this time. I felt that I was on the edge of needing to release some very strong emotions and, although I was afraid of losing control, I knew that it was important for me to approach this past life more directly through a one-to-one session. Also, I wanted to learn how that past life linked into my life now, and I felt that working with Paul individually could help me achieve that.

When I lay down to start my session, I could feel a mixture of feelings ranging from apprehension and fear to excitement. As I began to speak aloud about the experiences I was having, I could feel a swirling of emotions inside me. I knew that with Paul's help, I needed to approach some of the darkest moments of this life. It was from these places that my feelings wanted to erupt.

To begin with, I was sitting with my son and my male friend at the table in my hut, eating soup. Although I trusted my friend, I did not wish to tell him about the women circle that I attended. One reason for this was that I did not feel that he would understand what we were doing, and he might worry. But it was also dangerous to be associated with people doing those things and I wanted to protect him. It was difficult for me because the rituals that we did in this circle were very precious but it did not feel safe.

Paul asked me to focus upon the women in the circle that I did not trust. I became aware of one woman of whom I felt afraid. She had a role in the group as a leader, but I felt that her heart was cold. At Paul's insistence, I moved to the situation where I felt the most fear of her. This was an incident where she threatened the safety of my son if I did not obey her. There was something very dark about this woman, and I became very anxious about her threat.

It was soon after this that I made my last trip into the town. My body was releasing much emotion and fear. Further images emerged for me of the suffering I endured in the moments leading to my death.

I felt the men beating me after they had interrogated me in the stone building. Then I was put in another dark room by myself, all tied up. A man came into this room. He said that he wanted to help me, but he just wanted my body. I tried to move aside from his advances, but the ropes constricting me meant that I was helpless to stop him. Even though I tried to defend myself, he was stronger, and he raped me. But I would not submit willingly, and he didn't like that at all. He had his hands around my neck to strangle me. I knew that he wanted to kill me, but we both knew that he wasn't allowed to do so. Therefore he left me alive. Then I felt even more desperate. How could this happen to me? I felt so dirty, abused, and physically very weak.

But then I was being led with the other two women, one of whom I knew from the women circle, to the hill outside the town. People were shouting and throwing things at us. In some of their faces, I could also see fear and revulsion. But I could again only think of my son. Now I realised that I was concerned for his well being, not only because of my forthcoming death and absence from his life, but because of that woman and her threat to him?

As the burning commenced I felt fear, and then indignation and anger. In the regression I was shouting out, 'You cannot do that; I hate you; you don't have a right to do that...'

But then, as they lit the logs under me, I felt more that they didn't understand what they were doing. It was very hot, and I felt the fire like needles on my skin; it hurt very much. Somehow, though, I didn't suffer much from the fire, because I left my body very early. Four beings received me and they were so loving and kind.

As I continued to express concern for my son, Paul suggested that I move forward to a moment when I could observe what happened to my son. Then I noticed that my male friend was offering him comfort and taking care of him.

Finally Paul suggested for me to go to a place of peace, and I sensed the presence of a big blue-white being full of love. Very slowly I felt peace arising in me. Only then, I realised how tense and contracted my body had become during the regression. It took some moments to let myself relax. Accompanying the relaxation I felt lightness in my being, but I was also very exhausted, and dazed.

169

After Thoughts and Integration

In the days and weeks following this regression, I spent much time considering how this past life related to the life I was living now. Many thoughts came to me. What I released, especially in the final session with Paul, came from a very deep place within me. For some days, I had a fever and felt physically very weak. This indicated the need for me to be gentle with myself while everything was digested and assimilated.

The regression made me aware of a border that I have around my heart. This border is there to protect me from people who might hurt me, but it also prevents the love from flowing freely from my heart, and even for people reaching me from their hearts. At the end of that past life, I lost confidence in people and in the order of the world, suffering guilt, too, for having to leave my beloved son behind. Experiencing injustice, abuse and humiliation, when I only wanted to help people, I found very hard. It reminded me of my life now, when I have tended to feel guilty and responsible for things that are not actually my fault, and frustrated when I have known that I could not have behaved differently. I feel that the regression has helped to free me somewhat from the fears I felt toward other people regarding their judgement of me.

In my present life I have never been abused by men, and yet I have felt very sensitive and inhibited when in the company of loud or aggressive men. When I have been standing in a crowd of men, or even very close to them, I have felt very uncomfortable and unable to breathe normally. My instinct has been to want to get away as fast as possible.

When I was a child I was very shy within groups. If I was with a few people, then I felt OK. However, if it was a larger gathering with people that I did not know, I could feel very panicky. My response was to be very quiet and passive, just as I reacted in the past life.

At school, when I was about eleven, there was a girl in my class who had a lot of power. Nobody, even the boys, would dare to confront her or say anything against her. She could be very mean. After a while, I became one of her targets and I became very afraid of her. Over a period of some months, I suffered a lot through her intimidation. When Paul asked me if I could identify the soul of the woman who, in the past life, threatened my son, I knew immediately that it was this girl.

170

Later on, when I was fifteen, I went through a process whereby I was able to forgive myself for not standing up to her verbal attacks. Then I could forgive her for having hurt me. Doing this gave me a lot of peace in myself. I believe now that she has come once again into my present life as a test for me, and I am glad that I could find peace with her this time.

Another interesting link between that life and this is the prickly feeling that I have sometimes had when the weather is very hot, or when I have been in the company of a lot of people. In one situation, when I was ten years old, I was performing a play with my class in front of a lot of people in the assembly hall of my school. Feeling very nervous, we were about to start when my skin began to hurt, especially in the face, as if there would be a thousand needles prickling me. This was exactly the same feeling that I had in the past life regression, when the people burned me.

Increased Sensitivity

Since undergoing my regression, I have felt 'lighter'. For many nights afterwards, I had clear dreams that wanted to show me things, and feelings from within me that needed to be healed. In the course of my everyday life, I have felt more sensitive and vulnerable. This has been particularly apparent within my family, where I have felt very clearly aware of the dynamics of how the members of my family relate to each other. Somehow I have also felt less attached and more able to let go of things that formerly had bothered me.

I feel that the experience of this past life has given me a much deeper understanding of myself, and a broader perspective of the meaning of the situations and challenges that I have had to face. Slowly, I feel that the border around my heart is disappearing. My vulnerability, I believe, is an outcome of this, and I have also felt a little lost at times, as if I am in an open space.

What has been most strong in me since the past life is the desire and drive to serve and help people, and do healing within groups. In the past life, the impulse to do this awoke in me, but I was unable to fulfil my wishes to any great degree. I hope that in my present life, the opportunity will be given to me to go further with this. My intuition tells me that I will, and I feel a lot of joy at this possibility.

Chapter 18

Past Lives and Healing the Inner Child

When people recall memories of earlier times in their present life, through guided meditation or hypnosis, this is generally approached with a method called 'age regression'. In this way, people are able to recall memories from their present life that, with their normal consciousness, they might have forgotten. When undergoing age regression, it is possible to make use of outside sources to confirm the authenticity or otherwise of what is being experienced.

Our present life memories are stored in our subconscious minds. The process of regression then invokes specific memories from our subconscious minds, so that we can become consciously aware of them. Another way to access memories from our subconscious is when we dream, but dreams are usually mixed up with other experiences and information that we are processing internally. Regression under the guidance of a therapist can bring forth memories more systematically and without the intrusion of other experiences. However, the way that people perceive things when undergoing regression is very similar to dreaming.

Even familiar experiences, accessed through regression, will generally have more substance to them. Most of our conscious memories will have substantial subconscious aspects. These subconscious elements will be experienced more directly and emotionally through regression. Thus the experience of regression will have more of a living presence about it, than when we remember things in our usual manner.

Some people are more easily able to journey into their subconscious than others. Our subconscious mind operates in a very different way to our normal consciousness. To utilise our subconscious, we need to be passively aware so that we allow experiences existing within us to arise and be revealed. We can influence what comes forward by calling inwardly that which we seek. Usually our therapist will do this on our behalf.

Asking people to go further back into their memories easily extends age regression, resulting in the manifestation of past life memories. Of course, it is not easy to verify past life regression experiences as authentic. However, the experience of regressing to past lives appears just as real as reliving childhood memories. Both types of regression can display high levels of thought and emotional content, and stimulate strong bodily responses. Regression in both cases uses the imaginative faculty of our minds. The challenge for all of us when doing regression work is to be able to trust in the imaginative faculty of our minds - that this will bring forth 'true' experiences and not just something that we have created out of our desires.

When I am working with a client and I ask to go to the source of a problem, the inner consciousness of the person may come up with an experience from childhood just as often as from a past life. I define regression memories of childhood as inner child experiences, because they utilise the subconscious inner memory of having been a child. The inner child experience and events from past life memory can be manifestations of two layers concerning the root of a problem. In terms of my work with clients, allowing either experience to come to the surface so that we can work at it can have a healing and beneficial effect.

Inner child work and past life regression can both have a profoundly transformational effect upon our being. I feel that childhood memories and the experiences of past lives are part of a continuum, and one is not therefore more important than the other. Just as certain past lives can link and relate to each other, relationships can also exist between past lives and inner childhood experiences from our present life. Many threads worth exploring exist between the earlier experiences of our present life and what can be revealed as our past lives.

Although they may be part of the same continuum of consciousness, my approach to work with either inner child or past life problems is quite distinct. For both therapies, my essential aim is likely to be the same. My basic intention is to help that person to feel greater wholeness and integration of being. Generally this implies a need to visit particular memories where the problems existed at a more formative stage.

When I encounter a memory stemming from my client's childhood, I need to consider the consciousness of the child. Often, because of their dependency upon adults and their awe of the power of adults to impose their will, children will not necessarily feel able to express all that they are feeling in a particular situation. They might learn and copy patterns of behaviour from their parents, even though in their hearts they may not feel that this is how they wish to be. Children may take on beliefs about themselves because of what they are told even though these beliefs may not be true and could have a diminishing effect upon them.

The most important aspect of inner child therapy is helping people to untangle themselves from reactions and projections stemming from their child consciousness that could be to do with their parents, other people or whatever the problematic situation has been. That child consciousness can now identify with the adult consciousness and, with love and care, it may be possible for those two facets of consciousness to be united wherever there are blocks.

The child consciousness may be filled with fears and patterns that make such unity very difficult to achieve. For example, a woman who had an over protective mother, who didn't let her children go out and play except in strictly limited circumstances, may then have difficulties as an adult in relaxing and being able to enjoy leisurely activities. The child consciousness within that woman may be filled with an inner fear of her mother reaction if she stepped beyond the boundaries of what her mother allowed. This child may never have felt able to assert herself because of her fear concerning her mother's authority and power.

In a therapy situation it is useful to encourage an inner connection between that child consciousness and her adult self. With the help of the strength of the adult consciousness, the child may then be able to express her feelings to her mother in a way that she never felt able to do in the actual childhood. The child will not really be expressing these things to her mother, but to the representation of her mother that she has retained in her consciousness. This inner representation of her mother could be largely illusory or it might still correspond closely with the truth. But the adult woman will not want her own behaviour to be dictated by the fears and inhibitions that her child consciousness has retained.

By expressing feelings that have not yet been asserted, the child consciousness can begin to dismantle the projection of power that she felt her mother had over her. Quite a strong energy can be released as long suppressed feelings are let out, in turn making a significant difference to how the child consciousness perceives her situation. It can also naturally encourage her to feel more united with her adult self, and the desires of her adult self that have not been realised. It becomes possible to then nurture confidence within the child consciousness, so that she can do more of the activities that she really wants to do - without fear. At this point, I usually suggest that the adult consciousness invites the child consciousness into her heart. This is like 'coming home', a uniting of these different parts of the woman's being. In doing this, the woman can feel a great sense of peace and wholeness, that was missing until now.

Connecting with the child consciousness - helping to express what had previously been withheld, with the strength of the adult – leads to many useful therapeutic results. Much energetic fear can be released this way so that inner barriers are removed and the person can feel significantly happier. Initially the inner child in need of help requires much reassurance and acceptance from the adult consciousness, so that he or she can feel safe. Only when we feel safe can we allow any suppressed emotions attached to fear to be released.

Fear freezes energy within our systems that otherwise would flow and be part of our inner development. In this way, parts of our child consciousness can be frozen out by fear and those parts then stop developing. Those parts exist as units of living consciousness that have memory and other attributes. When they are frozen they become beyond our reach. Therefore, when we can connect with them again and give them adult strength to overcome their fear, bringing those missing parts into our hearts and being can help us to embrace qualities that we may have thought missing in us. We need some time for adjustment when we reconcile such parts into ourselves again.

One of my clients grew up in an atmosphere where his stepfather was very violent and controlling towards him. At some point, he closed up and decided that it was not safe to let anyone come close to him. Since then, even though he has had his share of relationships, he has always felt alone. It has also been his wish to keep people at a distance so that he could control his own interactions with them. When people disturbed him so that he felt vulnerable, he tended to lash out especially at other men. During the course of his life, he has hurt several men physically, and has acquired a reputation whereby people would be very wary about approaching him too closely.

A crucial event in his life has been the birth of his son. In his heart he has wanted to love his son and protect him. He has recognised that in his son, he perceives himself and the way that he was as a young child. Thus, he has started to question himself and ask how he can love himself.

In therapy my client has been able to share about aspects of his life and his feelings normally undisclosed to others. Through inner work it is clear that the tendency to lash out violently, and the fear of letting others come close, have their roots in other lives as well as in the present. But as he has shared more with me, and opened himself up to receiving healing, my client's body has started shaking. During our sessions, this shaking has grown from slight trembling to the extent where his body would sometimes be writhing uncontrollably. I have encouraged him to allow this process to take place and he has trusted me. I believe that the shaking has been a release of all the fear that he has stored and suppressed over the years. He has felt himself become lighter and acknowledged the progress that has been made. It seems that the aspect of his inner child consciousness that has been affected is the part that could allow him to reach out for closeness with others. Without that part functioning, he has lived a lonely life.

I have tried to approach those places in him where, in an altered state of consciousness, he would feel vulnerable to others coming close to him.

At these moments, he has felt the impulse to lash out and be violent. However, in his heart, he does not want to behave like that anymore. Instead, I have encouraged him to breathe with what he feels, and this has triggered further shaking and the release of fear.

My client knows that the work we are doing is helping him. At the time of writing, my work with him is ongoing. I am hopeful that at some point, the fear that he has stored will be fully released. Then, my client will hopefully allow that part of his child consciousness that wants to reach out for love much greater expression. I feel that he could then truly have the opportunity to build a life with much greater happiness than he has managed until now.

Therapeutic practices of healing associated with past life therapy are in many ways similar to inner child therapy but with some differences. In past life work there is a need to discover aspects of the experience that are hidden, as with inner child work. It is also essential to allow a space for the release of suppressed feelings, and the acknowledgement of limiting beliefs and attitudes. However, in past life work this usually takes place in the spirit realm, after the past life personality has died. Before this, it is necessary to go through the main stages of that particular life thoroughly and in depth. What people may receive, as healing in the spiritual realm, will reflect what has been discerned from the life itself.

With past life therapy, we are dealing with the perspective of a whole life including the childhood, and even the experience that follows after the physical life has ended. The scope of this is much greater than with inner child therapy, where the therapist's concern is focused upon the expression of child consciousness and its integration with the adult self.
From a broader perspective, the patterns of various lives may blend from one into another. Problems relating to our childhood experience may correspond with past life memories, where there have been challenges that were not met and that were not fully integrated at the time. There can also be polarities of experience that will give meaning to one's present circumstances. I will give an example to illustrate this.

Some time ago, I had a client who struggled with the fact that her father was an alcoholic. From her childhood right up to adult years, she had suffered much abuse and neglect as a result of this. When she did a past life regression with me, she discovered that in a recent past life, she had been an alcoholic man, and that one of her children then was the same soul as her present father. Such realisation did not change her present situation but perhaps helped her to begin to come to terms with it and accept her father rather than perpetuate bitterness and negativity towards him.

There can be situations that we confront in our childhood that have similarities with dynamics from certain past lives. The souls involved may be the same, or a set of circumstances from our childhood evokes feelings and thoughts that resonate with the past life. The reason that this past life is coming up could be because in that experience, the personality then did not deal with that particular situation well. Sometimes, patterns can extend themselves over several lives until the soul learns how to deal with them.

We bring attributes and subconscious memories from particular lives into our early life because these relate to the qualities that we need to express in order to grow. This can be the test for our soul that we are giving ourselves. It is up to us how we react to any given set of circumstances that we create for ourselves. When we consider our parents, brothers and sisters, our talents and gifts, our temper and all the various things about us, these may be attributes that we as souls have chosen. It is our free will to determine what we make of our life and how we respond to the challenges that confront us.

During the course of our life, if we spontaneously find that we are disturbed by thoughts, body sensations or images connected with a past life, it won't be an accident that this is happening. Something in our everyday life will have triggered this. In all likelihood, the theme of the past life may also have something to teach us about whatever issues we may be confronting in our life nowadays. We can welcome these memories because they can help us to learn our soul lessons. Similarly, we may be disturbed with thoughts and feelings associated with our childhood as well, with the same implications.

As we are confronted with life's challenges as souls, these are tests for our character. There are many different means as to how we are able to receive help to deal with our problems. Past life therapy and inner child therapy are just two approaches that can serve to prompt necessary inner change and transformation to take place.

Chapter 19

Ancient Connections from Our Past

Many people, when they first undertake past life regression access lives from the last few hundred years or so. Presumably, these comparatively recent lives have elements to them that are closer to what we need, to work out our present existences and therefore nearer to the forefront of our inner memories. But this is not always the case.

Sometimes people feel drawn to past life memory from a very ancient source, as a key to an issue that they are grappling with now. This work can be quite fascinating not only from the therapeutic standpoint but also because it brings forth experiences where people - in these past incarnations - can express behaviour and capabilities very different from those we exhibit today. The cultural setting of these lives can be of interest as models of societies quite distinct from our own.

Included here are case studies from two of my clients, Angelika and Nikki, to show how the spontaneous exploration of very ancient lives was relevant to each of them in their current situations, and also to use their experiences to illustrate some of the more interesting past life settings that can occur.

Angelika

My impression of Angelika is that she is a very serious and deep-thinking individual. Initially she made contact with me as a result of her having read the book that I co-authored with Lynda Braithwaite, *Atlantis - The Dark Continent*.

For many years Angelika had been seeking to gain spiritual knowledge and live in a spiritually oriented culture. Inside her she felt a deep sadness that she could not find this where she lived. After spending one and a half years in India, she decided to dedicate herself towards transferring aspects of old spiritual traditions into our western modern life. She felt quite alone in her efforts to do this, and frustrated that so many people appeared to be disrespectful towards what she considered to be the sacred and the beautiful. Angelika's instinct told her that her sadness and despair associated with this went deeper than her present life struggles. She was determined to seek for answers.

After attending what she called a 'releasing therapy' session with a woman who claimed to psychically tune into her past lives, Angelika was told that she had lived a traumatic life during the time of the destruction of Atlantis, and that this experience had affected her very negatively.

Until then, Angelika had known very little about Atlantis, but what this woman told her felt instinctively very right. Her enthusiasm was fired up to discover more about this subject. It was, of course, from here that she found my book; however she was interested enough to want to learn through her own experiences and not only from what other people told her.

Even though she had not met me, Angelika decided to attend my residential workshop in Scotland, and follow it up with an individual retreat with me where she could explore her past life experiences further. During this time she accessed three past lives that she was able to study in depth. They were all from very ancient sources. One of them was, as might have been expected, from Atlantis, but not the one from the time of the destruction. The other past lives were linked to this one, but from quite different places.

I would like to describe her experiences with reference to the account that she wrote for me.

Life 1

The first life that she accessed was the one in Atlantis. She started exploring this during the workshop, continuing it in our individual work. It was an oppressive life, one in which she was a male healer struggling with corrupt officials who wanted to use 'divine forces', as Angelika put it, for their own ends.

In her account she included descriptions of stone buildings, crowded streets, healing temples and a power-hungry government - all of which were only too familiar. I recognised the atmosphere of the life she depicted from research I had done when writing 'Atlantis - The Dark Continent', and sensed very strongly that it dated from the period leading up to the destruction of the land. Because of the sense of foreboding that she felt as this healer, it would not surprise me if it was the lifetime immediately adjacent to that incarnation where she was present during the fall of Atlantis.

As this healer, Angelika's soul was aspiring to be as morally righteous as he could be. His attitude became very hardened toward those that were perverting the sacred. This extended to his wife - he had no tolerance for her sympathy with the prevailing trends of the day. In fact an argument he had with her about this led to her death after he had physically assaulted her in anger. As time went on he became increasingly isolated and desperate.

The crucial events of this lifetime centred around the instances of horrific torture that he endured, as the officials tried to persuade him to work on their behalf. He steadfastly hung on to his righteous allegiance at the cost of his life, but felt completely alone, bitter and deserted in doing so. Although he felt that he had to be true to his principles, he could not understand why the divine forces could not have supported him more. Following his death, as he left the physical plane, it seemed to him that there was nothing sacred left to defend anywhere; it had all gone. This left in him a dreadful feeling of despondency and despair.

I tried to point out to Angelika how, in the hardness of his views, this healer's heart had closed down, and so he could not experience the support that was there for him spiritually.

Angelika, as she tried to analyse the situation mentally, could not understand how that healer could have acted differently and still have maintained his integrity. How could anyone allow the destructive forces to win and take control? Yet there was something about the way that the healer tried to hang on to the truth, and right way of doing things at all costs, that disturbed her.

Angelika was aware that in the work project for which she was responsible in Germany, there was again a situation where she felt that she had to hang on. It was as though, if she did not do all the things that were required to keep things going, then nobody else would. In this position, Angelika felt lonely and isolated.

Life 2

As she focussed upon these feelings in meditation, Angelika sensed that there was a wound around the theme of hanging onto what was precious, and a feeling associated with this, that was desperate and very alone. An image came to her of something bright blue, and she sensed that she could be in a cave or even in space. Nearby there were other beings surrounding her, and they were not very friendly.

This image was the entry point for Angelika to explore the second past life in her work with me. It was quite an extraordinary life in some ways because she was not human, and it did not feel to her or I that she was on Earth. We sensed that it was a very ancient life from a time when her soul was very young and placed in a different planetary system from our own. Yet it also became clear that the traumatic experience that she suffered then had made a deep imprint upon her soul.

In this regression she experienced herself initially as travelling through outer space. She did not sense that she had a physical body, but she did have some form of energy body. Somehow she was able to propel herself through space without needing a space ship. She felt very child-like, lively and curious about exploring the universe and various planetary systems. Landing on a planet, she noticed that it was coloured grey with some interesting dark bluish spots on it. She was drawn to a big indefinable object with a kind of entrance. Going in there, she felt that she was in a form of cave or labyrinth. Suddenly she could go no further and was caught. There were grey energy beings around her and she felt very frightened in their presence. She felt as though they could do anything they wanted to her and that they did not care what happened to her.

From many angles she sensed an electrical flash that they used like a lasso to trap her further. Now she could not move and felt that they were blowing more and more energy into her system. This feeling was unpleasant and filled her with horror. Her thought was that if she did not hang on with all her might then she might explode and fall into thousands of pieces. So urgent was the feeling that it reminded her very much of the desperate hanging on she had felt in the Atlantis regression.

At some point the explosion did take place. Her will to stop it was not enough. She saw dazzling white spots of light and thought that this would be her end. But then she found herself on the ground outside this labyrinth, still on this planet. Feeling shocked, she was glad at first to be alone. Then she sensed that something had changed. Inside what she felt to be her heart, there was a stone-like heaviness - something precious from within her was no longer there. They had taken it.

At once, her innocence and her joy in life were gone. Quickly she travelled back to her home planet, where she retreated and felt disillusioned for the rest of her existence as this being.

When she returned to normal consciousness from this experience, Angelika did not know quite what to make of this experience. The content of the regression went far beyond what she felt that she could have imagined was there. It disturbed her greatly that these beings could have taken something that was fundamental to her being.

It was a great relief to her when, shortly afterwards, it was suggested from a channelled source that, although something energetic was removed from her being in that incarnation, those beings could not reach her soul. A scar remained from that experience, but the missing energy had been retrieved long, long ago.

Life 3

Moving on from this, Angelika wanted to access a life that would be pertinent to the themes raised in the first two regressions, but also be relevant to her present situation. This led her into her third past life, an incarnation from ancient Egypt.

Ancient Egypt is a term usually assumed to refer to the Classical Egyptian civilisation that goes back to 3000-4000 BC. However, from my research into past lives, I believe that there was an earlier high civilisation of Egypt that began with the fall of Atlantis about 10000 BC. This society benefited from the practises and technologies that people from Atlantis had brought with them when Atlantis was destroyed. This civilisation lasted, I believe, for about three thousand years and then virtually died out, only to be resurrected again some thousands of years later.

The lifetime that Angelika accessed was, I think, from the earlier civilisation of Egypt, but interestingly it is still the most recent of the three incarnations that Angelika recalled.

In this experience, Angelika found herself to be the male son of a powerful political leader. As he grew up, he was taught about spiritual and psychic awareness in addition to the more secular leadership functions that he needed to learn.

He was initiated by his teacher whilst still a youth and, when a special crown was placed upon his head, he experienced a strong steady sun-like energy. His consciousness became very clear - focussed and expanded at the same time. The effect of this initiation was quite intoxicating for him. Becoming a member of a circle of initiates, the group in which he belonged regularly invoked Spiritual energy for rituals and to help with the well-being of the community. They had high ethical standards and rules for procedures so that the powers that they channelled would not be abused.

As his political power base was established, he became leader of this spiritual group. He enjoyed the sense of authority that his position gave him and keenly sought for others to respect his elevated status. Over a period of time, he increasingly identified what he perceived as being 'right' with a need to protect and 'hold on' to his position. Being the main keeper of the energies within the temple where he worked, he had unlimited opportunity to experiment with these. Although he was hesitant about doing this at first, he found that he could utilise the psychic powers he was able to invoke to help further his own ends.

Initially his intentions in doing this were quite innocent, but they grew less so the more he did it. At some point there was jealousy among the members about some privileges that were being administered. Disturbed by this he decided that he wanted to re-establish harmony; in private, he invoked the light energy, and with his mind he used his will to create a bond of harmony in the circle of his group, so that there would be no more dissension. The power flowed through him as he did this ritual, and he knew at its completion that it had been successful. This was the first step in a process where he increasingly used the energy as a tool for manipulation of others.

Angelika did not access all the instances where he, as this spiritual and political leader, had abused his powers. In the next stage of how this progressed, was a young man from his political circles who did not like him and who started to undermine his reputation. To counter this, he connected to the power of the energy source and created a ray of energy from his third eye. With his mind, he directed it like a laser beam to this young man's will. The ritual worked in that it disabled his rival's intentions, but this young man became mentally ill. His will was virtually destroyed and he could not function in any normal way any more.

Angelika's soul, as this leader, felt some regret about this but justified it as doing important work, feeling that the criticism levelled at him was not warranted. However, the more he utilised the powers to uphold his own position the more resentment and opposition grew against him. I'm sure that sensitive people were there, who could sense the darkness around him.

At some stage there were enemy troops attacking their community. In an extraordinary use of his powers, this leader invoked the energy he could utilise, and in his mind created an illusory fireball that would manifest in

187

front of his opponents as they moved to attack. The creation of this energy did actually frighten the enemy sufficiently for them to retreat from the battle. However, instead of being lauded for his achievements the leader instead attracted more resentment and resistance to his rule. He tried very much to appear to be good, and largely believed that what he was doing was for the good of all, but really he was using his will to try and control the forces operating around him and strengthen his position be doing so. It did not work.

A rival emerged, a man with charisma and integrity. This man inspired the masses and spoke out about the corruption of power at the head of government. The leader felt drawn to this man but also repelled by the threat that he posed. Soon he resolved that this man would have to go.

Using the energy in the middle of the night, the leader directed it as a force to still this man's heart. In the morning he was reported as dead. More and more people grew suspicious and the leader tried desperately to quell their will with his power. But one night a group of them came to his room, took him out and had him speared to death.

FuRtheR Thoughts

This lifetime shared many elements with the other two. It was obviously a darker life, one that prompted Angelika to question herself and her use of power and control. There was a sense of her soul in this incarnation needing to hold on to his position at all costs. In his isolation, this leader also believed that only he could do what was necessary for the people. There was some arrogance here. It appeared to me to be a case in all three lives, of needing to learn to trust in 'Thy Will' rather than 'my will' being done.

Such lessons are not necessarily easy to learn. All these lives presented themes that Angelika could recognise only too well as challenges facing her in her present life, especially in the area of her work. Following these regressions Angelika felt that she could breathe more easily. She felt the urge to let go of some activities in her life and give her self more time for contemplation.

From the evidence of these three lives, it is apparent that Angelika is quite an 'old' soul. She has probably had to cope with many experiences and learn many lessons over many lives. It would appear that she still has an agenda to fulfil on her soul path, and digesting these ancient experiences seems to be part of that.

All of Angelika's regressions were, I believe, quite authentic experiences. The way in which she was able to manipulate energies to kill people and affect battles in the Egyptian life, I have encountered before in other examples. It has been suggested that in the formation and placement of some of the temples and pyramids of ancient Egypt, directed psychic energy was used. I feel that such suggestions are not without foundation. In a regression that I went through from the earliest Egyptian period, I felt myself to be an overseer of the construction of one of these temples where such a process was enacted. I must have been around quite a bit in this early Egyptian time, for Angelika also identified my soul as one of the characters she encountered in her Egyptian lifetime. From my own bodily reactions, I believe that she was correct.

Regression experiences from Atlantis have been well documented in my book 'Atlantis - The Dark Continent', and tally well with Angelika's own report. As far as incarnating into other planetary systems is concerned, this is also an occurrence that is not so rare in my clients. There is the strong implication from some of these experiences that our Earthly civilisation may once have been seeded by beings who had travelled to our planet from other worlds.

Nikki

Nikki came with her partner to attend a residential workshop that I was leading. She was a bubbly, positive young woman in her twenties, full of vitality and enthusiasm. However, at the same time, I could sense her timidity and fear. It was interesting to me that someone of Nikki's age could be engaging upon a spiritual path already. Others in the group felt that she was fortunate to be making progress in this way whilst still so young. Yet Nikki also had problems that were no less pressing than the others', because of her age. She was clearly a deep thinker and her search for inner understanding was quite genuine.

The main issue that she presented centred on the struggles that she had in relation to her mother. When we came to do our past life regression, the energy dynamics of the difficulties existing between her soul and her mother's featured very prominently.

She was understandably nervous before entering the regression, but once in it, she immersed herself fully in the process. The past lifetime is very simple, and the account she gives reads almost like a fairy story with its content including elements such as mind control and draining energy. Yet, from my experience, I feel her regression is quite authentic and relates to a culture from our remote past where these capabilities really did exist. Below is her regression as recorded in her own words:

Nikki's Past Life

'...I am in a tower. It is cold and damp. The stones are cold to touch and I shiver. I am afraid, but also overcome with curiosity. I can see a faint light towards the top of the tower and I am drawn to it. I want to know what is there.

I look down and see myself in a long blue gown. It is edged in gold embroidery and it touches the floor so I am unable to see my feet. I gather my dress in my hands and begin to climb the winding stairs. My hair falls forward as I do so and I push it back over my shoulders. It is long, blond and falls heavily down my back. I stop to look behind me to see if anyone is there, but I am alone, even though I don't feel alone. I look upwards towards the light and my heart quickens. I am afraid, but I know I must go on.

I reach the top and see a brown, wooden door with no handle. I pause and again feel myself shiver. Light is shining from underneath the door and through the cracks in the wood, and I reach out my hand to push it open. I can see by my hand that I am young in age, but I am wearing a ring with a ruby stone for its centre and I know that I am married. Slowly, I peer inside.

I see a woman sitting towards the back of the room. She is wearing a black cloak and she is crouched over a stool. The room is round and there are two windows. It is dark outside and there is no moonlight. The only light I can see is from a candle that has been placed upon the floor in the

centre of the room. I look again at the woman. She is old, but I am unable to see her face.

I sense then, that we are not alone and that something else is present, watching. I look around me and hear movement in the shadows on my left, towards the floor – a rat, I think. I can just make out some eyes. It has stopped still now and is watching me in silence, hidden by a darkness that seems to creep around the edges of the room.

The woman continues to look down and I feel drawn by a power that surrounds her. I have to move closer to see her face and as I do so she looks up at me. I don't recognise her. She has white hair and I feel uneasy. I don't like her and get a sense of foreboding. She is smiling but it is not a friendly smile, rather a cruel, knowing one. She looks deep into my eyes and I feel like I can't move. I am very afraid now. A powerful force keeps me transfixed and I stand motionless. I begin to feel extremely weak, as though all my energy is being drained from me by this woman, but there is nothing that I can do to pull away. I am not strong enough and she just looks into my eyes, seeming to grow in strength and power.

I can hardly stand now. I feel incredibly weak and dizzy. I crumple to the floor and tears are flowing down my face. The woman continues to smile and the eyes are still watching from the shadows. I try to push up from the floor, but it is no use. I no longer have the energy. I realise then that it is too late. This woman has fed off my life's energy and now I am dying.

My body falls still as I let it go and look down upon the scene. The old woman is there staring and the eyes still watch from the shadows. Then, the old woman looks up and I begin to move away. She is laughing now, and I feel an incredible sadness as I think of my children, left now without their mother…'

It wasn't until the end of the regression with Paul that I learnt about the soul identity of the old woman. She was my mother – both in that lifetime and in this current one.

Afterwards, I was very tired physically. The experience, as I went through it, was emotionally taxing and left me feeling drained. Over the next days, I did a lot of thinking. Mine was quite a dark life. I learnt more about it when I ventured into a second regression to the same lifetime. It made me question about my relationships now, especially my relationship to my mother. There were dynamics in the experience where I was able to relate relationships now to then, so I questioned those things. I needed space to come to terms with them.

Further Thoughts

The theme of needing to assert her independence from her mother was very strong throughout this workshop. Nikki's past life experience further emphasised that. Afterwards, there was some improvement in her ability to relate to her mother, not to be overpowered by her, but I suspect that she may need to address this issue further when she is ready.

In accessing that lifetime, she had glimpses of other similar, more recent lives, but this one seemed to contain the most energy. The dynamic of the power struggle between these two souls was an issue that had been presented many times in various lifetimes, in an attempt for both of them to find balance and harmony, and perhaps to let each other go. In her present life Nikki was facing this test again. It is no wonder that the regression provoked her to be deeply thoughtful.

I intuited the setting of her past life to be ancient Lemuria. This was a highly developed civilisation that I believe to have pre-dated Atlantis, and it represented a fascinating but very dark culture. Some other clients have also accessed lives from this land. From my own regressions, I feel that it was a place where I had several incarnations. The existences of towers and psychic energy attack are two of the main features of Lemuria. It appears that it was a place where people cultivated the use of psychic energy to increase their personal power. People were able to leave their bodies and manipulate energy in all kinds of ways. They had many skills.

192

Unfortunately the use of psychic energy was much abused, resulting in a great deal of hurt and destruction. For a lot of souls, it was not a very nice place to be. I feel that the psychic depletion of the land ultimately destroyed it.

I feel that Nikki, like Angelika, is an old soul. Being aware of her sensitivity, she probably has a lot of latent psychic ability and healing potential that she could use for the benefit of others. Accessing some of her ancient lives, and especially the darker ones, could help her to gain a deeper understanding of this – and of her true path as an individual.

Chapter 20

Dealing with Sceptics

I do not only do past life regression with people who believe in it: some clients remain sceptical about whether reincarnation actually takes place; others, whilst feeling it to be true, doubt their own ability to access these memories - even when presented with the evidence of past life stories emerging from their inner consciousness.

We are all entitled to our own beliefs and it is certainly not my place as a therapist to try and manipulate these. The best approach we can have to our own belief systems is for us to be true to what we feel is right in our hearts. If we are open to testing and challenging our beliefs, we can learn about reality. In the end it is our choice, whatever we decide upon. Being on a spiritual path is largely about a commitment to discovering the truth. We are all going to have our own unique journey towards this.

The issue that I want to raise here concerns people who are either closed or sceptical with regards to reincarnation. Can people with this outlook gain anything worthwhile from pursuing past life therapy?

Human beings can be quite complex: a part of us may enthusiastically embrace the theory of reincarnation while another part of us wants nothing to do with it. An encounter with past life regression can provide the context for a struggle between these conflicting outlooks.

Clearly, past life regression therapy has the profound potential to challenge our existing beliefs on a very deep level. Even so, our beliefs are not going to change unless this is what we decide on and wish for.

Past life experiences can easily be interpreted as metaphors emerging from our inner consciousness that give us insights about our lives. Their origins remain a mystery if we are not prepared to believe that they are actual memories of past lives.

For regression therapy to be a worthwhile experience for sceptics, there needs to be an openness to exploring our inner consciousness, to try and release any preconditions or expectations about what we can allow to be there. If we remain closed to past life therapy as an idea, we can have an experience of regression that challenges our mental stability. We could then be very hostile towards it. In such a situation, I do not recommend that person to even try it.

I would like to include two case studies of people who, beforehand and afterwards, had sceptical attitudes towards the possibility of past lives. Yet in both examples - because of the positive expectancy that they brought into the experience - it appears to have helped them considerably in their lives.

Clare

I became acquainted with Clare in her forties. She was a softly spoken and very sensitive woman. The more I worked with her, the more she revealed to me about her hidden inner life, a part of her that she hardly dared to share with anyone. Her inner experiences had occupied a very precious part of her life, often as a substitute for substantial contact with other human beings. However, she has also carried within her much fear and confusion about her life and even her inner experiences. Having lived much of her life in isolation, she did not know how much she could trust others or even her own feelings and thoughts. In her early life she had endured much criticism and some disturbing experiences, and these had certainly left their mark.

I met Clare when she participated in a residential workshop that I was leading. Initially, I felt I had to encourage her to open up and to allow herself to reveal what was inside her to others. At times she was obviously afraid to do this but gradually she felt safe enough to begin to express more of herself. As she did this she became happier; it was like someone coming out of a shell. The group did not reject her as she had feared, but instead accepted her. The participants had their own fears and insecurities, and thus she experienced that she was not alone.

From our talks, it was clear that the issue of spiritual faith was unresolved for Clare. She had her own spiritual beliefs and a strong sense of reverence in her life, but it was deeply personal to her and she questioned herself about it frequently. The concept of reincarnation was not a foundation that she had considered as a framework for her beliefs. Therefore, the exploration of past life regression in the workshop provoked some strong reactions within Clare. The regression worked in a way that surprised her, and also challenged the previous boundaries that she had placed on her inner worlds. Below is her story.

Clare's Past Life Experience

Last Christmas, I was feeling very low, even desperate, as my whole life seemed to be falling apart and I could see no way forward. Some months previously, a friend had visited Paul for therapy and had told me about the past life regressions he had done at that time. When I contacted Paul, however, it was primarily because I was impressed at how this visit had enabled my friend to take the first steps towards improving his life. Past life regression was not uppermost in my thoughts. Having spoken to Paul, I chose to attend a course he was running a few weeks later. Although I had little idea what this course was about, I felt I needed to do something as soon as possible.

Paul had asked me if I was open to the ideas of reincarnation and past life regression. I replied that when I look at young children, it is hard not to believe in reincarnation because they are so much like themselves. As for memories of past lives, I thought them likely to be pictures of one's current situation, similar to dreams, rather than literal reality. In fact, I did not at that time consider these ideas of importance. They did not make me anxious – as the thought of hypnosis did for instance – because I felt that they were irrelevant to my life.

If I had had the faintest idea of what the course would involve, I would not have contemplated attending for a moment! It was intense and demanding, while also measured and paced - it was exhausting, rewarding and absolutely real.

I first began to suspect the reality of regression experiences after listening to the past life memories of another member of the group. These did not seem to me to be experiences that anyone could have made up, consciously or otherwise, so I found that I had to rethink my attitude to what was going on. Until then I had assumed that we were involved in various games and techniques to bring to our awareness matters that we might be in the habit of ignoring. It was an enormous relief to be in the company of people with whom I could acknowledge and respond to my inner thoughts and feelings, which usually I had felt that I needed to keep well hidden. Even so, my diary continued to be filled with such comments as "I do not believe any of this".

My life up until this point seemed to be like a series of ideas and memories that I recounted, like photographs or stories that I had been told. When I considered how I felt, I was not sure that I had lived at all. And when it came to my turn to attempt a past life regression, this feeling of falseness became so great that I could not begin. I felt that I would just be making it up. Paul suggested that I go along with the process anyway, and asked if I would be willing to continue with the story even if I felt that I was creating it myself. I agreed to this.

We approached the past life regression through a guided meditation in which we first created a safe place and a symbolic door. This safe place seemed much more real to me than the past life itself. I could move about there easily, feeling free and at home. It was somewhat surprising to me that I could open the door at all, and on returning bolted it securely and walked all around it just to be sure! In contrast, the time I spent through the symbolic door felt like a story that I was being told. Moreover, I was sure that these images related to someone else's life or to memories I had of books and films. In the notes that I made afterwards, I have written "not my life" three times.

I stepped through the door into a dark room and immediately felt that I had to decide which of the two people present I was going to be. Throughout the meditation, I had sensations relating to both characters.

197

Certain of these physical feelings were very real: the warmth of the paving stones beneath my feet, the coldness of the stone room, the weight on my arms and hands of chains, the stab of the knife. These images appeared to relate to a tale of human sacrifice in a stone city. Everyone around me seemed to believe that these sacrifices were necessary. Gradually, I became aware that it was my role to officiate during the ceremony itself and also to say who was to be sacrificed. I was very reluctant to fulfil these duties and allowed my authority to be taken over by the head of the guards. During the meditation, I also felt the responses of the man who was to be killed and to whom I felt extremely close. However, I never saw things through his eyes. Afterwards, I was hesitant about recounting this story: it seemed to me to be embarrassingly melodramatic. Why couldn't I have come up with something straight forward and ordinary?

These thoughts contributed to my reluctance to re-enter that life in the following regression. This time though, having agreed to Paul's suggestion to go along with it anyway, I knew that I was the young woman. Although I could feel physical sensations and see many details in colour, my awareness appeared to be limited to my immediate surroundings. When asked a question, I had to consider quite carefully what would be the most accurate reply and at one point, I sensed at the moment that I expressed it, that what I had said was inaccurate. It was as though I was imagining events, able to choose between various alternatives, and guided only by how my responses felt. Certain emotions were quite uncomfortable – feelings of loneliness and isolation, of not fulfilling my duty, of having to face other people's anger and impatience, of weakness in not either opposing or escaping from what was going on. Finally, I was the victim of the sacrifice. If anything made me feel that there might be some reality to all this, it was the moment when I was stabbed, because it happened so quickly, before I could imagine what would occur. After I had died in that life I laughed at the drama of it all, but I also realised that whatever I was supposed to learn had not been completed. I felt great fear that my time had been wasted and I would have to do this life again.

Some of my impressions seemed so bizarre that I did not at first recount them when asked. It appeared to me very important, however, that I should remember the details correctly. For instance at one point, Paul asked whether a certain person was a man or a woman. After deliberating for a while, I replied "not a man". He said, "a woman then", and I said nothing to this because I felt it was wrong but was unable to explain the wrongness. Later, when in discussion, I was telling the group how I changed nothing in that life, Paul said in passing that he sensed that the slave, for whom I had given my life, had been killed anyway. I felt complete shock because I had not realised this – I had died before it happened. So it seems I do consider this to be my story after all!

Many buried emotions were brought to the surface following this past life regression. I felt tired but content. That night I remembered details of my childhood that I had previously forgotten and understood how I had reacted to events at that time. The next day, I began to think how I am reacting now in the same way that I did in the past life. Since then, the significance of one of the episodes that I chose not to recount has also struck me and I have begun to give serious thought to the relevance of the emotional relationships in the story. These are difficult and painful thoughts. On my own, I doubt that I will follow them through.

Currently, I am holding on to two apparently contradictory beliefs: while I cannot deny the plausibility and coherence of other people's past lives, I feel that what I experienced myself was created by my mind to illustrate current dilemmas. It does not lack meaning because of that – quite the opposite. As time passes, I continue to gain insights into just how closely the past life mirrors my present situation, and I feel no stronger or more determined now than I did then, no better fitted to judge or influence things. Yet, at the same time, I am dismayed at the thought of how many lives I may have lived, to no avail.

What did I get out of it? Well, there is a growing sense of excitement that after all, there may be some purpose to the seemingly endless and meaningless mess of my life. I realise that allowing others to usurp my power may not be as harmless as I thought. And I look at other people in a new way – what if they are just involved in a complex story to learn certain truths? Rationally, I do not believe any more strongly that these past life memories are literally true, but (with help) I intend to live as if they are.

Author's Notes

My observation of Clare is that she gained a lot of confidence and affirmation for the workings of her inner mind, through this workshop. The past life regression was crucial because it entered into realms within her consciousness that she had never approached before (in this lifetime anyway!). What she discovered was that she could be aware of inner images, thoughts and feelings that were substantial, real and consistent with other people's experiences. The connection that she could feel with others went a long way towards resolving the inner isolation that had until then been so dominant in her life. There was a part of her that liked being distinct from others, so the fact that she did not share the same passionate belief in reincarnation as some of the other members in the group did not matter to her.

When I met Clare one year later, I noticed important developments in her character. Even though she had faced many challenges during that time, it was clear that her inner strength had increased and she had a much greater ability to relate to others and express what she felt to be true.

David

The main issue with David concerned his sexuality. For many years, he had not been able to express this side of his nature with a woman and it had clearly been frustrating for him. Now he had met a woman who was sexually very active and David had formed an obsessive relationship with her.

I was deeply gratified that David felt safe enough to share his problems with me. Clearly, past life regression and a belief in reincarnation had not figured in his life as anything of importance. Yet some weeks after I met him he came to me, seeking my help with regression to resolve his problems.

By bringing to the surface of his consciousness past life experiences where obsessive relationships featured in a similar fashion to the present experience, I feel that it became clear to David how his deeply held attitudes were like a stuck record needing to move on. Exactly how much influence the past life regression experiences had upon his condition is difficult to quantify. However, I suspect that it was quite substantial.

In David's case, I believe that past life regression served mainly as a metaphor for him to understand his life situation more fully. My impression is that the experiences he had gave him insights and understandings on a deep subconscious level, and contributed to him changing many of his inner beliefs and expectations of himself. It was as though a record had been winding around and around in the same place for a long, long time. He had to move on and his life needed to undergo some radical transformation. From what I have learned of his life after his work with me, it seems that he was ultimately successful in this quest. Below is his account of his past life work with me.

David's Story

What should have been a week in paradise had turned into the week from hell. I was expecting an intimate holiday with my lover – the beautiful woman with whom I was plotting a life down on the sunny South Coast of England. Instead, I was lying on the floor of a tent in a Dartmoor hippy camp writhing with emotional pain while the woman with whom I was in love lay in the next tent with another guy.

God knows why I didn't just walk straight out of the camp, punching my male rival in the face as I left. Maybe if I had, I wouldn't have needed "therapy". Where was my self-respect? There was definitely a kind of group psychology at work at the camp that meant that normal rules did not apply. After all, that was the point of being there. Maybe it was my behaviour that was unreasonable? Maybe she just needed more space? And anyway, how could I leave? If I walked out, our relationship would definitely be over. And, stricken with a kind of sickness that is sometimes regarded as love, how could I take that chance?

Paul Williamson was a participant at the camp, and was also offering both group and individual sessions of past life therapy. I had no prior experience of past life therapy and before that week at the camp, I would probably have dismissed it as a mere cranky curiosity. But now, along with all the emotional turmoil, I realised that I had been presented with a confusing sea of new and exciting possibilities. Who could tell what was true and what was false in such an atmosphere? And I knew that I needed help. What I know now – but didn't understand then – is that I needed help, not just in dealing with the fall-out of a destructive relationship, but in establishing myself on a new life path. There were ties to break with the past.

So I took part in my first group past life regression session with no idea of what I really needed, let alone whether or not past life therapy could help me find it. And to begin with, it didn't help at all! The group session took me nowhere. I could not get beyond my feelings of hurt, rejection and longing. Later on, I arranged an individual session at the camp with Paul. Sensibly, he did not even try to regress me and simply offered counselling and the opportunity to visit him for further therapy at his home in a few weeks time. That is how I found myself on the long drive to Lancaster. Attracted not so much by what past life regression had to offer, I was drawn by my feelings of trust towards one of its practitioners. He was definitely a healer – and if past life regression were his bag, then I would try it. I was desperate.

The first session began with an outpouring of anger. All the rage repressed at the camp came hurtling out of me. Fists were directed in a pillow rather than fists to a face – or to my own heart. Then we began the first full regression. Starting off with a relaxing meditation, we moved deeper into hypnosis and then I was guided through a door in my psyche into my past lives.

Images came in black and white – a cold and unfriendly place – and a frosty farewell from disapproving parents. Following that, a long journey on foot down a country lane whose bowing tree tops formed a tunnel channelling me towards a new life. Then emerging into colour there was the warm sun on my face. Sunflowers and hay bails. A beautiful lusty woman beckoning me into the barn...

After the session, questions overwhelmed me. Black and white merging into colour...? That's the oldest Hollywood trick in the book – how could my psyche be so corny? Why did all my past lives seem to result in me being spurned by a lover in favour of some other person or force? Was this really the most significant thing that had happened in all these lives? Or was it that I had lived many thousands of lives and what I needed now was to learn the lessons from these particular experiences? I was full of feelings of falseness. Was I really recounting lives that I had actually lived? Surely, I was just making this up? At best, couldn't I have been latching onto stories or dreams from deep in my subconscious that I needed to get in touch with? And did that matter as long as whatever was happening was helping me?

I cannot divorce this first real experience of past life regression from the environment in which it took place. During the long weekend I spent with Paul, his home was besieged by children from current and previous relationships. At mealtimes, it was like the tide coming in. Periods of frenetic and noisy activity, with crises erupting and subsiding were followed by calm as the tide of children swept out again. It created a kind of rhythm and a grounding for the past life regression sessions. Paul's stepdaughter was one of these children and her mature reflections on dealing with her estranged father, not to mention her boyfriend troubles, also made me think. Was I simply behaving like a lovelorn 17-year-old?

So did any revelations from my past lives help to free me from my infatuation and propel me to move forward on my new path? Well – not immediately. I was performing complex leaving rituals designed to symbolically sever the ties during the day and then walking a mile to the nearest payphone to call her up in the evening. But I am convinced that this was part of the process.

In the short term, after my past life regression weekend, I could eat and sleep properly again, something that I had not been able to do for weeks. This simple physical symbol of recovery was a huge step forward that enabled me to tackle other things. Six months on – and with lots of other new experiences under my belt - I am much happier. I am full of energy, feel positive about the future and have a wonderful new lover. In my better moments, I now understand that I can be loved.

Author's Notes

Both David and Clare approached their work with me with sincerity, building up a strong sense of trust in my ability to help them. I believe that the past life therapy worked for them because of this, although I do not think either of them could embrace a belief in reincarnation.

Trust, openness, positive expectancy and the willingness to explore are the most important tools for engaging in past life regression - regardless of the inner beliefs we hold.

Chapter 21

Past Lives and Our Energy Body

Once we engage in past life regression, it is natural to speculate about our personal history as souls. We want to know how many lives we have lived on earth, and about other souls with whom we have been associated. We are curious as to how far along our path of lives we have come, and whether we still need to keep returning to the earth for more lives. We probably have numerous questions regarding the soul lessons we have learnt in the past, and what it is that we still need to learn. These are not mere intellectual questions.

My supposition is that generally, people interested in tracing past life histories have been around for a long time. People with short histories do not have so much to discover and so, I don't imagine that the interest is there. They are more involved in enlarging their experience for the future. When seekers begin their inner journeys to discover their past, they may find that it is much more vast than they anticipated.

Through the cycles of reincarnation, we give ourselves a multitude of tests so that eventually we learn to cope reasonably well with the various life situations we face as human beings in the physical world. The essence of this process, as I have already stated, is about learning to love. We stumble many times as we try to grapple with particular tasks that we have given ourselves. However, as we succeed with our goals, we gain knowledge and broaden our experience and ability to serve as souls.

From the experiences of many of my clients, and from channelled teachings, it is apparent that there is a spiritual realm where we go when we die, and from where we come before we are born. This realm is a place for us of great love. Here we gain nourishment and perspective upon our existence. Being in spirit is the seed place from which we propel ourselves into each physical incarnation. Even in our physical world we carry within us the memory of the love that we have felt in spirit; naturally we want to connect with that love in the course of our everyday lives. This yearning to be reunited with the love we have known in spirit has the capacity to give meaning and direction to our activities on earth.

We give ourselves many types of tests to face on the physical plane. Especially in the early stages of our evolution we do not have much wisdom to direct us as to what we need. This is where our guides come into the picture. Before a given lifetime, they can help us to decide what lessons are appropriate for our soul being in a given lifetime, so together we can make our plans about how we want to progress.

Our first lives might be quite basic, concerned with survival and learning what it is like to be a human being. We might be quite clumsy in the way that we go about things. As we grow and learn through experience, our soul may become ready and willing to take on more complicated tasks. With some of these we make mistakes and repeat certain lessons until we can appreciate their meaning for us, and act appropriately. As our souls grow, we experience situations on the physical plane in greater depth, especially when we open the channels within us, so that we feel connected with our inner self.

There may be lives when we do not test ourselves or build in any substantial challenges for us to face, so that we can enjoy a life on the physical in relative peace. These might be 'good' lives or quite mundane lives where things work out pretty much as we would expect and we do not need to make much in the way of adjustment inside ourselves in order to survive. But these are not lives that most of us would choose very often, unless we want to avoid some issue that needs to be resolved.

As souls we want to learn, and to do that we have to face challenges. From a spiritual perspective, some of those souls that we love most might be the ones that put themselves in a very challenging relationship to us to test how we cope with it. Our closest loved ones in spirit may be our enemies in some lives, and we need to respond to this as part of our learning as a soul. Do we choose the path of love and acceptance, or do we submit to our anger, jealousies and fears, letting these emotions dominate our actions? We are not going to always get it right and the mistakes we make are likely to leave wounds inside us.

The shadow of previous lives that we have lived stay connected to our energy systems as we go into further lives. Unresolved issues remain attached to us on a subconscious energetic level. When we are able to achieve a balance or equilibrium relative to the issues of those past lives, these patterns dissolve into the experience of our greater soul and are not needed as part of our tests on earth any more.

For example, if we have lived many lives where we have hurt people, we may feel a strong repugnance against wanting to cause any injury to others. Although at times we might feel rage, inside we probably feel a desperate urge to control this. Sometimes we succeed and sometimes we do not. Until, as a soul, we feel comfortable getting on with people, even in adverse conditions, this repugnance against violence is likely to continue to lurk in the background and exist as a fear inside of us. It could be that we need to be especially kind to particular souls that we have hurt in the past as a way of making up for this. At some point in our soul development, we may feel quietly content that we didn't need to be aggressive to others any more, and the problems connected with this issue will fade gently into our greater soul being. It will be like a ripple effect that gradually becomes calmer until it is still.

Our Energy Body

Permeating and extending outwards from our physical body, we have an energy body. This is usually called our aura. Some people can see this aura as various subtle colours mingling together. People have auras and other life forms also have auras too. Subconsciously, we are quite aware of other people's auras. If we are in a room where somebody is angry, for instance, we might sense that anger without the person concerned saying anything, because of the anger existing in that person's aura. Spiritual healers are able to feel the vibrations of another's energy field through their hands. In our energy body we carry our thoughts, emotions, beliefs and memories. I believe that these exist in our energy bodies rather than in our brains. Our brain can pick up information from our energy body, but our consciousness exists independently of our brains. If it did not, then all would be lost when our physical body dies. I believe that our energy body survives our physical deaths.

Our energy body connects with our physical body at quite specific places. The main centres where this connection occurs are called the energy chakras. By focussing upon places in our physical body and letting ourselves drift into an altered state, we become aware of memories that may be stored in the aspect of our energy body that is associated with that place in our physical being.

As an example, in a particular past lifetime, we could have suffered a shocking injury to our arm. There may be trauma associated with this injury that we did not resolve in that lifetime. In our current lifetime then, the remnants of this past life trauma may still be lingering in our energy field. We will not perceive it with our normal analytical thinking processes. The place where we are most likely to become aware of it will probably be when we concentrate our attention upon our arm. We could be disturbed by something connected to that arm. By moving our consciousness there, we might spontaneously go into an altered state of awareness where the feelings and thoughts associated with this experience begin to emerge. As this becomes stronger, we may feel strange sensations in our arm. If we accept these feelings and allow them to develop further, trauma of the past life might start to release itself through us and we will relive that memory.

Our energetic body connects to our physical body. Where there is some disturbance in our physical body, it probably corresponds to something going on in our energetic body. We learn to train ourselves to become alert to the messages and patterns existing in our energy body, by asking inner questions, listening and opening our awareness to any form of sensation that we feel in our physical body.

Understanding the energy body is a science in its own right. In terms of past lives, we sometimes access these experiences most readily by breathing into a particular place in our energetic body, and opening our perception to what it tells us. The placement in our body as to where we need to concentrate our attention is meaningful, and we can learn much by studying this.

There are some places in our body that act as energetic gateways into past life experiences. These are called the energy chakras. Here I discuss them in detail, and how they serve to help us access past lives with specific themes and learning.

The Chakras as Pathways to Past Lives

Although there are many thousands of energy chakras connected to our physical body, there are seven significant ones that have most influence over us. Each of these corresponds with the different modes of expression available to us. The seven main chakras all have their function, together connecting with each other, and are the main vehicles through which our personalities experience life.

Ideally we need the chakra system of our bodies to be functioning in balance and harmony. However, this does not always happen. Confronting specific challenges in our lives puts demands and strains upon particular chakras. Because of this other chakras compensate in an effort to keep our energy system in equilibrium. Our energy body is continually in motion, with adjustments being made and alterations happening to our chakras according to the thoughts and feelings and physical effort that we project.

Fear tends to close down the functioning of aspects of our energy system. If this happens other parts of our being become more active to compensate. For instance, if we are afraid that we might be rejected, we probably feel a contraction in our chest. While this is taking place, the energy systems associated with our stomachs and head may become overactive. While we try to cope with feeling rejected, we might feel a strong urge to eat chocolate or some other comfort food, and our heads might be buzzing with thoughts that we cannot control.

It could be that in a given lifetime, we as souls may choose to develop our experience by relating mainly to the functioning of just one or maybe two of the chakras. We become preoccupied with the issues connected with these chakras, providing us with the theme for our experience in that lifetime.

In doing past life regression, if we breathe into one of the chakra centres of our body, we may find images and thoughts arising from past lives where we were working on themes relating to that chakra. There can be a link between some energy disturbance in one of our chakras, and memories of lifetimes where the functioning of this chakra was being developed or challenged in some way. If we suffered in these lifetimes and did not learn our lessons, there may be a wound in our being connected with this chakra. In our present lifetime, we could be giving ourselves another chance to learn this lesson. By going into the experience of those past lifetimes associated with such an energetic wound, we appreciate more fully the task that is there for us now. Pain and energy disturbances felt in particular chakras is our soul's way of alerting us to something that we need to bring to consciousness. Whether we agree to do this or ignore those impulses is up to us.

The chakras are all linked with each other. I do not believe that learning associated with any particular chakra necessarily denotes more advanced learning, than development connected with another chakra. I feel that all the chakras have a multitude of dimensions where there may be opportunities for learning. They each have their role and their own importance in the scheme of things. Ultimately, as souls, we need to have gone through sufficient developmental experiences with each of the chakra levels before we are ready to move on.

While we still experience ourselves as souls in spirit, I believe that we choose particular dispositions as the base from which we may need to apply ourselves in any given lifetime. The disposition that we choose can then slant our energies in a certain direction and this is how we focus our attention - through the workings of one or possibly more of the main chakras. For that lifetime, the workings of the chakra we have chosen provides the leading experience from which we can try to feel balanced and in harmony with other aspects of our being, and the functioning of the other chakras. We become attuned to the vibrations of that chakra and our reactions to challenges that we face will be centred upon it.

Learning how to cope with the experience of rejection is a lesson that is likely to be centred upon the heart chakra. At an early stage of our soul evolution, we might choose a scenario where someone that we love leaves us for another. We are challenged to come to terms with this and accept it. As we gain maturity as a soul, we test ourselves further by creating a similar situation compounded with a childhood where our parents underwent a painful separation. To test ourselves even more, we choose a disposition for ourselves where we are born with an obsessive personality, tending to strong emotional reactions to disturbances of any kind. In each case we have to learn to keep our hearts open to love and acceptance rather than closing our hearts down in hatred and despair. If we do not manage it, then we probably need to come back and try again.

I would like now to outline some of the predominant experiences and qualities that I have observed, connected with each chakra and their possible relationship to past life experiences.

The Crown Chakra

Starting at the top of the seven main chakras, the energy chakra situated just above the head is referred to as the crown chakra. Energetically, this chakra is associated with our faith and our openness to our higher self, to 'God' and to our guides and angels. From here, we reach out for help and guidance and we receive impulses from spirit corresponding with our soul urges and our path forward.

When this chakra is blocked, we are cutting ourselves off from spiritual help. At those times, we have probably decided that the only way to live our lives is according to our own will. We could be angry with 'God' or 'Spirit', feeling that there is nothing outside our own will that can help us. Physically, people experience a blockage to this chakra as a band across the top of their head or a depressed feeling there.

In terms of past lives, the development of this chakra might include tests that we give ourselves involving our faith. We may put ourselves in adverse situations where we easily doubt that there is any help available from spiritual sources to support us. The only way that we can resolve such a situation might be through asking for inner help and listening to guidance. If we succeed in this, we could then find a sense of peace and understanding whereby we are able to help others gain spiritual understanding too. In a lifetime where we do not address this challenge we may feel very depressed, unhappy and isolated. This can have a lot of negative consequences. Without spiritual guidance and support, we easily become lost in our own thought processes and confused about what we need to do next. We build our own perception of the world around us, that has very little to do with true reality, but is merely of our own creation.

My partner Eleyna had a constant feeling of pressure at the top of her head when she first started coming to me for therapy. At the time she was suffering from depression. Inwardly she was very sensitive and drawn to spiritual experiences. But her life until then had been very bleak. At an earlier age she had made a decision that had blocked out spirit from her mind. Now with her rational intelligence she questioned whether spiritual experiences were mere fantasy, doubting whether giving these experiences credibility would be of any use to her.

Finally, after some months of argument, discussion and therapy, Eleyna went through the memory of a past life in Victorian times. In this lifetime a young boy suffered and lost his faith in 'God'. Later, because of the inner difficulties he felt, the aggression and hostility he stored inside found a very destructive outlet. As a man, he became a murderer. When Eleyna connected with that vulnerable young boy who needed help but was unable to find it, her compassion for this past life personality was awakened. Soon afterwards, she had a spiritual experience during one of our sessions. Here she had a direct experience of the love of spirit in a form which she could no longer doubt, and she knew that spirit was in her life. From this moment onwards, the pain and depression at the top of her head was gone.

The Third Eye or Brow Chakra

Situated in the centre of our forehead, this chakra is associated with thought, intuition and psychic perception. The lessons connected with this chakra have to do with trust.

With our third eye centre we manifest experiences through our thoughts. We direct and try to control the universe that we live in using this faculty. When we are open to listen to other influences, we can see visions and 'know' what is going on around us by opening our third eye.

People become anxious and afraid when they are not able to control aspects of their lives in the way they wish to. This brings worry and tension around the head area. When the third eye chakra is blocked, this is usually because of negative thoughts and inner expectations that are not in accordance with reality. People may fear the worst and go about creating scenarios in their minds that satisfy these fears. When such people are confronted with a challenge, they magnify and distort any difficult aspects so that they can decide that the challenge is quite insurmountable. Of course, this is not always the case at all.

People develop their capacity to manifest experiences that they want through positive thinking and through visioning the results they are trying to achieve. Our thoughts reach outward like a beacon in front of us, attracting experiences to us by the nature of what we are thinking. When we are afraid of things going wrong, these thoughts also attract certain forms of response into our lives and because of fear, we tend not to even recognise help when it comes our way.

We can also make mistakes with our third eye chakra. If we think that we want one thing, when from our soul perspective we need something else, then we may not achieve what we seek. Even with positive thinking, under these circumstances, the universe will most likely give us signals to try and persuade us to seek another course. However, if we persist in following an action that is contrary to our soul needs, it can lead to much difficulty and frustration. In our present society, we talk about 'control freaks', people who try and direct their lives like this. But the universe will not be subject to someone's personal will.

The third eye chakra is to do with our personal power and our personal capacity to make our own decisions. For this chakra to be operating in harmony with our overall needs, it needs the crown chakra (guidance) and our heart (compassion for self and others), to be open. Then decisions that we make could well be wise and constructive. Unfortunately, this harmony is not always present.

If we are having trouble finding peace in our lives, the best methods of helping our third eye chakra are through meditation and affirmations. When we meditate, we endeavour to listen to our inner needs and experience stillness. This helps us open up to guidance. Affirmations are positive statements that we think, and feed to our inner consciousness. Even if we do not fully believe them, by repeating them, they have influence. By practising affirmations, we train our thought processes to be more positive and expect outcomes in our lives that are conducive to our happiness. Affirmations we use to suggest that our hearts are open and that we are able to trust the universe to support us, help us to achieve the inner harmony that we need.

Sometimes, we say of certain people that they are 'caught up in their heads'. They may be people who try to analyse every nuance of what they experience, to work out their own solutions to problems. Here, the third eye chakra is over-active to the exclusion of other chakras. People with highly developed mental intelligence may feel that they do not need help from any one else or any other source to go forward in life. If there is a distortion, the person concerned is resistant to receiving help. Superficially, this appears to be a form of arrogance. However, underlying that, it is more likely that such people are afraid. They might believe that if they did not take matters into their own hands, things will not work out for them. In other words, it is an issue of trust.

In terms of past life experience where lessons connected to this chakra form the main theme, I feel that these are likely to be lives of inner conflict. There may be a strong sense in these life stories of how the person thinks that things should be. Then things may turn out differently from how that person wants. The challenge for the person will be to reconcile the thoughts of how they think things should be with the reality, and to accept this reality. Such a challenge may have various strengths of difficulty.

214

With reference to one of my own past life experiences, I have mentioned in my first book, 'Healing Journeys', a life where I felt myself to be a leader of a temple in very early ancient Greece. I loved the temple life and my part in it and wanted to preserve it. However, there were invaders that wanted to destroy it all. I felt very much attached to all aspects of this life and passionately did not wish for it to be damaged in any way. The truth in this situation is, I believe, that this particular temple civilisation had served its purpose and now needed to come to an end. My personal purpose was to trust and to release it. This was difficult for me, and I became angry that I could not have what I wanted. The focus of this struggle, as I perceive it, was in the third eye chakra where I could not reconcile the thoughts of what I wanted with what was actually happening. During the regression, I felt an acute pain in my forehead while the images of the invasion came to me. The past life contained lessons for me in my present life, about the need to let go and allow things to end when the time is right.

The Throat Chakra

Situated around the area of the throat and neck, the function of this chakra is to do with speech and creative expression. Through an active throat chakra, we express our will. When we develop this chakra, we are working on our capacity for leadership and our ability to assert ourselves. Situated between the head and heart, it has the potential to combine and synthesise the energies of our thoughts and feelings. However, if there is not a clear energy flow between the thoughts of our third eye chakra, and the feelings of our heart, then this can block the functioning of our throat chakra. There may be distortions in either the third eye chakra or the heart chakra that cause the block. People may feel a lump in their throats or some sense of constriction when they need to speak, as symptoms that this chakra needs attention.

There can be a conflict between how people feel that they should act (head) and what they feel is right (heart), leading to uncertainty of expression. From the throat chakra comes the urge to express our truth. We may be afraid that we will be hurt or someone else close to us will be negatively affected by what we have to express. This inhibits us from being honest because we do not feel safe. It could be that there is pressure from others to compromise our self-expression and therefore, a fear of speaking out.

In past lives, we typically find that experiences connected with the development of the throat chakra are lives in which the personality has something important that must be expressed, but there are challenges that make the fulfilment of that expression difficult. The main tests surrounding this chakra are then to do with courage and honesty.

Recently, I was working with a woman who complained that every time she meditated, she felt a pain in her throat. One day, she managed to confide in me how as a child, she had been sexually abused by a member of her family. She had felt a great sense of shame about this and had told nobody. Her concern was particularly for her relationship with her husband, and she was afraid of how he would react if he knew about it. They shared an honest and very open relationship, but this secret haunted her and affected her sense of self-worth in the relationship. I urged her to share the story of this part of her life with her husband, and even though it was very difficult for her, she did so. He reacted with compassion and this helped her a great deal. After this, her throat felt easier and her meditations became deeper and more meaningful for her.

If we feel blocked from expressing our truth under certain circumstances, this indicates a past life experience in our subconscious memory that resonates with this issue. In a similar situation from the past, we might have failed to act and assert ourselves in the way that was needed at the time.

With reference to the example that I have just given, of my client who was abused as a child, I feel that it is very likely that she has past lives in her memory where this was also an issue. It could have been that she has had lives where she was both abused and ones where she was the abuser. The learning associated with this would be about learning to honour her needs sufficiently as well as the needs of others. In her present life, by expressing what she was feeling to her husband, rather than hiding it, was an act of being compassionate with herself. It helped her to unlock the feelings of love that she wanted to express to others that previously had felt blocked. She had to overcome her fear to do that.

216

The throat chakra becomes blocked when people feel bad about themselves for some reason. This stops them from being assertive and wanting to expose themselves to others. Going through a past life where this is an issue, it is necessary to trace the roots of these negative thoughts. People only feel bad about themselves because of some misconception that they have acquired in a situation where they found it hard to cope. When this is traced, there can be a lot of fear about accessing the beliefs and feelings involved. Bringing those dark thoughts and feelings to the surface is difficult, especially where they concern shame and guilt. However, it is necessary to do this in order to clear the block. Once this takes place, the person is better prepared to appreciate the truth of the situation, and to voice this. Voicing inner truths has a vital function in clearing and healing blocks relating to fear of any kind.

When people start feeling bad about themselves, they easily manifest situations where bad things seem to happen to them. We attract energies to us by the way that we feel and think inside. In terms of past lives, I have often observed with experiences that have resulted in deaths by hanging or strangulation, that these have usually been lives where self-expression was the main issue. The person may have been challenged to express some essential truth but did not do so because of fears and doubts relating to self-worth.

It is important for people to feel able to express themselves and their own truth, so that they can love themselves even with their own weaknesses. This is a key ingredient for people to learn in order to open their throat chakra.

Words are not the only form of self-expression connected to the throat chakra. Being an artist, a musician, a fine craftsman or a dancer will also demand an open and flowing throat chakra. This energy centre appears to me to be most essentially about expressing the beauty of the soul and of life itself. To be successful creatively people need to love themselves, and recognise the spark of beauty and wellspring of love that is in them and in everything else.

The Heart Chakra

The next chakra, situated in the centre of our chest, is known as the heart chakra. Our heart chakra functions according to our capacity to give and receive love. We learn with our heart chakra about loving in the most personal sense, loving other human beings and ourselves. However, we also have the potential in our hearts to learn about love in its most universal aspect. I believe that, if we can open our hearts sufficiently, we can appreciate our connection with all other life forms.

I have already suggested that our soul grows and evolves through its capacity to channel love. Therefore I feel that the development of our heart chakra is fundamental to us gaining spiritual awareness but also expressing our individuality as human beings.

You may notice, as a seeker, that when you feel very loving and content, your chest will probably feel warm and expansive. You will feel the energy there. Conversely, on occasions where you feel unloved and separate from others you may feel a pain or constriction in your heart area.

When our heart is closed we will feel a sense of alienation and separation from others. This can bring quite an awful feeling of isolation and emptiness that we try to cover up. Sometimes souls try to compensate for feelings of loneliness engendered by a closed heart, by seeking power over others to feel some sort of connection with the world around them. When people believe that they are unloved, it may not matter how much attention other people give them; until they are willing and ready to open their heart, they continue to feel empty inside.

Soul tests that people give themselves concerning the heart chakra are usually those where some rejection or challenge comes along that will tempt the person to close down the heart. The lesson, of course, will be about keeping the heart open.

When we are born into physical reality, we face the restriction of awareness and love that physical existence imposes. This is a test for the heart chakra of the soul. For sensitive people, this can be much more acute. Often, from within the soul, there can be a reluctance to be born.

218

Such an attitude stems from the memory of previous painful experiences in other lives. This affects the functioning of the heart chakra from the very beginning. If we say 'no' to life rather than 'yes', it makes a difference. Such resistance affects the outlook and belief patterns that people have when approaching challenges, and may make life much more difficult than it would be otherwise.

In one of my own past lives I chose to become a samurai. During my childhood in this life, I suffered difficulties with my parents and my father in particular. He was very violent towards both my mother and I, and I did not like the strong reactions that he engendered in me. I did not want to be bothered by such turbulent feelings in my heart. So I trained to become a cold and clinical killer in service to the emperor. I took on this role and performed it well for some years. At some point though, I came across a mother and child that I needed to kill. As the woman looked up at me with imploring eyes, something melted in my heart. She reminded me of my own mother. I could not kill her. Instead I killed myself.

I believe that the soul test that I gave myself in that life was to see if I could unlock my compassion, even when my heart had been closed down to an extreme degree as it is when people took on that training to become a samurai warrior. This was quite a strong test. In that lifetime, I constructed walls around my heart so that I would not feel what I did to people. It did not feel very pleasant. But I never lost completely that longing in my heart for love, to give and receive love.

Typically, tests for the heart chakra are centred on relationships and the need for us to act with integrity. When we love somebody, we quite easily acquire the mistaken belief that the only love that will satisfy us in our life needs to come from that person. If the person that we love is more interested in someone else or not so concerned with us, this affects the openness of our heart. To feel that we cannot obtain the love that we need can be quite devastating.

It is not very comfortable to feel a lack of love within our heart. We can feel a pain in our chest or an emptiness that may be unbearable. Rather than open our hearts to receive that love, from sources that could supply it to us, we are likely to believe that this is not possible. Then we are inclined to construct walls or barriers around our heart to protect ourselves so that we do not feel our own pain. These walls just serve to isolate us even further from our world. Without access to the love we need, our thought patterns most probably become quite negative. We become inclined to either judge ourselves harshly or lash out at others and blame them for our predicament. Ultimately, it is only us that can take down those walls.

If the person from where we expect to receive the love we need does not give it, then the love we feel may turn to hate. In our hearts we may feel starved of love and therefore want to project the terrible feelings that this engenders onto that other person. This outlook can be very destructive.

Because as human beings we are naturally motivated to involve ourselves with other people, our companions serve us as the ground upon which we can learn the lessons of love. Men and women need each other to propagate children. Certainly when a child is born it needs its parents' love. So there is a great need for us to have our hearts open, if not for our own sakes, then for others.

When our heart is opened sufficiently, we recognise that love exists in all life forms and that the universe supports us to be how we need to be. There is no lack of love except in our own minds. For us as souls to reach a state of maturity where we can accept that fully, I believe, is one of the main aims of our existence.

The Solar Plexus Chakra

Situated just below the heart chakra, this chakra is associated with the central nervous system and the adrenal gland. Its main function is to do with issues of safety and our responses to fear. With our sympathetic nervous system, we react to threatening situations with either fight or flight. The solar plexus chakra is energetically the focal area from which we sense instinctively whether or not a situation feels safe to us. Lives predominantly concerned with the development of the solar plexus chakra typically involve battles of one sort or another.

People can live on the rush of adrenaline. It can produce the thrills and excitement of confronting danger. Such feelings can be extremely addictive. Once people are on the roller coaster of seeking further adrenaline 'fixes', they tend to have little care about whether they live or die. The lessons associated with this chakra are about learning to value life. I feel that life will only be appreciated while the adrenaline gland is activated in moderation.

The solar plexus chakra is like a sensory antenna that reaches out from us to determine if the environment around us is safe. Therefore, it is a place in our energy field where we may be very vulnerable to attack. We can pick up thoughts and emotions with the sensing organism of our solar plexus. If someone is critical or negative towards us, we may pick this up instinctively with our solar plexus chakra. Because of this, we can react negatively through our nervous system without consciously realising why.

People sometimes fold their arms around their solar plexus chakra to protect themselves from fear in situations where they feel uneasy. In ancient times, priests would cover their solar plexus with specific metals or hardened material so the emotions and thoughts of those around them would not affect them. I imagine that the purpose of the armour worn by soldiers was not only to protect the soldier from physical attack but also to cover the solar plexus and heart areas - this would stop the soldier from feeling fear and for caring about the enemy.

I have remembered a life where I was living in the midst of a network of aggressive tribes, all jockeying for position and power. The life was situated somewhere in Eastern Europe around the middle ages. I know that I have had many earlier lives involving fighting, but somehow this one was different. All my life, I was trained to learn to be a warrior. When it was time for me to go to battle for the first time, and I was advancing with my two young friends, something made me turn away and I could not fight. My father was the chief of this tribe, and when he later came and found me, he accused me of being a coward. I was so confused inside because the way that I acted was contrary to everything that I had been taught. Therefore, I could not contradict my father. He killed me, with a spear through my solar plexus. I could feel the pain.

Later, as I was able to reflect upon that life, I could feel that my actions were not so much cowardice but actually the assertion of my individuality where my soul impulse was to choose non-aggression in the midst of tremendous instinctive peer pressure to fight. The main challenge of this life was focussed upon my solar plexus centre and to do with confronting various fears within me. I realised in the experience after my death that it was actually a very strong and positive life, even though it ended tragically.

Fear generates stress in our nervous system. Stress can magnify fears out of all sensible proportions and affects the way we react to situations. Instinctively, we want to avoid such uncomfortable nervous responses. To remain steady when our nervous system is pumping with adrenaline, and going into overdrive, demands a strong will and a clear inner knowing about our way forward. In my experience, it helps more if we can breathe with our fears, trying to accept them rather than struggle against them. When we try to suppress our fears, they probably get worse, and we become increasingly afraid of the fear itself. This makes our nervous reactions even more out of our control, resulting in panic.

When the solar plexus chakra is disturbed, we feel very anxious and vulnerable. In this condition we need to feel comforted, reassured and loved. Whether the sources of the fear come from our present lifetime or the past, we need to feel safe to know what to do with that fear. I believe that it helps us much more if we can approach our fears rather than try to run away from them. Even though we do not want to do this, I feel that it is the only way to overcome our fears. Fear can be built up in layers by the resonance of many similar experiences. Our solar plexus instinctively reacts to what it considers to be perceived threats. Going to the source of that fear to identify what is happening - letting our body react by shaking or shivering - helps. By accepting the source of our fear, we are able to let it go, and put it in the past where it belongs.

The Sacral Chakra

The next chakra is known as the sacral chakra and is situated in the region of our lower abdomen. It is connected to our sexuality, our desires and urge for personal power. When a woman becomes pregnant, this chakra opens to allow the soul of the baby to enter into her energy field. It is therefore an energy centre associated with the manifestation of life and I believe that this is true on other levels as well as the birth of human life.

It is within this chakra that our appetites for what we instinctively want are formed and expressed. The lesson with this chakra is about learning to become aware of what we need from deep inside, rather than what we want with our desire nature. It is in our soul interests to express those inner needs in our actions and wants as much as possible.

It is not always easy for us to attune to our deeper inner needs. The feelings of what we desire can influence us very strongly. If we feel that we cannot have something that we want, rather than listening inside, we become passive and decide that we can't get what we want, thus becoming victims of somebody else's control. Alternatively, we become more determined to have what we want, closing our minds from any other alternative.

Very often, the desires of our sacral chakra centre on our relationships with others. If we want another person very much, we become tied to that person, feeling as though that person is ours. From our sacral chakra we can are inclined to become possessive. If the object of our affections turns away from us, we become jealous. If the one we desire chooses someone else, we might become envious of that person.

The appetites of our sacral chakra may also prompt us to become materially acquisitive. We could have urges to want to be rich or fashionable. Alternatively, we might wish to attain a position where we have power over others. By trying to meet the desires of our sacral chakra, we are seeking to satisfy our urges. Of course, some appetites are never satisfied. The more we try to satisfy them, the stronger and more urgent they become, leading to greed and abuse of power on many levels. If our sacral chakra operates in a flowing connection with our heart, and if our heart is open, then we may be able to perceive our true inner needs without many problems. However, if our heart is closed or disturbed in some way, and if the connection between these two energy centres is not flowing, then the expression of wants from the second chakra may not be in harmony with the needs of the soul.

When our heart is closed, we are not open to considering and respecting another's needs. We are also unable to tune into our own true needs. This is the type of situation where sexual abuse and other distortions of the sacral chakra occur. In the example of sexual abuse we may seek gratification through sexual interaction with someone's body. Unless this is a shared experience of love, the sense of gratification and fulfilment may feel empty afterwards, resulting in the further desire for more such experiences. There may be the illusion that such experiences are the only way to mask the feeling of emptiness. Thus, the problems of addictions are created through distortions related to the sacral chakra, from where we gain our appetites.

Because of the instinctive nature of how we perceive things through our sacral chakra, it is not very easy to control the impulses prompting us to act from this source. Desire can feed upon desire, and become more and more dominant in our outlook. Therefore, addictions like drug taking and alcohol abuse also perpetuate themselves in association with the disproportionate functioning of this chakra.

If we do not feel good about our desires, we might try to suppress them. It is unlikely that we will be successful in doing this. We will probably still seek out what we desire, in spite of the attempts of our will to thwart us. I feel that the best way to deal with distortions relating to desire is to seek a deeper appreciation of our true needs.

We also feel impotent if we do not believe that we can get what we want. This can be as much of a problem as when our desires are overly strong. Our desires can be very much influenced by our beliefs. Therefore, in past life work related to this chakra, it is very important to learn as much as possible, about the core belief that has led to a certain set of conditions manifesting themselves.

In terms of the evolution of our soul, we need to learn to consider others as much as ourselves. When we don't do that, we have to return in other lives to experience what it is like when others do not consider us. Because the appetites of the sacral chakra can be so strong, it is a challenge for all of us as souls to bring its functioning into balance with the other aspects of our being.

When I explored one of my past lives, I discovered that I was an aboriginal woman. While still a teenager, my male partner whom I loved and wanted very much died when a snake bit him. I was shocked and very distressed by his death. Part of me wanted to die so that I could be with him. Yet inside me was the impulse to train my psychic gifts so that I could be the medicine woman of the tribe. I did not know what to do.

In this situation I suppose that I could have reacted in many ways. I felt the impulse to be angry at the creator force for allowing this to happen. For the rest of my life I could have lashed out in frustration for not being able to fulfil my desire to live with my partner. But I did not want to hurt others. In the end, I did train and become the medicine woman of the tribe, but in a way where I remained detached from the people I helped. I did my work out of a sense of duty, wanting my life to be over so that I could join my partner. The desire I felt to love and care for my partner could have been transmuted into a love and care for all the people in the tribe. But in this life, I could not let go of my desires to be with this man.

Subsequently, in the next life I again was in a situation where I had shamanistic gifts. Once more, I experienced personal tragedy, losing people that I desired and loved. This time, I was able to shift the focus of my attention. Despite numerous challenges, this was a life that I dedicated to serving the people. Consequently, I expect that the lessons of the previous life were now learned so I could move on to new challenges.

The Base Chakra

The last chakra that I want to consider is called the base or root chakra and is situated at the lower end of our body. This chakra has links with our legs and feet and is to do with our connection with the earth and our sense of belonging with our clan or family group.

When we are born into physical incarnation, we retain contact through our crown chakra with the spirit world where a large portion of our soul remains during our life. However, the 'Spirit of the Earth', which provides the material for our physical lives to take place, also holds us. Through our base chakra being open, we feel ourselves at home on the earth. The Spirit of the Earth prompts us to experience passion and beauty so that we want to live our physical lives to the full.

I believe that the crown chakra and the base chakra are equally important. When we are alive in physical incarnation, we need to embrace the physical aspects of life fully. By engaging in physical life, our soul has the opportunity to learn its lessons. But it does not serve us to become lost in the physical so that we are totally separated from our souls. Thus, an equal balance is needed between these two aspects of our being so that we can be in harmony with our needs.

When our base chakra is closed, we may not feel any point in living. We can feel disconnected with a sense of meaninglessness for all that we do.

In many native cultures, the base chakra is very open. People from these cultures often go around without shoes and feel the vibration of the earth directly. They are sensitive to their environment and feel the interconnectedness of all life. Within the concrete jungles that we live in our western society, it is much harder for us to feel this.

I believe that the main lessons of the base chakra are about being grounded and appreciating the life that we have on earth, even when it is difficult. For all of us, there is the temptation when things get tough to decide that we don't want to be here.

One component in the evolution of our souls is that we become equipped to meet all variety of challenges from our lives on earth. When we do not meet a challenge successfully, we might decide to try and opt out. This usually involves releasing our hold on earth, so that our base chakra shuts down. In extreme cases this can involve suicide.

Without our base chakra being open, we are unable to live our lives as our soul has chosen. When our crown chakra is closed we cannot recognise our challenges truly.

To honour our base chakra, we also need to honour our physical body and look after it. It is sometimes said that our body is our temple. We need to be able to appreciate ourselves, whatever difficulties we have been through.

In terms of past lives, tests for the base chakra are often centred on our sense of home and belonging. We might have a lifetime where we are very attached to our family, say, and then lose them in some way. Alternatively, we might have needed to move from a place where we felt secure and happy. The challenge in these sorts of scenarios is to let go and open up to putting down roots in some new situation. If we cannot release our attachments, we may fall into a big hole of despair and close down. We could then have to face similar challenges in another incarnation in an effort to do better.

There could be a purpose in us needing to release a family bond, for instance. We may need to embrace the family of humanity rather than just our blood family, especially if we have chosen a path of service, with the aim of helping others. Being confined in our attentions to our immediate family group could limit us, denying us the opportunity to reach out to others possible. Understandably we feel reluctant and perhaps resistant to give up something that feels precious to us. The test is for us to trust that our needs are met - and let go anyway.

Moving home may be a test where we need to learn to embrace the earth as our home, and not just one small portion of it. Again, the challenge is to move beyond limiting circumstances. We may be afraid of leaving the familiar. However we only feel pain while we resist the change that is being asked of us. Letting go of attachment is not easily achieved, especially if we need to stay open to putting down new roots. Some allowance needs to be made for the grieving process associated with any loss. But the act of release might be what is expected of us, so that we can learn to be more fully in the flow of life. For our base chakra to be open, it is our task to accept our life as it is.

We are given the earth as a place to express ourselves. With our free will, we can do what we like. It is common in our modern world to want to exploit others, or our world, as an effort to try and gain some form of advantage. But engaging in abuse essentially causes us pain, as the nature of the energy that we put out returns to us.

The earth provides the food that we eat, the water that we drink and the air that we breathe. Without the earth we would not physically exist. As we appreciate what the earth gives to us, we feel a need to be responsible for our actions. We do not exist in isolation. When we pollute or exploit the earth, this hurts, but the earth still loves us.

When we abuse the earth or indeed, abuse other people, it feels awful when we open to the truth of what we have done. But life goes on. When we realise that we have done something abusive, we want to behave differently. This is when compassion starts to grow within us.

Past life regression helps us learn about our potential strengths and weaknesses. When we come across a very dark life, the horror of can make us cringe. How could we behave in such a way? When the energy of that feeds through us, we grow, and we learn that we are no different essentially from anyone else. The earth is our playground to learn these lessons. We can feel truly nourished by the earth as much as from spirit. That is the path of our souls.

Our Energy Body as a Whole

The various chakras link together. The functioning of one influences another. Studying the chakras individually helps us to become aware of how multifaceted our experience can be. We are complex beings. To be able to control the workings of our own energy system, we need to become very self-aware. Our energy body operates at many subtle levels. Influences from our past lives are centred in specific places within our energy body. However, there is only so much that we can digest at any given moment. I feel that the best we can do is to learn to listen inwardly to our energy body in all its aspects, so that we can appreciate what it wants to communicate with us. If we ask it for help, impulses can come into our awareness that support us to learn.

Chapter 22

Karmic Patterns

The traditional notion of 'Karma' is a concept dating back to ancient times. The basic premise of teachings about karma is along the lines of 'what we sow with our actions, thoughts and feelings, so we will reap'. Hence, whatever energy we direct outwards is reflected and returned to us, so we can learn from it if we wish. In terms of reincarnation, the theory is that if we do not reap all that we sow in one lifetime, it carries over into the next, or some subsequent experience.

It is commonly assumed that karma proceeds along the lines of 'an eye for an eye', so that literally what we do to others will be returned to us and done to us exactly in the same manner, either in the life that we are living or a subsequent life. Therefore, if we murder someone in one lifetime, in some future time we will be murdered in very similar circumstances, to balance out what we did to that other person. However, in my own experience, I have observed karma to be much more subtle than that.

I would like to outline my own thoughts as to how karma operates, illustrating these with discoveries that I have made during my own regressions.

Since my teenage years, I have considered karma to be an irrefutable law of divine justice, something that made life ultimately and fundamentally fair, however human beings regard it. Underlying our sense of reality, I have felt that our universe is a meaningful and loving place where all our actions have consequences, and where all life is evolving towards oneness and unique expressions of love.

Elsewhere in this book, I have suggested that human souls are basically sparks of divine energy. To become human, we have been given the gift of free will. This gift enables us to make our own decisions, but also separates us from our divine consciousness. When we become human souls we begin the task of undergoing a journey so that we can be consciously reunited with our divine essence, embracing all life with love and becoming eventually as 'God'.

With our free will, we make decisions allowing us to either become closer to our divine essence or to feel more separated from it. When we feel more separated from our divine essence, our life feels darker and we can feel a greater sense of isolation as a result.

Our free will engenders that karma. While our actions are in harmony with our deeper inner needs, and the needs of other people and life forms with which we are connected, we can proceed in peace. However, when we deviate from that harmony in our thoughts and actions, some compensatory impulse is needed to restore the balance. Living on our planet earth makes it very difficult for us to be in total harmony with ourselves and with all life around us. Therefore, with our life in motion, there are always things for us to work out while we are in physical incarnation.

Once we start to act in ways that are not in tune with greater needs of the whole, we will feel less connected to our Spiritual self, and therefore more alone. This process is reflected in the different stages of growth as we go through life. We start as babies and young children, with innocence and a weakening connection with what may be called universal love. From the beginning, we have an insatiable curiosity to explore and learn. But as we learn, we become more self-conscious and self-interested, and through that orientation, less aware of how everything is connected. As we enter puberty, the world no longer appears to be a perfect place and we feel bound to develop our individuality and self-consciousness. Then, when we live through our adulthood, we feel an increasing yearning to want to combine our sense of individuality with a desire to know 'God' and our relationship with all beings.

Feeling alone can be very difficult for us because in essence we do not want to feel that way. However, as well as our yearning to be united with our divine essence, there is also the yearning to experience life as fully separated from this divine essence as possible. It is as though we can only experience the full meaning and scope of existence, if we as souls allow ourselves to experience a state of what appears to be almost complete darkness.

Along our journey as souls, it appears to me that we separate ourselves from the state of unity where we feel at one with all life, and seek instead to embrace the darkness. From there, we aim to bring light and love into those dark places so we can bring that awareness home to our spiritual essence. This implies that as souls we strive to learn to be able to cope with every facet of human existence. Such a journey needs many, many lifetimes, I believe. Also, the expression of our existence is somehow unique and individual. For us to be able to celebrate our uniqueness is an important step upon our way. By learning to accept the dark, we build our individuality. This is the positive side of accepting a state of aloneness. To my own mind, love is as much about building our individuality as it is about embracing union with life.

The principles of seeking individuality on the one hand, and wanting to embrace life and nurture our connection with it on the other, can easily appear to be in conflict with each other. They are like the active and passive principles or the masculine and the feminine. I feel that karma is a process that strives to help us bring these impulses into harmony within us.

We can only learn as souls by knowing the consequences of what we do. Therefore, we have to perceive and feel the results of our actions. As we go through successive incarnations, we develop our capacity for self-consciousness. The more we experience of life, the more our maturity, as a soul evolves. While we continue to learn, there may be certain triggers prompting us to act in a manner that continually throws us off balance. It is our task to rectify those imbalances. We have many rough edges as souls that need polishing before we reach a state of being whereby we can advance beyond the need for physical incarnation. In the meantime, we continue to be given challenges that we have to meet, to test our capacity to act truly.

Karma manifests in many forms. If we cause hurt to another human being by not offering sufficient respect to that person, the only way we learn is through being able to feel what it is like when we are similarly disrespected. This is one aspect of karma in action; it is like a mirror reflecting back to us what we have directed outwards.

When we experience difficulties in our lives, we are inclined to speculate about what we did to deserve this. We might feel that our circumstances must have been determined by karma that we have created in the past. However, this is not necessarily the case. People tend to believe that when 'bad' things are happening to them, they must be being punished for what they did wrong in the past. But we need to cope with our challenges and accept them, rather than feel sorry for ourselves.

We may choose to take on some new challenge as a soul, and the circumstances we face could have nothing to do with the past. We might have confronted similar situations in the past to those we are going through now, and the energy of those events may impinge on what is happening. But it does not help to feel that some aspect of our lives is a punishment: we do not learn from opportunities that circumstances bring us with that attitude.

We may need to cleanse ourselves from the energies relating to that past, because in our souls it is not our wish to repeat things but to move on and mature. Therefore, if we are stuck in some pattern of action that we have repeated many times, we may be inclined to do the same thing again because of the familiarity of it. If we recognise the pattern from the past and fully acknowledge it, we will not feel the same pull to perpetuate what we have done. We will feel liberated to make a new choice.

The choices we make as souls test us to our limits. Through past life regression we learn about ourselves, and explore patterns that we have created in our existence to get to where we are today. Regression experiences often seem to give merely a tiny piece in what is the very elaborate and many-layered fabric of our soul being.

Learning about Karma through Regression

Regression sessions often indicate karmic patterns because the experiences that emerge from one past lifetime might relate to another lifetime, where a theme has been developed and encountered again. Sometimes it can be very clear when this has taken place.

At the end of a past life session, when appropriate, I ask my client's consciousness to reveal an experience to give a reason for my client going through that particular life. This can give some very interesting responses. Typically, my clients gain a glimpse of another past life where the other polarity of experience was in evidence. For example, if my client had gone through a past life of being a victim of abuse, the answering experience may be one of another lifetime where he or she was the perpetrator of abuse.

One other past life experience might not be enough to answer all the issues brought up in a particular session. Quite frequently, it is more complex. Past life regression sessions reveal bits and pieces of karmic puzzles, but do not usually address all of it.

From my own study, I have come across past lifetimes that I would call 'turn around' lives. These lifetimes can be very significant because they relate to experiences where some limiting pattern was altered and the soul started to act differently. These lives can be very healing when they remove a difficulty or restriction that was in place in that soul's mind.

For instance, if the soul goes through a series of lifetimes where, whenever they feel rejected, they become vengeful towards the person they hold responsible, this might be difficult to overcome. Finally, after many lifetimes, that soul may be confronted with an experience of rejection in a lifetime where, instead of being vengeful, they release the person that they feel is betraying them, and are able to let go more graciously. This is a turn around lifetime. After it, this particular pattern would hopefully lose its force. The lifetimes building up to this turn around probably contribute considerable tension to the soul while the pattern becomes further engrained. Each time the soul does not turn around adds a feeling of failure and the sense that things have to be done differently.

Unfortunately, I have noticed that turn around lives do not occur very frequently in past life regressions. It is probably the case that we learn more through witnessing where we went wrong rather than when we went right. If we are in danger of repeating a pattern from the past, where we went out of balance, then we will need to be reminded of the mistake that we once made - rather than when we put it right again. Thus, unless I ask for them during a regression session, such lives do not tend to come forward. But without these 'turn around' lives being visible, a very important element in the whole picture of karma will be missing.

It could be suggested that past life regression is a tool to help people in their present lives to work through patterns that are no longer in harmony with their deeper needs. In that way, our present lives can become turn around lives.

Coming across past lives that were turn around experiences has made me more determined to do my own study of past lives, so that I can understand the mechanism of karma more comprehensively. This has led to me setting up what I have called my 'soul line experiment'.

For a long time, I have been interested learning how karma operates specifically within the experience of the soul over the space of several lifetimes. Recently, I began to explore my own past lives in an attempt to gain knowledge of my own karmic patterns. The results of this experiment have been both illuminating and fascinating for me, and I would like to share some aspects of what I have discovered.

I am uncertain as to how typical my own experiences are when compared to other souls. From learning a little about my soul, I do feel that I have had urges, strengths and weaknesses that may not be exactly the same as everyone. However, my hunch is that all souls have to cope with quite similar dilemmas. Therefore, what I have discovered about my own soul, could resonate with others as well.

My Soul Line Experiment

As I have indicated, since my teenage years I have been curious to find out about my own past lives. Over the years I have explored many of my lives through regression. I have also gained awareness of some of my lives through the experiences of others, people who feel on a soul level that they have known me before.

To go into regression myself, I have used the Spirit guide of my colleague, Lynda. This guide's name is Albani. By placing Lynda into trance. I could access Albani, who would lead me into regression.

One morning, I awoke with the impulse that I wanted to gain a record of all my past lives, or as many of them as I could manage, going back in order from the present time. Later that day, I asked Albani, if she could help me to accomplish this. I knew that it would be too time consuming and emotionally demanding to go through each one as a full regression. What I wished was to gain a brief overview of each one including details of the type of character that I was, the circumstances and setting of the life, its principal challenges and the manner of my death and approximate age at passing. It became clear as I discussed this, that I would need to do this in stages. I did not know how easy it would be to pick up all these details. Nor could I be certain whether I would be able to give a comprehensive account of each life without missing any. But I was quite determined to try.

As I began my first session, I was feeling quite nervous, but Albani outlined a visualisation that proved to be very effective. From a safe initial place, I needed to open a door and there in front of me was a line of light, my soul line going far off into the distance. Every so often, along this line, I could see a circle of light that represented another incarnation. I could step from one to the next, experiencing details of each one in turn before moving on to another one. My starting point was my present life as Paul. At the completion of the session I could come back through the door and return that way.

With Albani's guidance, I found as I stepped into each circle, that impressions would come to me and I was able to answer all the questions that I had set up for myself. The results were very interesting.

Immediately after each session I would write down the impressions that had come to me, and then I could study them. I found that I could manage about six to eight lives in one session.

As I slowly began to travel back through the ages, I was quite amazed by the impressions that had come to me. Some of the lives were familiar to me through my previous work, but many were not. As I inwardly stepped onto each circle, I found that I had no forethought about what that particular life would be. But I had to trust that what was revealed to my mind would be accurate.

When I examined my findings, I began to sense some of the inter-relationships between lives. I could feel how the energy from some lives, even some from quite a way back, was feeding into my present life. This gave me much cause for thought. There were lives that felt as if they did not have anything to do with my present circumstances. As I looked further I observed that some lives seemed to be in clumps, where a specific theme was being explored over several lives and mistakes worked out.

It was interesting for me to place past lives that were already familiar to me in this soul line. The lives that I knew were either life times that I had accessed myself, when I had previously gone through regression, or else lives where I had been identified by others from their own regressions. These lives made more sense to me, now that I could observe them in the context of other lives around them.

Exploring my soul line was quite a concentrated experience. I hoped that I had remembered all my lives in the correct order, and I feel confident that it is largely accurate. However, one evening as I meditated impressions came to me quite spontaneously of a clump of lives that I had omitted. Once included with the others, the overall pattern of the lives then felt more complete. On a couple of other occasions single lives came to me that I had overlooked. So, I suppose it is an ongoing process to gain a full knowledge of all these lives.

At the time of writing, I have recorded details of over one hundred lives stretching back over 4000 years to about 2000 BC. Several of these lives were very short, and I have estimated that there have been gaps averaging about 10-12 years between each lifetime. Obviously, I have packed the lives in, one after the other, without much space in between. Instinctively, I sense that most people have had greater gaps between their lives over this period than I have chosen. I suppose that my soul has been quite eager to gain further earthly experiences.

When I reached this point at about 2000 BC, I decided to pause and study some of the specific lives that had come up in more depth and detail. I was also very interested to study my karmic relationship over this period with various people who had been important for me in my life now.

Albani showed me a technique that I could use to examine particular relationships that I had shared with certain souls. Again, the method that she suggested proved to be very effective. By imagining a distinct colour for each person that I chose, I could sense where on my soul line the connection with that other soul was most intense and significant. By following this exploration, I began to observe patterns within lives and interweaving between them that was again, quite fascinating.

The various lifetimes on my soul line expressed many qualities. There were lives that appeared to be very positive and others that were dark, where I felt that I had been cruel and unkind. The most obvious finding with the lives was to be seen in the great variety of the experiences.

Eventually, I tried with a couple of my clients to apply the same method to explore their soul line and found that the way that their lives inter-related to each other tallied with the findings on my own soul line.

Now I would like to share specifically about some of the patterns that I have discovered within my soul line. Hopefully, this may give some indications about how karma can work its way out for souls. It is a field of enquiry that could be carried on much further.

My Karmic Relationship with Eleyna

The first pattern of links between lifetimes that I have discerned from my soul line, that I want to share, concerns my karmic relationship with my wife Eleyna. It is typical for human souls to have a number of other souls with whom they continue a relationship over the course of many, many lifetimes. In my case, I sense that Eleyna's soul is the one with whom I have shared the closest relationship, and I feel that we have travelled our way through various lives together for a very long period of time. Although we are very close, and I feel that she has been my partner much more frequently than with any other soul, I do not regard her as my soul mate or anything like that. I more feel that we are fellow pilgrims that love each other and want to help each other to grow, each having our own lessons to learn.

I have noticed that Eleyna has not featured in all the lives from my soul line, from what I have discovered so far, but I do feel that she has been in most of them. With her soul being so close to me, it would be easy to imagine that we should be partners every life that we live and therefore live happily ever after. But it doesn't seem to have worked that way. If we shared a harmonious relationship every lifetime, we would not learn through each other, but would probably become entrenched in certain patterns and not grow. It feels more that the kind of relationship we have shared has often been challenging, so that we have been tested to learn something substantial through the power of our interactions. Because we are so close as souls, any interaction between us in a given lifetime has tended to affect us very deeply, more so than with other souls. Therefore, some of the scenarios that we have set up for ourselves in particular lifetimes have severely tested the personalities that we have become, to determine if we can find the way through our difficulties to experience love. I notice from the soul line that sometimes we appear to have succeeded and other times we have not.

With Eleyna's soul, I feel that there has often been a high degree of co-operation and working together. There have been other souls with whom I have tended to share a more antagonistic relationship, so I feel that there has been like a kind of dance for certain souls in the way that we have met through numerous incarnations.

In the next chapter I wish to write in more depth and detail about the nature of soul relationships. However, I think you can assume that in your personal environments of today, there are probably many people whose souls you have met before in other lives. As a seeker you may be able to sense souls with whom you have been associated on a long-term basis, and even the dynamics of how that relationship may have manifested in the past.

For instance, as souls we may set a situation up for ourselves where we will be attracted to form a relationship with someone, whose soul may have been involved with us in very difficult and abusive circumstances in a previous life. We will probably not be aware of that initially when we meet them again. But as we get to know them, some of the old feelings may seep through, and it will test us as to how we deal with those feelings and what sort of relationship we are able to build this time.

From my own soul line I would like to give an example of relationship karma based on four consecutive lives where in each one, I shared a close relationship with Eleyna's soul. In each of these lives there were quite strong challenges, and apart from the last one, I don't think that I did very well in meeting those challenges. Therefore I created a need for manifesting balancing situations so that I could learn.

I believe that the impetus for the situations that we created in these lives came from earlier experiences, mainly in Egypt where Eleyna had lived some lives in which she had been quite heartless and cruel. Therefore, I believe she had needed to choose, as a soul, some lives where she could experience being the recipient of someone else being cold and heartless towards her, as a balance. However, in the first of the lives I am going to discuss, I feel that I overplayed my hand and treated her much more badly than was necessary. This then had consequences for me.

In this life, I was a domineering, abusive, rough man who was married to Eleyna's soul. I had an emotionally deprived childhood with a father who beat me and reacted to this by becoming very closed and unfeeling. Anyway, I regarded my wife as an impediment and treated her like dirt, eventually killing her so that I could be with another woman who seemed to have more money and be living in better material circumstances. This woman, incidentally, poisoned me later on. Experiencing this regression, I felt as though I was totally blocked from expressing any love. Inside, I had an anger and determination that I had to get my own way so that no one would hurt me. I didn't like myself for it, and projected my own self-hate into the way that I related to my wife.

Some years earlier, Eleyna had regressed to this lifetime at a time when she was afraid that I might dominate her. Going through this regression helped to cleanse her of this fear and she could forgive me. But for her, it was very hard to understand how I could treat her in this fashion during this incarnation.

Looking to the next lifetime, it was possible to see how the karma that I incurred from this first experience was worked out. It was actually quite subtle, and not the brutal tit for tat experience that may have been expected.

In this next lifetime, I was female and Eleyna's soul was my male lover. In this life, I fell passionately in love with Eleyna's soul and could not consider how my life would be without him. He actually treated me kindly, with no cruelty at all. At some point though, my lover went away on a boat trip, and I knew that I would never see him again. I believe that his boat capsized in a storm. In any case, I decided that I couldn't cope without him and so I committed suicide by cutting open my wrists.

After the first experience, when I treated Eleyna's soul like dirt and didn't want her, in this one, her soul consumed me as being all-important and precious. In the first experience, she was dependant upon me for her survival and I killed her. The next life was one where I felt emotionally dependant upon her, as my male lover, for my survival, then he was gone. This is obviously the other polarity that I had to experience. I didn't do very well though. I felt this time that I couldn't live without her. By committing suicide, I did not value my own life sufficiently, and I allowed what happened to Eleyna's soul to affect me so that I reacted with very negative responses and actions. In two lives, I had gone from one extreme to the other. In that life, I believe that Eleyna's soul had acted to serve me and try to help me to learn my lesson. Because I did not, this precipitated further experiences.

The next life introduced additional themes that again might have had their roots in earlier lives. In this experience, I was an unhappily married man. Eleyna's soul came into my life as a young and vulnerable woman who fell in love with me. She was of a lower class than me, and with me being in the position of power I could have treated her like dirt, as I had done in the first life that I discussed. However, this time I did manage to open my heart to her. In our interactions, I treated her with sensitivity and kindness and loved her far more than my wife. However, I was not a totally honourable man. When my wife found out about my affair, she vowed for revenge. My young companion was brought before the courts charged with improper behaviour. The test for me was about whether I would be willing to defend Eleyna's soul in court, uphold my integrity and risk my own position or not. In the event, I did not defend her and she was subsequently stoned to death. As it sunk into my awareness about my cowardice, I could not live with myself and I ended my life by hanging myself.

On Eleyna's side, there was also a wound that carried over from this lifetime. She felt bitterness that I had not spoken up for her at a time when she needed it. This is another past life that Eleyna, herself, has also experienced in regression, and she found it very harrowing. Again, though, it related to issues that she was experiencing at the time when she was afraid that I would not support her sufficiently. Going through this regression helped her to reduce her fear.

In the final life of this sequence, I was a young woman having an affair with a married man (Eleyna's soul). This life was like a mirror to the previous life. On this occasion I was stoned to death and my lover did not support me, but the emotional dynamics were completely different. Although I have not been through this regression and only got a brief overview of it, I believe that in this experience there was a degree of peace and acceptance on my part about my fate. I sense that I had some religious faith that helped me. I was able to let go, and release my attachment to being with him, and open myself to fate. Also, I feel that Eleyna's personality in that life was sorry about what happened and did not react in an extreme way, unlike the previous lives where for each of us, our emotions had been very disturbed. Therefore, I feel that our responses in this life helped to resolve the karma that we had built up, particularly on my side, so that we could move on.

These lives were obviously more complex than I have been able to portray them and there were other souls involved. But I think that it is possible from the description I have given to see how polarities of experience may be presented as another form of the same lesson for a soul to learn. In the instance of these lives, I was quite a slow learner.

Some of the strands of karma from these lives did not appear to have been cleared and addressed in the last life of this sequence. From my soul line, there is another life, some hundreds of years on from these experiences that I feel has a link with the second of these lives that I have discussed. In this life, I was a Roman administrator in Britain in the early years of Roman occupation. I married one of the local Celtic women (Eleyna's soul once again). My wife found it difficult to adjust to the new conditions and became addicted to alcohol. Although I tried very hard to help her, and loved her very much, eventually she was killed from an alcohol-related accident. Although I missed my wife terribly this time round, I did not end my own life but carried on. My life felt very lonely after that, but I did learn that I could live without Eleyna's soul from a situation where she left me in tragic circumstances. Therefore, I feel that this experience helped to heal the earlier past life experience where I felt that my lover had abandoned me. By the time of this Roman experience, I had become stronger. Even though I was infatuated with Eleyna's soul and loved her passionately in both experiences, in the later life I felt more able to stand on my own feet, even when I was bereft of Eleyna's companionship. This was obviously a good growing experience for me.

Karma Involving the Development of Character

I would like to outline the karmic patterns I have observed from another sequence of lives, this time involving various souls who were helping me to learn a lesson. The theme of learning in this sequence concerns my soul learning to combine an occupation with spiritual matters and having respect for others' more earthly personal needs at the same time.

It was the first of these lives where most of the mistakes were made. The karma that was generated came about because of a soul challenge that I did not meet. I was living in India and was brought up in a cloistered monastery to become both the spiritual and secular leader of a large community of people. My fellow monks and I were very much removed from being confronted with the everyday needs of the people who lived outside the monastery. I was not prepared by my living environment to deal with these problems. At the same time, I came to feel my own position as somewhat elevated and expected that my authority would be unquestioned. In the most part, I was quite a gentle man and enjoyed the spiritual practices that formed the main part of my life. But when a woman stirred up protest against my leadership and complained that the people's needs and rights were being ignored, I felt completely affronted. In my anger, I had this woman stoned to death. Immediately, I realised that I had done something very wrong. My test had been to let this woman in, so that the barriers between the monastic life and the life of the people could be broken down. Then, the energies of each of these aspects of community life could have fed each other. What I had done to this woman went against all the teachings of my spiritual practises. With my closest companions, I confessed to them my regret and went up into the mountains to try and atone for my mistake. Feeling despair, I decided consciously to leave my body and so I died.

In my next lifetime, I set up a quite similar scenario for myself to test myself again. This time, I was born into the ruling family of a city and province in Italy. My upbringing was quite insulated from being exposed to the needs of the 'common' people. Whereas in the previous lifetime, I had been brought up with a regime of spiritual practises and discipline to adhere to, in this experience the emphasis was more about learning the secular mechanisms of power. I suppose that the potential was there for me to have become a ruler removed from the needs of the people, as in my previous life. But this time, I faced a challenge that I met successfully and this completely changed the route of this life.

My wife became very ill and was dying. I was distraught, and wanted to do anything to help her get better. My desire to help her enabled me to discover that I had healing powers in my hands and, because I accepted and utilised this ability, she recovered. After that, I was much more caring, making it my business to learn about the needs of the people. I lived the rest of that life as a compassionate and caring ruler.

This life did much, to resolve the karma that had been built up from the previous life, and gave my soul character additional maturity. However, I am aware that not all the issues from the first life were addressed in this second experience.

The next life of this sequence, I believe, occurred some hundreds of years later. In this lifetime, I was a teenage girl, very impressionable, and inspired by my mother to want to seek God through the church. In the village where I lived there was a monastery, and I wanted to be part of this monastery and satisfy my thirst for spiritual experience and knowledge. The monastery was closed to women but, through my insistence, I was allowed to sweep and clean the chapel when the monks were not conducting services there. One monk took me into his confidence. I trusted him and he sexually abused me. Following this incident, the monk concerned made sure that from then on I was excluded from the monastery.

The pain of this was too much for me to bear. My desire to enter the monastery had become an obsession. One day, I climbed over the walls and slit my wrists while I lay on one of the gravestones, ensuring that my blood would forever be in the grounds of the monastery.

This was not a very nice life, but I suppose that it helped me to appreciate the pain that the woman from the first life must have felt when she was excluded. The determination that I felt for my blood to soak into the grounds of the monastery ensured that my next lifetime would be again centred on a monastic experience. This time, I would be trying to put things right.

The scenario of the life immediately following this one was very much like the first life. I was male and spent most of my life in the insular, cloistered environment of a monastery, rising in position until I became the Abbott of this monastery. Now I don't know all the details of this story because I have only had a brief overview of it, but I sense that during the course of this past life, I initiated reforms to open up the monastery to the outside community. By doing this, my soul completed the purpose that I had first set out for myself in the earlier life from India. Therefore, I feel that the karma engendered from this sequence of experiences was then resolved.

Karmic Lives of Service

Among the various lives that I have come across from studying my soul line, so far, there have also been some very short lives. In some of these, I sense that my purpose was more to be present for the sake of some other soul's lesson, rather than for any obvious benefit relating to my own learning. These appear to have been lives of service to others. I believe that most of us as souls engage in this type of life periodically, especially as a means to try and help another soul that we may love. Things don't always work out the way that they have been planned though.

In one life from a sequence, where I feel I was trying to serve and help others, I found myself as a young man who felt passionately drawn to want to help some lepers in a leper colony in India. I had some healing ability and tried to provide comfort and support to these people. At some point, I too contracted the disease. I feel that my purpose in that life was to open myself for others to help me, but nobody did. I suffered from complete rejection and a horrible death where my body gradually became rotten and fell to pieces. From the experience of having suffered so much rejection, I stopped believing in myself. This precipitated further the onset of the disease. The karma in this lifetime occurred straight away rather than in a future lifetime. Through feeling so rejected by others and letting that eat away at me, I became emotionally crippled inside. By doing this, I was distracted from my purpose, and suffered accordingly.

A couple of years ago, I regressed to a life when I suffered from acute sciatica and was afraid of dying. Going through this past life experience actually helped me to feel calmer about my ordeal with the sciatica. My close friends helped me to feel that I was not alone and this enabled me gradually to build up my strength again. I know that my lesson at that time was about me learning to believe in myself, so it had a lot of resonance with the past life. The event that had triggered the sciatica was the break up of my marriage, an experience that led me to fundamentally question and doubt my self-worth.

Another Karmic Sequence

The next set of lives illustrating the workings of karma that I would like to share commenced again with a life where I was cruel. In this experience I was a trader who spent most of my time at sea. People were transported in my boat and I treated them as slaves. I was big and strong and seemed to take delight in causing hardship and suffering to others. As a child I had suffered cruelty from my father, and now was quite happy to impose that upon others. From one image I saw, I was using a whip to hurt people on my boat. Eventually, I was killed in a mutiny, dying quite young.

During that life, my compassionate side was completely suppressed and I think that there was considerable karma for me to make up. I got lost in the enjoyment of imposing power upon others. The next three lives seem to relate directly to my experience as this trader.

In the following life, I found myself forced into a monastery (yet again!) from a very early age. This monastery was a very cruel place and I was treated there just like a slave! Within these conditions I found it very hard to endure my life. After a time, I stopped eating and consequently wasted away to my death.

My impression from this experience is that I died too early, and that it had been intended for me to experience the hardship of this place for a while longer to make up for my actions in the previous life.

In my next existence, then, I only lived to be two years old. I was born male, and suffered continual abuse and cruelty until I died.

Even after this, I do not think that the karma was fully met. My next life was in Scotland at the time of the Picts. Again, it was a very, very hard and desolate life. I was not kind to my wife in this existence, and so things carried on into my next life where I was a young woman dominated and abused by her husband. Because I largely accepted my fate in this experience, I feel that the karma from the earlier trader life was finally laid to rest.

A Good Life

During the course of my soul line explorations, I became aware of a female spiritual being who wanted to help me. Her energy was very gentle, but also very wise. She had a much stronger presence than my personal guide, Sebastian, and I believe that she came from a higher spiritual plane. During one of my sessions, the name came to me quite clearly that she was called Eurydice. As my communication with her developed, I learnt that she had once been my personal guide for many thousands of years in ancient times, but since then had moved on. I even believe that I was associated with her physically a long time ago before the time when she was my guide when I was at a much younger stage of my soul development.

While Sebastian was there as a support for me in the trials and tribulations of my everyday life, I sensed that Eurydice wanted to assist me with my deeper soul growth and gaining further knowledge of my soul.

During one of our conversations, the topic came up about what entailed a good life in terms of soul growth. I asked for her opinion about which lifetime had been my best in this regard over the past two thousand years. The answer Eurydice gave quite astonished me.

I suppose the most obvious choice of what entailed a very good life would be one where I was happy and being very caring and helpful towards many people. But the lifetime that Eurydice picked out was nothing like that. It was an incarnation that I lived in Sweden about 1700 AD, where I had been an alcoholic.

For some years, I had been aware of this particular experience, and felt this past life to be very strong in its energy, but I could not quite understand what made it so significant for me. Shortly afterwards, I had a regression to go into this lifetime in more depth; things became much clearer.

In this past life, I was born with an extremely sensitive nature into an extended family situation living in a large farmhouse. From the very beginning of my life, I was sexually and physically abused on a daily basis by nearly all the various adults around me, including my mother and father. I had to endure mental cruelty, emotional deprivation and torture. There was no love from anybody except my sister and one or two servants who also suffered with the abuse. My only refuge was with nature, the trees, the lake and the wild animals. I could sense their divinity and they became my friends.

Through it all, I did not give up and I did not become vindictive, even though I suffered hugely. In my later years, I turned to alcohol as a means of escape from the turbulence of feelings inside me. One day in my late twenties I stumbled onto a rake that pierced me, and I died.

I am aware that over many, many lifetimes, especially in earlier times, I had taken on roles of leadership and wrestled with issues of control. In this life, I had no control over anything, and I was abused constantly, yet I largely accepted it and survived. The learning for me was immense.

When I considered it in the spiritual realm, I realised that this had been a chosen life. There had been no obligation for me to work out negativity with the other people in that life. I had entered that life as an act of service towards the others involved, to give them an opportunity to find compassion in their hearts. Primarily I wanted to test myself as a soul, and my ability to cope in such a difficult environment.

Facing Our Karmic Responsibilities

Many other examples exist that I could chose from my soul line to illustrate the nature of soul growth and the operation of cause and effect. If we move from considering my personal experience to what happens for humanity in general, there are numerous examples of karma working in our lives. Someone who is very kind to us may feel a compulsion to be that away because they were cruel to us in another life. We may feel compelled to want to help someone else because of the way that we acted in a previous life. Everything has a reason and a purpose in our lives.

Our lives can be very complex with many sub-themes of behavioural difficulties and relationship dramas. I suppose that there could be many past lives influencing us. It does not appear to me to be a very straightforward task for us to delineate and judge what our precise karmic needs are at a given moment. There can be many movements within our character suggesting different actions. All I feel that we can do is to open ourselves to our hearts and instincts, listening as deeply within as we can, and asking for inner guidance when we need it. The best that we can do is to be as honest as we can and express our truth.

In the soul line that I have been studying from my past lives, I have gained a lot of knowledge of my past experiences and the patterns of karma that I have tried to work out previously. Such knowledge gives me insight, but does not necessarily make it easier to live my present life. I feel that I perhaps now know more of the things that can help guide my actions. But in the my present life experience, I still need to make choices and overcome my fears so that I can act appropriately when I am called upon to do so. And this is the challenge that we all have to meet.

Chapter 23

Soul Relationships

In the course of our daily lives, we meet many people. When we believe in reincarnation, we are inclined to wonder who we have known before in previous lives. Some of our acquaintances we may have met on many occasions, in numerous incarnations – whereas we might be meeting others for the first time. We could encounter someone in the street who has learnt all the lessons needed as a soul on earth, who is ready to advance beyond the need for earthly incarnations. Other people could be just at the beginning of their cycle of lifetimes. We are not necessarily going to discern truthful answers to enquiries that we have about these matters. Yet I feel that they are valid questions to ask.

If we are interacting with two people, one of these people might be a soul that has been our lover on many occasions in the past, while the other could be someone on a soul level that is quite new to us. Then, presuming that we had knowledge about our history with those souls, we could well be much more interested in the first person than the second. But our inner task might be to love and respect these two people equally. This would be a challenge for us to resolve.

On the other hand, if we gain knowledge concerning the history of our soul link with somebody with whom we are in contact, this could help us appreciate more deeply the dynamics involved in the relationship, so that we can learn to deal with it better. Such knowledge could potentially be of great benefit.

When we undergo past life regression, we begin to gain knowledge of where we have known other souls before. Some people can do this much more easily than others. I believe that, if we have an interest in learning about these things, we can trust that, at the right moment, such information will be given to us.

The desire to learn about our soul history, and the nature of our soul relationships with others, goes right to the heart of our search to discover our essential being. If we gain knowledge of this sort, it is up to us to choose to deal with this information responsibly.

From my own research into past lives, including the work I have done with my own soul line and from regression work with many hundreds of people, I have begun to draw some conclusions about the nature of soul relationships. There is also much that still remains a mystery to me.

With regards to people in our everyday life - our family, friends and enemies - I feel that, unless we are a very young soul, we are likely to have met most of those people as souls in a number of lives. Some of those lives could have been lives where our interaction with these individual souls was congenial and others where it was difficult.

Our relationship with souls that we know can take on many shapes and forms. We can be male or female; the relationship can be close or antagonistic. Basically we try to help each other as souls to grow, mature, and experience all the various aspects of life.

Soul Mates

If we consider our closest relationships, one question that very often people ask is about whether they have a soul mate, someone with whom they could be perfectly compatible. I do not believe that such a thing easily exists.

When we are first created as a self-conscious soul, I believe that we are created as an individual. As we undergo our journey as a soul, we have to make our decisions as individuals and we have to meet our challenges also on that basis. However, we are learning the lessons of love and so we are striving towards ever-greater union with others. The force of love prompts us to keep meeting with certain souls, because we want to evolve together and help each other.

We could decide at some stage in our soul journey that we always want to be with some other soul, and such a decision will influence the course of our evolution. But such a decision is up to us and does not imply, say, that we are a being that has been split in two, eternally in search of reuniting with our other half.

Soul Link Patterns

There are many different relationship patterns that we could adopt as souls as we proceed on our journey. We could choose to evolve mainly as a soul on our own, with perhaps some other souls with whom we would interact spasmodically. Alternatively, we could link ourselves with one other soul and have that soul as the main focus of our attention, with some further souls having a subsidiary interest. In another variation, we might choose to unite with a group of other souls and work with these souls mainly as a means to gain further experience, and thus feel ourselves as part of a soul group. The patterns can be quite complex, and we can also decide to change the focus of our soul relationships at different phases of our evolution.

From what I have been able to discern from my research into my own soul history, there is quite a large circle of souls with whom I choose to interact. Some of these souls, I believe, have been around in incarnation for at least as long as I have, and we try to help each other in our struggles to progress. I feel that we have quite often associated with each other as a group. However, there are other souls with whom I have an equally strong link in which, with them, we have built our relationship through the strength of our individual interactions.

I am also aware of souls with whom I have once had a very close relationship, but with whom I have only had infrequent associations more recently. It seems that the main purpose of these relationships has been fulfilled in the past. But I suppose it to be also possible that those souls may draw closer to me again at some moment in the future.

As souls, we have different levels of maturity. It may be helpful to us to associate primarily with a group of souls that have a similar degree of maturity as ourselves. The balance of giving and taking is more likely to be achieved between these souls, in theory at least. But we have the ability to form a love link with any other being, human or otherwise. So we can also choose to associate with souls that have more or less maturity than ourselves, as we wish. Once a love link is established it continues throughout eternity

Sometimes, when a soul reaches the point where they do not need to incarnate upon the earth anymore, that soul may choose to become the spiritual guide of another soul whom they love very much, so that they can continue their association. There are cases, of course, where this may not be appropriate, and the soul in incarnation on earth may need a guide with whom they are less familiar.

I believe that my present spiritual guide, Sebastian, is a soul that I have met in physical incarnation in more than one of my previous lives. He has told me that we knew each other well in ancient Greece.

The main point that I wish to make is that with love, all kinds of creative possibilities can open up. It is up to us to create the soul relationship patterns that feel right to us.

Soul Vows

It is quite common for us as souls to make commitments to other souls, either while we are in earthly incarnation, or when we are in spirit. Sometimes, these commitments are so strong that they extend over many lifetimes or even the whole course of our earthly incarnations and beyond. I call these kinds of commitments 'soul vows'.

It is well to remember that in the spirit phase of our incarnations we still have choice: it is here that we are much more aware of the larger perspective of our soul journey. Therefore any vows that we make while in spirit are likely to have a lot of power and endurance.

At an earlier stage of my own soul journey, I made several vows that are still operating in lives currently. In one of the ancient civilisations before Atlantis, many thousands of years ago, I believe that I went through a series of very bleak and dark lives where I killed and hurt many, many people. As the pattern of these lives continued, I desperately tried to find a way out. Finally, to my great relief, I entered a life where I had similar severe challenges to those that I had been working on, but this time I managed to meet those challenges positively and act compassionately so that I made a difference to the lives of many. Thus, I started to turn the pattern around. It was such a relief to me to be able to begin to free myself from this darkness that I desperately wanted to make amends with those souls who had been most negatively affected by my actions. With some of those souls, I made some passionate soul vows following that positive life, where I promised to try to help them from then on.

One of these vows, I believe, was with my wife and partner, Eleyna. I think that it was then that we decided that we wanted to live our incarnations very closely allied and to support each other through our incarnations. I believe that her soul was instrumental in helping me to turn the pattern of destructiveness around, and I helped her soul too. From this very intense experience, I feel that we decided that we had the potential to make a worthwhile team. After that time we became very closely associated. But she was not the only one.

Following that lifetime, there were several other souls towards whom I felt a sense of responsibility to try to support them and guide them, where I could, out of a sense of love for them and how much I had hurt them. My resolve with these vows has been tested many times, and I have not always been successful. Such vows are made from love though, making them very different from the more negative oaths and curses that are also possible.

Negative Vows and Soul Entrapments

Let us consider the nature of negative vows and curses. At the end of a lifetime where a soul has suffered very badly at the hands of another, that soul may vow to make life 'hell' for the one that perpetuated the suffering. In a similar fashion, a soul may endeavour to curse another soul. These are vows made whilst in earthly incarnation, not in the spiritual realms. Usually, when vows of this nature are expressed, the souls concerned will work very hard in spirit to try and find scenarios whereby, in the immediate lives to follow, these vows are resolved and rescinded. Otherwise the effects upon the relationship of the two souls concerned can be very damaging, very quickly.

When people gather hatred into their hearts concerning another soul, it can result in lifetime after lifetime of conflict and bitter recriminations. If only one of the souls is reacting negatively, it may be possible to start a process of healing, for both souls to learn from these interactions. But it does need for both souls to be willing to change, before things can finally be worked out. However, when both souls continue to want to slug it out, this can go on for many, many lives. These lives can be full of emptiness, resentment and regret.

Not all souls are compatible with each other. As souls we all have our own vibration of being, with unique interests, dispositions and inclinations. With some souls we will find ourselves much more easily in harmony than with others. This is something that is also true in spirit. We may gain an affinity with another soul by loving them and receiving their love throughout the ages. But some souls may quite naturally pull in other directions and not be suited for us in terms of close interaction.

If we find ourselves in an intractable conflict with another soul, there are two possibilities as to how we could best move forward with this. If we deeply love this soul, we may need to find peace through togetherness and acceptance. We might need to work out our rough edges with that soul by being willing to become closer to them.

However, it is also possible that we may have become entangled with the other soul without realising the consequences of what we were doing. In this case, especially if this is a soul with whom we are basically incompatible, we may need to let go, and stop reacting to provocation, so that we can free ourselves to concentrate our attentions more upon those souls with whom we do have an affinity. This is where we need guidance to help us to make wise decisions.

Another trap that we can get into as souls on our path in relationship to other souls is when we become infatuated. This state can come into being when we are afraid that we could not live without that other soul in our lives. We may want that soul very much too. The problem with infatuation is that our attention is drawn very much to the soul with whom we are fixated. Our appreciation of other souls in terms of their worth and value diminishes, and our expectations of the soul with whom we are fixated is far too great for that soul to fulfil. Therefore, this state of being is likely to create anger and possible violence because the soul concerned cannot get what they want.

The resolution to this problem can be attained through the soul that is infatuated learning to let go. It can only be through detachment that infatuation can transform itself into true love. The lesson of unconditional love is one of the most important tasks for us to achieve as souls. But I also believe that it is one of the most challenging tests for us to pass through as well.

When we hold onto fear, it can prove a trap in terms of our relationships with other souls. By being afraid, we want to withdraw, and can then feel very lonely and isolated. While we are in physical incarnation, I believe that we are meant to interact, so that we can learn to love each other. Fear prompts us not to do this, and therefore always works contrary to our soul needs. The person who is afraid needs to let love in and also express their love to find relief from this problem.

The other main entrapment for souls that I want to mention is guilt. When we blame ourselves for something that we feel that we have done wrong, then we also stop being true to ourselves. Our actions will be affected by what we feel we need to do to make up ground with the ones that we might have let down or hurt. If we blame ourselves too much we may feel that nothing that we ever do could be enough to make up for what we did.

This is a rather self-defeating attitude. In fact, in any situation where we feel that we might have done wrong, we need to leave it up to 'God' to rebalance the dynamics that need some sort of karmic response. We cannot change what we did. We are better off concentrating on what we are doing now, and to make the best of it.

The Power of Love

I believe that the universe we inhabit as souls is full of the most amazing creativity and potential in terms of expressing ourselves. We can only wonder at it. In essence, it is love that gives us these possibilities. We really have the power to create our own destiny in whatever way that we want. Of course, we need to learn how to do that, and this could be the main purpose of physical incarnation - to teach us about this. It is natural for us to want to become like God, or as God, because God is love to my belief. And that God force is inside us waiting to be realised.

When we are in physical incarnation, we tend to lose sight of all this while we struggle around in our limitations and self-absorbed problems. But it is love that we want and need. It is important that we learn to trust, and have faith that we are being looked after. Even when our life appears to be very bleak, then I believe that we have every reason to be hopeful.

Past life regression can help us to reconnect with love, especially when we undergo the experience of death and passing into the spiritual realm. By doing this kind of work, we can open the doors to the true nature of our inner reality. There is a dramatic contrast between the love that people experience in the spiritual realm, and the pain and suffering that characterise physical incarnation.

Often that pain and suffering is only really a delusion, although we will of course feel it very acutely. Our fellow souls are there to help us learn about what is true, and we are there to help them too. In the spiritual realm, we can make our plans and intentions. In the physical realm, we have to carry them out.

Chapter 24

An Experiment in Simultaneous Regression

One of the most intriguing aspects of past life regression is the reality of shared memory.

It is possible for a person to acquire knowledge of one of their past lives, to identify someone they know as a soul featuring in that past life as a character that they met then, and for that other person to have a memory of the same experience from the perspective of this other character. This has happened so many times in my work that I believe it to be intrinsic to the process and therefore achievable for anyone undergoing regression to perceive if they can open to it.

The consequences of this phenomenon imply that past life regression is not merely an expression of someone's isolated imagination, but something that does impinge upon others. A conclusion can be drawn that we are all inwardly connected, and we can speculate that everything that we do in our present lives now links with the actions of others on levels that most of us can only barely conceive.

A group of familiar souls

People that we encounter in our everyday lives could well be souls that we have known before. Meeting those people could have a purpose in terms of furthering a soul relationship or providing a challenge for each other. There is meaning and reason for every moment in our existence.

Sometimes, events may bring a group of people together because at some deeper level the souls concerned had chosen that at a particular juncture in their lives, they would meet and explore their relationship together and accomplish some task. On a conscious level those people might have no idea of the threads that are prompting this gathering, but nonetheless, will be guided to fulfil what had been inwardly decided.

The following study concerns a group of nine people who came from diverse backgrounds and locations to participate in a workshop that I was leading in Scotland. Most of them were not previously acquainted with each other. However, as the workshop proceeded, many of them had a growing sense of familiarity with the other members of the group, as if they had known each other at some deeper level before. When we started doing past life regression, this was borne out and members of the group became aware of a great variety of connections with the others that were there. Many strong friendships developed within the group in a very short space of time.

From the willingness and enthusiasm of this group, I suggested in one of our evenings that we try an experiment in simultaneous regression where more than one of the group could regress to a past lifetime where they felt they had met, at the same time.

Setting up the experiment
To begin the evening, I led a meditation for everyone, in which they could each access a life where they had met at least one other member of the group and identify them. By this stage of the week, they were all so used to doing inner processes that this task was no problem, and with the exception of one group member who was not present, they were all able to come up with lives where they felt that this had happened.

Next, I chose three of these lives to work upon further. With each of these in turn, I asked the person who had accessed the memory in the meditation to lie in the middle of the floor and for those that s/he identified as further participants in the past life to lie down too, so they all lay next to each other. Then it was a matter of directing them all to a couple of critical events from moments when they were together and encouraging them to express their own reality of the situation simultaneously.

The results were quite dramatic. In each of the lives chosen, there were three or four group members involved. So, all eight group members featured in at least one of the simultaneous regressions. After they had finished, I asked them each to write an account of what they had experienced. From this base, I would like to represent a description of what happened.

Regression 1 - A Native American life

In the group meditation, Larry was aware of himself as living in a small Native American encampment. He was a young boy, aged eight or nine years. Larry sensed that he was in a happy and loving family environment, with father, mother and a sister, who was a few years older than him.

In the scene where he entered, he was collecting water from the nearby river and playing around with his sister.

As I moved the meditation on to a later significant event, Larry saw riders approaching on horseback, shouting aggressively. In a scene of panic, his mother grabbed him and his sister and ran desperately to escape from the raiders. Larry saw his mother impaled with a spear through her left shoulder as they were running. As she fell to the floor, she released her grip on the two children and died. Larry had no knowledge of what then happened to his father, his sister or himself and came out of the past life at that point.

In terms of soul identification, Larry immediately recognised all three members of his Native American family as being group members of the workshop. In particular, he sensed that Janie was his mother, Jacqui his father and Shona his sister.

All three of these group members had reacted to Larry's sharing with various feelings, visions and bodily sensations and had a positive expectancy that they were involved in Larry's past life experience.

The next step was to lay the four of them down together so that they could regress together. There was no need for any long, involved induction. With a few clear instructions, they were all fully engrossed in the experience.

Initially, I suggested for them to enter at that moment when the little boy and girl are by the river collecting water. Although I did ask questions to establish the scene, there was much information that was left unsaid. Yet afterwards, when the four of them compared notes, what the four of them had seen in their vision about the setting of the place tallied exactly.

With it being his second excursion into this memory, Larry's recollection of the events was much more detailed than the first time that he did it. He placed himself by the encampment, which was solely for the family. The dwelling where they lived consisted of a single animal skin tepee. Next to the camp, there was a shallow, fast flowing river that was bordered by rocks and boulders. Behind the camp was a cluster of trees and a grassy slope.

He and his sister were at the river where they had been sent to fetch water for their mother. He noticed that his sister was carrying a bowl with coloured beads around the edge, and that he was splashing his sister.

Although I was questioning the others, Larry later reported that he continued to view events in harmony with the way they did.

Shona could see her younger brother smiling mischievously while in the river splashing her. She sensed herself to be carrying a wooden water carrier on her shoulder, feeling happy. Although not spoken, she commented in her personal account that she could see mountains with snow on them in the distance. This is something that they all saw independently, although none of them mentioned it.

In her account, Janie wrote about the weather, that the sky was bright blue, the air clear, the sun shining and hot. She was aware of the children playing in the river, laughing and splashing. Next, she called the children to bring the water for the meal. She was preparing a meal, cutting meat from the proceeds of what her husband had caught with his hunting.

There was a pot on the fire, and she sensed that her husband was behind the tepee, either sharpening knives/spears or cutting animal skin. She could feel a deep feeling of contentment, close family bond and tremendous love.

Jacqui, in her account echoed details that the others had given. As that father/husband, she was very much aware how they lived on their own. He had been out hunting and being with the family felt very safe and peaceful.

In these tranquil moments, all four of them felt happiness and a deep sense of belonging with each other.

From this situation of peace, I then directed them forward to the occasion when the raiders came. Immediately, as they lay on the floor, all four of them showed visible signs of agitation.

There was a sudden shout from Jacqui as the father of 'Get the children'. They all seemed to respond to this and their bodies, particularly Janie's, were writhing around with shallow breathing, as if in panic.

Larry wrote in his account how he heard the hooves and shouting from the approaching tribesmen. Then, looking up, he could see his mother running towards him, attempting to gather him up in her arms.

Janie had a sense that the attack could have come from members of her own tribe. There was a vague feeling of unease inside her about why, as a family, they were living on their own.

As the mother, Janie was aware of the thundering sound of horses that were hurtling towards them. She sensed that they might have been expecting her to be alone with the children and were surprised by her husband's presence. After her husband shouted to her, she felt herself grab both the children, one in each arm. In desperation, she struggled to reach the protective boulders by the river. Then she felt a spear pierce her left shoulder and the children were ripped from her arms. As this happened, she howled to her ancestors in Spirit to protect her family and especially the children. This was a sound she made aloud. Her body convulsed and she felt that this cry came from deep inside of her, from her soul. It felt to her like no other noise or cry that she had made in her life. For her, it was like an ancient cry to the universe.

The life in her body withdrew. She felt no pain and was aware of leaving her physical body. Instinctively, she knew that her children were both dead and her husband was still alive. The riders on their horses left the encampment as quickly as they had come.

Following on from this deeply emotional experience, Janie felt inwardly cleansed and exhausted. For a considerable time, she felt a burning pain in her left shoulder.

In his experience, Larry was aware of having been trampled to death by the horses. His body jerked violently during these moments. For some time later, his back ached. However, as the son, Larry was very concerned about the fate of his father. Why had he not died like the rest of them? It became apparent to him that his father had escaped, but why had he not tried to protect them? This is what he would have expected his father to do.

In Spirit, he met with the others, who tried to assure him that there was nothing more that his father could have done, but this left a feeling of unease in Larry.

For Jacqui as the father, she felt that he had left the campsite after the rest of his family had been killed and had afterwards continued to live for a considerable time on his own. With this realisation, Jacqui too, felt quite uncomfortable.

Coming out of the meditation, they were all visibly affected with many lingering feelings. In particular, Jacqui found it difficult to come to terms with it all. Throughout the following day, she had a horrible pain in her heart with the thought that as that father, he had not adequately said goodbye to his family.

In the meantime, Larry also wrestled with turbulent inner feelings about it, but this was resolved for him in a later meditation when he was drawn back to that life at a point after death but before passing into the light. He saw the familiar grassy slopes of the hillside near to the encampment and a solitary but beautiful tree. There was the sound of the river, but all else was silent. Then he was at the site of a burial mound and could see his father riding off into the distance. Larry was happy to see his father alive and well and that he had returned to deal with their physical remains. He then heard his sister tell him that it was time to leave and together they all went to the light.

Later that evening, Larry was giving Jacqui some healing. He placed one hand on her heart charka and one hand on her back. Suddenly, she became aware of a small Native American boy to her right hand side. Then his father appeared, a tall handsome man. As the healing continued, they remained there together. Immediately, Jacqui felt relief in her heart centre and had a deep sense of father and son having made their peace.

My instincts told me that in that lifetime, Jacqui's soul had pursued a path of revenge after his family's death. When I confronted Jacqui about this, her own senses told her that this was true. She felt that he had ended up as a very bitter man.
A family trauma

Throughout the week, Neil had struggled to obtain comprehensive images from inner journeys that he had undertaken. He had persisted though, and had learned that even quite sparse perceptions could yield experiences of considerable meaning for him.

From the meditation on this evening, he sensed that he was standing on the edge of a cliff looking at his sister who was sitting on the edge of a rock pool busily playing with the life forms that were there. They were both children, and he felt protective towards his sister, who felt to be younger than him. Neil was aware of another figure that was there. He could not see her face but had a strong sensation that it was his mother.

When asked to identify the other characters from this scene, Neil identified Shona as being his sister and Jacqui as his mother. As soon as this was spoken, Jacqui and Shona felt certain that his identifications were accurate. There was a vague notion of another member of the group, Sue, being involved, but they could not agree in what context. Sue, herself, felt quite strongly, that she was there, so eventually she was included in the group when they lay down to do the group regression.

Initially, I suggested that it was that occasion when they were by the rock pool. Jacqui was aware of a bright, blue sky with a sunny breeze. She felt happiness and contentment as the mother, having the children there with her, running and playing together. Shona could feel herself as the younger sister, playing and laughing. It was an obviously tranquil scene.

I wondered about Sue's part in their lives, and so to explore this, I suggested to them that it was now a moment when they were at home with all the various people that lived there. Immediately, Jacqui's and Shona's bodies showed signs of agitation, while Sue's body stiffened. At the mention of the house, Neil sensed some dark presence. It became clear that this was a large family situation with numerous children clambering around. I asked about the father, and by their reaction, it was evident that this was a source of difficulty for both Jacqui as mother and Shona as the young sister. When questioned about this, mother had to admit that her husband was abusive.

At the mention of the father, Sue had felt an inner energy surging through her body, like hot fire. She was the father, and felt so angry. Sue was drumming her finger on the floor impatiently. While doing this, she felt herself as him, sitting at the kitchen table, waiting for his wife and two children to be back from the beach. As Sue listened to Jacqui, as mother, tremble with fear as she spoke about how her husband beat her, the whole scene opened up before Sue's eyes. The table where he was sitting was rectangular shaped, beefy legged, and covered with a green checked cloth. There was what looked like a Belfast sink and a back door.

I suggested that they move forward to the worst moment of abuse and hostility from this father. The tension mounted. Jacqui, as mother, was pleading with her husband not to hurt her. Shona, as sister, felt herself to be under the table with Neil, her brother. She shouted out to her brother, 'Don't listen to him' when he started laughing at his father. But then, her body shook and shivered violently as her father's aggression proceeded.

She felt herself to be hugging her brother tightly from under the table, while Neil, as brother, felt a tremendous urge to protect his sister.

In her account, Sue felt herself, as the husband, move towards his wife and grab her by the neck. He hit her hard and pitched her up and lashed into her, again and again, until finally, he hit her head onto the sink and killed her. Then there was silence.

Initially, Jacqui had the perception that she had survived this attack and had lived on afterwards with the children, without her husband. Sue and Shona were adamant the she had been killed.

As she sensed her mother being killed, Shona felt a huge rage fill her whole body and she felt as though she would explode. After she came out of the experience, she continued to shake uncontrollably, and it was only after she was encouraged to squeeze a cushion and yell with all her force that she was able to let the rage out of her body.

Sue felt complete horror about the deed that she had committed. Jacqui had become a close friend of hers and the thought of hurting her was utterly abhorrent to Sue. To help her to complete her part in the drama, I led Sue through to her past life death in that experience. It was a dark, dark place, silently cold, and knowingly a space to rest achingly, to contemplate about his past.

That night, Sue felt ill and shaken by what she had remembered. The next day, I was able to help her by reassuring her that the experience was from a long time ago and well and truly in the past now. By leading her into that dark place again, I kept moving her forward until she was able to come out of there and accept the light. Then she could feel peace.

I believe that the reason Jacqui felt that she had survived was more a wish fulfilment than fact, because she had felt so strongly the urge to provide for her children and be there for them. When I challenged her about this and she meditated upon it, she felt that the later perception she had had of herself in that life was actually her funeral, where her children had lovingly cared for her body, and in fact she had died as the others had indicated.

Death in Rome

In her meditation, Dawn was in the stands of a Roman Amphitheatre. She was feeling devastated and angry. Below her, her young lover was about to be torn apart by the lions because she loved him. She sensed herself to be a young teenage girl of high birth. Looking over her left shoulder, there was a man sitting beside her that was connected to her. This man was responsible for her loved one's death. He smiled at her coldly and raised a hand. She hated him. Then she was watching for her lover in those last desperate moments before he would be taken into the ring. She felt shocked.

Then she felt herself in another scene where she was standing and watching a parade. The senator was being lifted up in exultation by the crowds. She felt contempt for him.

When asked, Dawn identified other group members, Lynda as the senator and Larry as her young lover. Both of them felt the connections were accurate although Lynda felt very uneasy about admitting hers.

In the group regression, I went through various scenes to explore the relationship of the two young lovers. Larry recounted how he felt an urge to reach out and hold Dawn's hand. Instinctively, he knew that they were sweethearts. He could envisage the two of them holding hands in a garden with marble pillars and climbing plants. He also knew that his love for her was forbidden as she was betrothed to a senator.

Larry described Dawn's appearance as being an early teenager, around fifteen years of age, with long, light brown hair in ringlets. There was a white ribbon in her hair and she was very beautiful.

Larry then felt anxious as he believed that they had been seen together in the garden, having heard someone running away.

Later, after being moved on, Larry felt himself being held by two people in a darkened enclosure before being pushed out into the amphitheatre where he saw two lions. He then felt himself being chased and mauled by a lion's claws before being pulled to the floor and savaged by them until he died. His last moments of life felt very real to him, and he could feel each slash of the claws in his back. As he was about to die, he shouted very loudly, 'No'. Throughout the regression, Larry felt a great hatred for the senator.

For Lynda, as she began to access the memories from this lifetime, she immediately felt a change in her personality. She became cold, dispassionate and completely detached from the events that she, as this man, had set in motion. Members of the group commented about how her voice changed, taking on qualities of expressionless arrogance, that was cold and cruel, rather than the usual lyrical tones that was more familiar to us.

Lynda, as the senator, perceived that the young woman was betrothed to be married to him, against her wishes. She was in love with a young man who was a Christian, which was outlawed then. To follow that faith meant death. Lynda was aware in her mind of the young man being mauled by lions. She heard his screams of agony and these were echoed by Larry's screams beside her. However, as the senator there were no emotions of sympathy as he watched this young man torn apart, his girlfriend sobbing alongside of her. Instead, it offered him some grim satisfaction and affirmation of his position and power.

For Lynda, this was a tough and dark experience, one she needed later to go through more thoroughly to cleanse herself of it.

Dawn was aware that she died not so long after her lover. In Spirit, she was reunited with him. The feelings of love were very pure and almost overwhelming for her.

Feedback by the group members of their experiences

Many of the group needed help to digest and integrate their individual experiences from this evening, but the general comment was one of amazement about how enthralling, engrossing and believable the shared memory experiences had been. There was strong and very deep bonding that occurred between group members from this experience, and in the days and weeks that followed, several of them continued to spark memories from each other of further past lives where they had been linked too.

Even in lives where antagonism had been evident, this did not impair the relationships that existed. For instance, the friendship between Jacqui and Sue continued to deepen and flourish in spite of the very difficult past life encounter that they had shared. Jacqui had explored some of her own dark side in regression and could appreciate that the underlying thread of her connection with Sue was one of love. Likewise, Larry's connection with Lynda has developed into one of trusting friendship, even though he suffered at her hands when he was the Roman Senator in the Roman life.

Altogether, it was a very satisfying experiment for all concerned.

Chapter 25

Doing Your Own Regression

In this chapter, I would like to present a possible meditation that you can record and use, to help you gain some glimpses into your own past lives. This meditation can also be used in conjunction with any therapy you may be having, if memories from a past life have emerged. In this case, the meditation helps you to elaborate upon any memories that have appeared, and put these into context for whatever you need to learn.

To utilise this meditation, I suggest that you record the script onto a cassette. You may need to experiment with the length and speed of delivery until it feels right for you. It is advisable to speak quite slowly into the recorder with sizeable pauses after most sentences. Alternatively, you may choose to work with a companion who can read the script aloud for you.

It is best if you find somewhere quiet to do the regression, a place where you are unlikely to be disturbed. You can lie down or sit in a comfortable chair, as you prefer. For the purposes of recording your experience, it is useful to have pen and paper by your side for when you return from the meditation. It is helpful to make a note of all the thoughts, impressions and feelings that you have during the regression, however fleeting. Remember that the regression experiences that you have, are likely to be quite dream-like, and tend to fade quickly from your consciousness once the meditation is over. Therefore it might be helpful to note down even vague imagery.

It could be some time afterwards that the significance of a particular image comes to you. Therefore, writing down as much as you can remember, even things that seem irrelevant, will honour those impressions. This provides a space so that afterwards, when you are ready, you are receptive to the insights given to you. Otherwise much may be forgotten and passed over.

As further preparation for the meditation, you might wish to become clear about any issue or theme for which you would like answers or help through the past life experience. I suggest that you write this down as a form of acknowledgement of your intention in the meditation. Once you have done this, you can proceed.

Past Life Regression Meditation

To begin this meditation, just sit or lie comfortably. Have your eyes closed and take three deep breaths. With each deep breath, imagine that you are breathing away any tension or nervousness that you may be feeling. Breathe in peace so that you find yourself to be relaxing, going deeper and deeper within. Just let go and allow your self to drift into a very satisfying inner state of being.

As you go deeper and deeper, imagine there is a very pleasant wave of relaxation flowing through your body. Experience this relaxation flowing down from the top of your head, through your shoulders, your neck, down through your shoulders, arms and hands, through your chest and abdomen, your back and thighs, right down your legs to your feet. Soon your whole body is filled with this pleasant feeling of relaxation. Just let yourself go deeper and deeper.

Then, as you relax even more, focus upon your eyes and the muscles around your eyelids. Just imagine as if your eyelids are very, very relaxed. You could even try to open them and find that they just want to stay closed.

So relax your body and allow your mind to be at peace, to feel more and more at peace...
(Pause)

Imagine now that you are going down ten steps to a very deep part of your consciousness, to a place where you become increasingly receptive to the memory of one of your past lives to be revealed to you.

Going down the first step now, going deeper... Then the second, going deeper and deeper... Treading the third step and then the fourth, all the time becoming more inwardly receptive.... Now coming down the fifth and the sixth steps, feeling more and more relaxed... The seventh and the eighth.... Now the ninth step, going even deeper... Then the bottom step... Move forward from here as you are ready to go on.
(Pause)

Now I want you to imagine you are standing in a meadow, a very beautiful, nourishing meadow. Just sense this meadow. Be aware of the grass, any flowers, bushes and trees. Feel the air around you, with the sky above you and the Earth beneath your feet. Smell the aromas around you. Let yourself explore this meadow so that it becomes for you a very safe and familiar place.

As you proceed with the meditation, if you feel at any time that you need support, you can always return to this safe place and breathe in the fresh, nurturing air as you are doing now.

But the purpose of this meditation is for you to connect with the memory of one of your past lives. So I ask your inner consciousness to select for you one such life that would be appropriate for you to experience at the present time. At this point you may become mindful again of the particular question or issue that you wish to address through the past life experience. Ask inwardly for help with this if you are in doubt.
(Pause)

Then I would like you to become aware of a door. This is the door that when opened will lead you to an experience of this particular past life that your inner consciousness has chosen. Approach this door now. If you do not see it, then sense it as if it is there. Check inside yourself if you can really choose to enter into the memory of this past life. If it feels right to you, then prepare to open the door. I am going to proceed as if you have decided to go ahead. Otherwise, stay in the meadow for the duration of the meditation.

On the count of three, I would like you to open the door and step through to the experience of the past life on the other side. Let yourself do this. So one, opening the door, two, stepping forward, and three, you are now in the past life. You are in some moment from this past life. Sense your body, your environment and what you are doing.
(Pause)

As you perceive yourself more fully, you will be able to let thoughts, feelings and images of the story from this life to unfold. You will perceive accurately and truthfully what is appropriate and healing for you to learn from this experience at this time.

Start to become aware of yourself and your situation. Notice the ground under your feet and what is around you. Is the ground hard or soft? Be aware of your feet and sense whether you are wearing shoes, boots or sandals or if your feet are bare? As you become aware of that, notice more about your body. Sense the clothes that you may be wearing. You might be able to sense whether you are male or female? Also, get an idea if you are old or young, strong or weak, just generally how you are feeling in your body?

Notice now whether you are inside or outside? (Pause) Are there people with you or are you on your own? (Pause) What are you doing? (Pause) And how do you feel about your activities? (Pause) As you become more and more aware of all those details, also experience the emotions and thoughts that you are having. (Pause) What is your position or responsibility within the group or society where you live? (Pause) How do you feel about that? (Pause) What is occupying you right now?

In a moment, I would like you to let the experience of this life move forward so that you experience what happens next. Try to let yourself experience the happenings of this past life by being the person you were then, feeling and knowing things as that person.
(Pause)

What are you experiencing now? What is happening to you? How are you reacting? Go right through the event that you are now experiencing. Be aware of what is truly significant for you in this scene. Be aware of other people that may be there and anyone with whom you are relating. How does it feel to relate to those people? Just let the feelings come to the surface that might be there.
(Pause)

Now you are becoming aware of the place where you live around this time. Experience your self there and notice any other significant people with whom you share the space of this dwelling. (Pause) How do you feel within your home? Do you feel comfortable or uncomfortable? (Pause) Be aware of the quality of the relationships you share within your home. (Pause) If you are on your own there, notice how that feels.
(Pause)

Next, experience yourself doing the main activity of your everyday life. Notice if you are doing that on your own, or with others? (Pause) Let the details of this activity become very clear to you. What responsibility do you hold, if any? (Pause) Be aware of any aspect of this activity that you dislike or find difficult? (Pause) What inspires you about it? (Pause) Let yourself experience some moment when you are engaged in this activity that is important for you in some way.
(Pause)

Now I would like you to go to some important earlier time in this lifetime. It is one of those significant formative experiences that shape your life. Be aware of that event now. If there are any other people involved with this experience, become aware of those people. Sense how they relate with you and how you react with them. Let any emotions that are involved come to the surface so you can identify them. Is there anything that is going on making you feel afraid? Go right through the important phases of this event until it is all over. Be aware in your thoughts of any important decisions that you make, any attitude that you adopt that affects how things turn out.
(Longer pause)

Next, I would like you to become aware of a relationship that you have in this lifetime that makes some important difference to your life. Just become aware of that person now, and some important interaction that happens between you. (Pause) Is this person male or female? (Pause) How do you relate to that person? (Pause) Sense the quality of this relationship as it develops. You may be even able to perceive how the relationship unfolds over the course of this lifetime. Be aware of the strongest moment of contact between you and how you move on from that. (Pause) Also, sense if there is any trauma involved within the relationship. (Pause) There may be a moment where things change, where you are confronted with something in connection with this other person. If so, let your self become aware of the event where this takes place. Sense the emotions that you feel for this other person.
(Longer pause)

In every lifetime, we make a soul plan of how we wish that lifetime to be. As you further explore this past lifetime, become aware of one particular event that brings out the most significant challenge that you face in this past lifetime. (Pause) What is the nature of this challenge? (Pause) Do you have any religious or Spiritual faith to help you? (Pause) Experience how you react at key moments when this challenge is presented to you. (Pause) Go through one such event connected with this challenge now. If there are any strong emotions that you feel with regards to that, sense these feelings and let them flow through you.
(Longer pause)

There could be a moment in this lifetime where you are offered the chance to turn things around, especially if you have strayed from your purpose. If this is so, be aware of that event now and the decision that you make. Be aware of the environment around you and any people who are interacting with you. Notice the ramifications of that decision and how you feel about it.
(Longer pause)

Also, there could be some significant moment of achievement for you in this lifetime. If this is the case, go to the moment when you attain this. (Pause) What is the nature of this achievement? (Pause) Be aware of your circumstances as you reach this point in your life. Do you feel pride

or regret at this attainment? (Pause) Is there something that you have neglected or do you feel satisfied with yourself?
(Longer pause)

Now it is later, and you are approaching the moment of your death in that lifetime. Notice your circumstances. (Pause) You may be in a position to reflect upon the life that you have lived. How do you feel about that? (Pause) Do you want to die, or is this something that is being forced upon you? (Pause) Do you feel fulfilled by the experiences of this lifetime or does it feel as if it has been wasted? (Pause) What contribution have you made to the lives of others? (Pause) Go right through the details of your death. Experience anyone else who is involved. (Pause) Proceed to the very moment of your last breath. (Pause) And what happens after that?
(Longer pause)

Be aware of what you experience following on from your death. Notice what happens to your consciousness when you leave the body. (Pause) What thoughts and feelings do you carry with you following your death? (Pause) Is there anyone there to help you?
(Longer pause)

Now it may be possible for you to gain a perspective upon that lifetime. What did you learn and achieve through that experience? (Pause) What were your main mistakes? (Pause) How do you feel now that this lifetime is all over?
(Longer pause)

You may need to go through some form of cleansing experience, and if so, let this take place now. Learn all that you need to learn, even if this involves others. Surrender to this experience so that it may help and heal you.
(Longer pause)

If there is any wise being there to help you, open your awareness to this being, and take in any 'truth' and perceptions that you need to assimilate. The understandings we need to integrate following a lifetime can be obvious but are sometimes quite subtle. Let your self learn what you need

to learn. Doing this, you feel stronger and more complete.
(Longer pause)

Now you might be able to experience something of how this past lifetime links with the present lifetime that you are living now. (Pause) Be aware of any similar patterns, relationships. (Pause) There may be even soul connections, souls featuring in both lifetimes. You could open to an awareness of this now. (Pause) What can you learn from that past lifetime that has relevance to your life now? (Pause) Just take in any understandings that you gain. (Pause) How are you coping with those challenges in your present experience? (Pause) What could you do better? (Pause) Let your inner consciousness make adjustments to your perception so that you can learn what is necessary for you.
(Longer pause)

In a few moments, you will be able to complete this meditation for today. So, only when you are ready, find your way to the door, go through and close it firmly behind you. Remember all the details of the impressions that you have gained. For some moments, feel yourself enjoying the meadow once again, letting this help you to adjust to your present life body and consciousness once more.
(Longer pause)

So being very gentle with yourself, and only when you are ready, bring your self back to normal everyday consciousness and open your eyes. Take some time to write any notes or draw any impressions that may have come to you. Allow yourself to rest sufficiently before you engage in further activity.

Afterthoughts
When doing this meditation, you may find yourself gaining detailed information and vivid images, or what comes to you might feel to be more limited. Your capacity to access past life memory can vary according to what is occupying you in your everyday life. There could well be times in your life when past life memory is very close to the surface for you, and other times when it is very remote. It could be worthwhile to have somebody present with whom you can share the

experience, especially if anything that emerges in the meditation disturbs you. Once more, I suggest that you trust your own instincts about this.

The scripted meditation I have outlined could well be a satisfactory method for you to get a 'taster' of past life regression. However, to gain the full benefits of this work in depth, I recommend that you seek the guidance and help of a therapist. You will then be able to surrender to the experience more fully, and gain the safety and support that you need.

Chapter 26

Conclusions

Throughout the course of this book I have attempted to make an honest appraisal of past life regression based on my own personal experience of it. My intention has been to give an enthusiastic account of the many aspects of this work with its potential for personal growth and gaining self-knowledge. At the same time, I have not wanted to disguise or deny possible pitfalls or difficulties that can be encountered with those who want to engage in regression processes. What I have tried to concentrate upon is facets of the work that I feel to be of general interest to seekers, and also that which I have found most relevant in my practice as a therapist. I have shared personally about many of my own experiences and those of some my clients.

Upon reflection I recognise that if we consider past life regression to be a field of research there is still much to be discovered. There are areas of study relating to regression that I have not dwelled upon in this book. Included in these are topics such as parallel lives, future lives, Spirit possession and animal incarnations. For those who are drawn to these interests, I am sure that there are other books where they are explored extensively.

People need to find their own meaning in inner experiences, and there are many valid routes of past life enquiry that exist beyond what I have tried to portray. I tend to take a more traditional view that we live distinct lives, one after another. What I have tried to communicate concerns the areas of past life regression that feel important to me. My hope is to create openings in the understanding of past life regression for beginners and also those with some experience, people who want guidance as to what they can expect from this work.

Personally, I find past life regression absolutely fascinating. It gives me pleasure to share my knowledge of it. In terms of my own inner search, learning about past life regression has been, and continues to be, an important component of my Spiritual path, and has taught me much.

Studying this volume, I hope that there may be benefit to be gained from what I have written. However, I would suggest that ultimately, although books can bring forth knowledge that can give a useful foundation to any endeavour, reading about subjects is no substitute for experiencing them.

Past life regression has huge potential to help us gain wisdom about the essence of our life and also the inner freedom to express ourselves more fully. It is a path that needs courage to be undertaken, but I know that it does not appeal to everyone. My abiding wish is that this book will inspire those of you who are interested, and help you to feel safe enough to embark on this great adventure into your own soul's journey.

Author Contact

You can contact the author at

P O Box 121
Lancaster
LA1 5GS
England

Please enclose an SAE if writing from within the UK, or two
International Reply Coupons from elsewhere

Soul Pathways Paul Williamson

As souls, before we are born, we agree to take on certain challenges during our incarnations on Earth. Meeting these challenges may prove to be very demanding and testing for our character. We can be confronted with situations where we feel rejection, guilt, isolation, loss of trust and many other difficult emotions. It may seem easier to seek to escape or avoid what our soul has set out for us to do. Yet, when we can ask for help and reach within to learn about our inner truth, we can feel stronger. We may still need to endure suffering and come to terms with experiences where we feel that we have fallen short of what may have been wise and right. However, by being open to discover what is within, even when this may be uncomfortable, this may begin a process of healing and finding peace. In this, his third book, Paul Williamson has gathered some very frank and open accounts of people's life stories. These express, through intimate personal sharing, details of fundamental human problems, which are common to us all. By exploring the underlying conditions of these problems, Paul has tried to communicate thoughts and ideas that people may use to gain understanding of their own dilemmas. Sensitively written, this book is intended to help readers to find their own `soul pathway', so that they can emerge from experiences of inner darkness in their lives, to a life that is happier, richer and filled with hope. ISBN 186163 1812   £13.95

Healing Journeys Paul Williamson

Paul Williamson is a Past Life Therapist, Hypnotherapist and Healer. Here, he tells about his own unfolding spiritual path and what he has discovered about past lives, healing the inner child, channelling, spiritual healing and earth healing. Using numerous case studies, Paul shares his approaches to therapy and methods of healing that have helped people from their inner experiences to find peace and well-being. Within these stories, Paul charts some fascinating possibilities about the nature of our inner reality. From this, Paul affirms the relevance and importance of honouring the inner spiritual dimension of our being, so that if we can find peace within, then this could help us find greater meaning in our external lives, and help us to create a happier, healthier society too. Told simply and from the heart, this book shares many touching human and spiritual experiences that will interest seekers everywhere. These experiences can be truly called "Healing Journeys". ISBN 186163 100 6

Atlantis The Dark Continent Paul Williamson & Linda Braithwaite

The legendary civilisation of Atlantis is a topic that can evoke feelings of awe and mystery. Paul has investigated experiences of people's lives on Atlantis using regression, and now firmly believes that Atlantis did exist. Through careful research, and by using the shared soul memory of four people, Paul and Linda have compiled a fascinating account of the history of Atlantis from the times of the first settlements through to its destruction. Included are detailed living transcripts of regression sessions and channelled teachings. These experiences detail aspects of the healing and psychic power, and various forms of corruption in which people from Atlantis became involved. There are sharings of the psychological learning and scars that were left upon souls who became obsessed with power. From the tragedies and mistakes of these times, for the many millions who lived then, there may be lessons that can be learned. For those who have hidden within them, soul memories of having lived on Atlantis, this book may stimulate a recollection of those long lost times. ISBN 186163 1308   £12.95

FREE DETAILED CATALOGUE

Capall Bann is owned and run by people actively involved in many of the areas in which we publish. A detailed illustrated catalogue is available on request, SAE or International Postal Coupon appreciated. **Titles can be ordered direct from Capall Bann, post free in the UK** (cheque or PO with order) or from good bookshops and specialist outlets.

A Breath Behind Time, Terri Hector
Angels and Goddesses - Celtic Christianity & Paganism, M. Howard
Arthur - The Legend Unveiled, C Johnson & E Lung
Astrology The Inner Eye - A Guide in Everyday Language, E Smith
Auguries and Omens - The Magical Lore of Birds, Yvonne Aburrow
Asyniur - Womens Mysteries in the Northern Tradition, S McGrath
Beginnings - Geomancy, Builder's Rites & Electional Astrology in the
    European Tradition, Nigel Pennick
Between Earth and Sky, Julia Day
Book of the Veil , Peter Paddon
Caer Sidhe - Celtic Astrology and Astronomy, Michael Bayley
Call of the Horned Piper, Nigel Jackson
Cat's Company, Ann Walker
Celtic Faery Shamanism, Catrin James
Celtic Faery Shamanism - The Wisdom of the Otherworld, Catrin James
Celtic Lore & Druidic Ritual, Rhiannon Ryall
Celtic Sacrifice - Pre Christian Ritual & Religion, Marion Pearce
Celtic Saints and the Glastonbury Zodiac, Mary Caine
Circle and the Square, Jack Gale
Come Back To Life, Jenny Smedley
Compleat Vampyre - The Vampyre Shaman, Nigel Jackson
Creating Form From the Mist - The Wisdom of Women in Celtic Myth and
    Culture, Lynne Sinclair-Wood
Crystal Clear - A Guide to Quartz Crystal, Jennifer Dent
Crystal Doorways, Simon & Sue Lilly
Crossing the Borderlines - Guising, Masking & Ritual Animal Disguise in the
    European Tradition, Nigel Pennick
Dragons of the West, Nigel Pennick
Earth Dance - A Year of Pagan Rituals, Jan Brodie
Earth Harmony - Places of Power, Holiness & Healing, Nigel Pennick
Earth Magic, Margaret McArthur
Eildon Tree (The) Romany Language & Lore, Michael Hoadley

Enchanted Forest - The Magical Lore of Trees, Yvonne Aburrow
Eternal Priestess, Sage Weston
Eternally Yours Faithfully, Roy Radford & Evelyn Gregory
Everything You Always Wanted To Know About Your Body, But So Far
    Nobody's Been Able To Tell You, Chris Thomas & D Baker
Face of the Deep - Healing Body & Soul, Penny Allen
Fairies and Nature Spirits, Teresa Moorey
Fairies in the Irish Tradition, Molly Gowen
Familiars - Animal Powers of Britain, Anna Franklin
Flower Wisdom, Katherine Kear
Fool's First Steps, (The) Chris Thomas
Forest Paths - Tree Divination, Brian Harrison, Ill. S. Rouse
From Past to Future Life, Dr Roger Webber
Gardening For Wildlife Ron Wilson
God Year, The, Nigel Pennick & Helen Field
Goddess on the Cross, Dr George Young
Goddess Year, The, Nigel Pennick & Helen Field
Goddesses, Guardians & Groves, Jack Gale
Handbook For Pagan Healers, Liz Joan
Handbook of Fairies, Ronan Coghlan
Healing Book, The, Chris Thomas and Diane Baker
Healing Homes, Jennifer Dent
Healing Journeys, Paul Williamson
Healing Stones, Sue Philips
Herb Craft - Shamanic & Ritual Use of Herbs, Lavender & Franklin
Hidden Heritage - Exploring Ancient Essex, Terry Johnson
Hub of the Wheel, Skytoucher
In Search of Herne the Hunter, Eric Fitch
Inner Celtia, Alan Richardson & David Annwn
Inner Mysteries of the Goths, Nigel Pennick
Inner Space Workbook - Develop Thru Tarot, C Summers & J Vayne
Intuitive Journey, Ann Walker Isis - African Queen, Akkadia Ford
Journey Home, The, Chris Thomas
Kecks, Keddles & Kesh - Celtic Lang & The Cog Almanac, Bayley
Language of the Psycards, Berenice
Legend of Robin Hood, The, Richard Rutherford-Moore
Lid Off the Cauldron, Patricia Crowther
Light From the Shadows - Modern Traditional Witchcraft, Gwyn
Living Tarot, Ann Walker
Lore of the Sacred Horse, Marion Davies
Lost Lands & Sunken Cities (2nd ed.), Nigel Pennick
Magic of Herbs - A Complete Home Herbal, Rhiannon Ryall
Magical Guardians - Exploring the Spirit and Nature of Trees, Philip Heselton
Magical History of the Horse, Janet Farrar & Virginia Russell
Magical Lore of Animals, Yvonne Aburrow
Magical Lore of Cats, Marion Davies

Magical Lore of Herbs, Marion Davies
Magick Without Peers, Ariadne Rainbird & David Rankine
Masks of Misrule - Horned God & His Cult in Europe, Nigel Jackson
Medicine For The Coming Age, Lisa Sand MD
Medium Rare - Reminiscences of a Clairvoyant, Muriel Renard
Menopausal Woman on the Run, Jaki da Costa
Mind Massage - 60 Creative Visualisations, Marlene Maundrill
Mirrors of Magic - Evoking the Spirit of the Dewponds, P Heselton
Moon Mysteries, Jan Brodie
Mysteries of the Runes, Michael Howard
Mystic Life of Animals, Ann Walker
New Celtic Oracle The, Nigel Pennick & Nigel Jackson
Oracle of Geomancy, Nigel Pennick
Pagan Feasts - Seasonal Food for the 8 Festivals, Franklin & Phillips
Patchwork of Magic - Living in a Pagan World, Julia Day
Pathworking - A Practical Book of Guided Meditations, Pete Jennings
Personal Power, Anna Franklin
Pickingill Papers - The Origins of Gardnerian Wicca, Bill Liddell
Pillars of Tubal Cain, Nigel Jackson
Places of Pilgrimage and Healing, Adrian Cooper
Planet EArth - The Universe's Experiment, Chris Thomas
Practical Divining, Richard Foord
Practical Meditation, Steve Hounsome
Practical Spirituality, Steve Hounsome
Psychic Self Defence - Real Solutions, Jan Brodie
Real Fairies, David Tame
Reality - How It Works & Why It Mostly Doesn't, Rik Dent
Romany Tapestry, Michael Houghton
Runic Astrology, Nigel Pennick
Sacred Animals, Gordon MacLellan
Sacred Celtic Animals, Marion Davies, Ill. Simon Rouse
Sacred Dorset - On the Path of the Dragon, Peter Knight
Sacred Grove - The Mysteries of the Forest, Yvonne Aburrow
Sacred Geometry, Nigel Pennick
Sacred Nature, Ancient Wisdom & Modern Meanings, A Cooper
Sacred Ring - Pagan Origins of British Folk Festivals, M. Howard
Season of Sorcery - On Becoming a Wisewoman, Poppy Palin
Seasonal Magic - Diary of a Village Witch, Paddy Slade
Secret Places of the Goddess, Philip Heselton
Secret Signs & Sigils, Nigel Pennick
Self Enlightenment, Mayan O'Brien
Spirits of the Air, Jaq D Hawkins
Spirits of the Earth, Jaq D Hawkins
Spirits of the Earth, Jaq D Hawkins
Stony Gaze, Investigating Celtic Heads John Billingsley
Stumbling Through the Undergrowth , Mark Kirwan-Heyhoe

Subterranean Kingdom, The, revised 2nd ed, Nigel Pennick
Symbols of Ancient Gods, Rhiannon Ryall
Talking to the Earth, Gordon MacLellan
Talking With Nature, Julie Hood
Taming the Wolf - Full Moon Meditations, Steve Hounsome
Teachings of the Wisewomen, Rhiannon Ryall
The Other Kingdoms Speak, Helena Hawley
Tree: Essence of Healing, Simon & Sue Lilly
Tree: Essence, Spirit & Teacher, Simon & Sue Lilly
Tree Seer, Simon & Sue Lilly
Through the Veil, Peter Paddon
Torch and the Spear, Patrick Regan
Understanding Chaos Magic, Jaq D Hawkins
Vortex - The End of History, Mary Russell
Warp and Weft - In Search of the I-Ching, William de Fancourt
Warriors at the Edge of Time, Jan Fry
Water Witches, Tony Steele
Way of the Magus, Michael Howard
Weaving a Web of Magic, Rhiannon Ryall
West Country Wicca, Rhiannon Ryall
Wheel of the Year, Teresa Moorey & Jane Brideson
Wildwitch - The Craft of the Natural Psychic, Poppy Palin
Wildwood King , Philip Kane
Witches of Oz, Matthew & Julia Philips
Wondrous Land - The Faery Faith of Ireland by Dr Kay Mullin
Working With the Merlin, Geoff Hughes
Understanding Past Lives, Dilys Gater
Understanding Second Sight, Dilys Gater
Understanding Spirit Guides, Dilys Gater
Understanding Star Children, Dilys Gater
The Urban Shaman, Dilys Gater
Your Talking Pet, Ann Walker

FREE detailed catalogue and FREE 'Inspiration' magazine

Contact: Capall Bann Publishing, Auton Farm, Milverton, Somerset, TA4 1NE